STREAMS OF LIVING WATER

Lectionary Devotional
For Cycle B

STREAMS OF LIVING WATER

*Lectionary Devotional
For Cycle B*

STEPHEN P. MCCUTCHAN

ARPress

ILLUMINATING IDEAS,
EMPOWERING VOICES

ARPress
45 Dan Road Suite 5
Canton MA 02021
Hotline: 1(888) 821-0229
Fax: 1(508) 545-7580

Ordering Information:
Quantity sales.Special discounts are available on quantity purchases by corporations, associations, and others.For details, contact the publisher at the address above.

Printed in the United States of America.

ISBN-13:   Paperback   979-8-89330-011-6
              eBook   979-8-89330-012-3

Library of Congress Control Number: 2024901008

Dedication

I dedicate this Devotional Year B book on behalf of the hard working clergy who daily confront the challenges of our time. May this book offer rich resources in support of your work. May you be blessed as you contribute your gifts on behalf of those called by God. May your ministry be filled with God's blessings and personal satisfaction.

In addition to the clergy who offer their gifts and faith to nurture their congregations. I also dedicate this volume to my wife, Sandra, who up until her death in November 2019 was my chief editor and support in all of my writings. She encouraged me when I was down and counseled me when I was anxious or confused. While I miss her deeply, I feel that my 53 years with her enabled me to maintain faith and integrity that supported both my ministry and writing. I was blessed by our marriage and that gratitude has enabled me to continue to journey through my time of grief.

Table Of Contents

Spiritual Nurture
For Pastors

As a pastor, you are called by God to offer spiritual guidance to the people entrusted to you. The psalmist describes those who delight in the law of the Lord as being "like trees planted by streams of water which yield their fruit in its season, and their leaves do not wither" (Psalm 1:3). There was a thirst that drew us to the faith and eventually to the ministry.

The challenge we face is to not allow the incessant demands placed upon us in the ministry to deny us the time to stop and refresh ourselves by that stream of living water that initially attracted us. We do not take the time to allow God to make us lie down in green pastures and lead us beside still waters to restore our souls.

As Jesus said to the Samaritan woman, "Everyone who drinks of this water will be thirsty again, but those who drink of the water that I will give them will never be thirsty. The water that I will give will become in them a spring of water gushing up to eternal life" (John 4:13-14). It is critical that pastors, despite the seemingly inhuman demands that are placed upon them, not lose touch with that refreshing water that feeds their souls.

This book is offered in support of your ministry. It is intended to support you in your profession by encouraging you to take time for regular prayer and devotions so that God might continually touch your life and speak to you through scripture.

The structure of the book builds on two features of our professional life — the structure of worship and the provision of the Revised Common Lectionary. The basic structure of most experiences of worship include the offering of praise, confession of sins, being nurtured by the word, offering prayers of thanksgiving and intercession, and experiencing the benediction or the blessing of God. The Revised

1

Common Lectionary offers four readings normally drawn from the Hebrew scriptures, the psalms, the gospels, and the epistles.

At the beginning of the book, you are offered five formats for your time of prayer. The first one focuses on the praise of God. The second focuses on the confession of sins and assurance of forgiveness. The third is directed toward a time of thanksgiving. The fourth offers you the opportunity for offering prayers of intercession. Finally, there is a time to receive the blessing of God or the benediction. Following these formats for devotions, there is a series of brief meditations on each of the scriptures proposed by the lectionary for the following Sunday.

The intention is that you would find at least five times during the week to take time for prayer and meditation for half an hour or more. You would begin the week with a time of praise. Next you would have an opportunity to confess those burdens that are bothering you and experience the grace of a forgiving God. The third day would allow you to spend some time offering your thanksgiving for all that God provides you. On the fourth day you would have an opportunity to focus on the needs of your congregation or the society around you. And on the fifth day, you can rest in the blessing of God who has called you to ministry. During this time, you will also be nurtured each day by the scriptures that form the basis of your worship on the following Sunday. I recognize that some may find it more helpful to alter the calendar and use the lectionary readings that will provide the basis of the worship several weeks in advance so that your meditation might also stimulate your thinking with respect to the sermon that you will need to prepare. You may find it helpful to have a pad of paper to capture the thoughts that occur to you.

The appropriate time to use this devotional will vary with the schedule of each individual. Many find that an early morning time can be set aside and is usually not disturbed, but for others it is an appropriate way to end the day. I also would suggest two other alternatives that have proved helpful to me. Most hospitals have chapels, and if you carry this devotional with you, you could often find a brief time after a hospital visit to nurture yourself in the chapel. Also, I have found a remarkable sanctuary in fast-food restaurants. I order a minimal meal, take it to the most remote corner in the restaurant, and allow the meal to be a spiritual experience that slows down my eating and feeds me with some bread of heaven. No pattern fits all personalities, and I encourage you to explore what time may best fit your pattern and personality. I have deliberately chosen to create just five formats for prayer under the assumption that there will be at least two days each week that do not fit into this rhythm. However, if you are fortunate enough to have a sixth or seventh time, you can simply choose to repeat any of the offered formats.

My hope is that the flexibility of the formats and the opportunity to reflect on the lectionary scriptures will encourage you to be good to yourself and strengthen that connection with God that has drawn you into your calling. God's call in your life was not a mistake, and the church needs your gifts in response to the hunger of God's people. May God strengthen you for the journey that lies ahead.

Spiritual Nurture
For Mainline Christians

The presence of Mother Teresa and her witness has inspired many Christians and even non-Christians because of the powerful simplicity of her witness. In 2007, a book, *Mother Teresa: Come Be My Light*, was released that included some of her most private letters that revealed her own spiritual struggle and some of her darkest periods of doubt. To combine this revealing glimpse into her soul with the visible witness of her life of service to the less fortunate is an empowering gift for the ordinary believer. The agony of the Garden of Gethsemane (Matthew 26:36-46) is the honest agony of the most faithful Christian. The soulful cry of abandonment from the cross (Mark 15:33-34) belongs to all of us. We do not have to be afraid of our moments of doubt or disbelief.

Like the agony of the father who cried out to Jesus, "I believe, help my unbelief" (Mark 9:24), it is natural for us to long for a belief that seems beyond our grasp. Yet it is comforting to understand that we are not alone in such a difficult journey. The question is what we do when we are experiencing a difficult period of time in our faith journey. When you read through the psalms, you are constantly hearing the psalmist recall what God had done for his people in the past. For example, in Psalm 22 the psalmist cries out in the midst of his agony: "In you our ancestors trusted; they trusted, and you delivered them. To you they cried, and were saved; in you they trusted, and were not put to shame" (Psalm 22:4-5). It does not require much imagination to realize that the psalmist is rehearsing the memory of God's faithfulness in the past in order to provide him or her courage for the future. Again the witness of Mother Teresa is a help to us. Even during her darkest periods, she did not abandon the disciplines that made connection with the memory of those times when faith had been strong for her.

One of the treasures that God has provided for us to sustain us not only in the mountaintop experiences of faith but also in the valleys of doubt is the discipline of scriptures and prayer. It is the wisdom of the church to have provided us a lectionary to guide us in being immersed in the wisdom of the story of the faith. Here we recall how God has worked in the lives of people in the past so that we can have the courage to await God's presence in our future. Our doubts and even our periods of disbelief are not a barrier to our journey.

Many otherwise very good and sensitive people have, in the words of the prophet Jeremiah, lost contact with "the fountain of living water, and dug out cisterns for themselves, cracked cisterns that can hold no water" (Jeremiah 2:12). It is the intention of this book to draw upon the wisdom of the church's discipline of the lectionary to provide you with streams of living water that can nourish you on your journey.

It is easy to feel lost and unimportant in the pressured society in which we live. Power and confidence come to those who feel as if their life is filled with meaning and that their contribution is part of something greater than themselves. The Christian story is fundamentally about God who created everything that exists, who has become personally involved in the flow of time and history to accomplish a glorious purpose, and who calls you to be part of the unfolding of that story in this universe. Your life is not insignificant but is intended to be a paragraph in the divine story that God is unfolding. Even the mistakes and missteps you take do not need to be wasted but can be redeemed by God through Christ in the telling of this all-important story.

To feel our own connection with God's story, we need to reconnect with the Spirit that is animating the true meaning of our lives. We need to feel a personal connection with the God of our salvation. A major gift by which God invites us to stay connected with the divine purpose is that of prayer and scripture. For many Christians, those very practices have fallen into disuse or have become a routine that is devoid of power. This book is intended to provide you a means by which to reenergize your prayer life and to hear God speaking to you through scripture. It is intended to support you by encouraging you to take time for regular prayer and devotions so that God might continually touch your life and speak to you.

5

The structure of the book builds on two features common to many Christians in mainline churches — the structure of worship and the provision of the Revised Common Lectionary. Whether your church uses the lectionary or not, the format can still be used. You will discover that it will help you feel connected with the wider body of the church that reaches across the world. The basic structure of most experiences of worship include the offering of praise, confessing of our sins, being nurtured by the word, offering prayers of thanksgiving and intercession, and experiencing the benediction or the blessing of God. The Revised Common Lectionary offers four readings normally drawn from the Hebrew scriptures, the psalms, the gospels, and the epistles.

At the beginning of this book, you are offered five formats for your time of prayer. The first one focuses on the praise of God. The second focuses on the confession of sins and the assurance of forgiveness. The third is directed toward a time of thanksgiving. The fourth offers you the opportunity for offering prayers of intercession. Finally, there is a time to receive the blessing of God or the benediction. Following these formats for devotion, there is a series of brief meditations on each of the scriptures proposed by the lectionary for the following Sunday.

The intention is that you will find at least five times during the week to take time for prayer and meditation for half an hour or more. You will begin the week with a time of praise. Next you will have an opportunity to confess those burdens that are bothering you and experience the grace of a forgiving God. The third day will allow you to spend some time offering your thanksgiving for all that God provides you. On the fourth day you will have an opportunity to focus on the needs of your congregation or the society around you. And on the fifth day, you can rest in the blessing of God who has called you to the faith. During this time you will also be nurtured each day by the scriptures that will likely form the basis of your worship on the following Sunday.

The appropriate time to use this devotional will vary with the schedule of each individual. Many find that an early morning time can be set aside and is usually not disturbed, but for others, especially those with children, other times will be more appropriate. It may be an appropriate way to end the day, but there are some who feel so drained by the pressures of life that it is hard to focus when they are so tired. So, before you conclude that your life just does not allow for such a discipline, let me suggest a few other opportunities. First, many of you drive to work in your own car, and often you can plan to arrive at your parking space in time to have some extra time alone before you enter your place of work. While it may seem shocking at first, let me further suggest that a perfect place to find alone time at many places of work is the stall in the restroom facilities. Also, I have found a remarkable sanctuary in fast-food restaurants. I order a minimal meal, take it to the most remote corner in the restaurant, and allow the meal to be a spiritual experience that slows down my eating and feeds me with some bread of heaven. No pattern fits all personalities, and I encourage you to explore what time may best fit your pattern and personality. I have deliberately chosen to create just five formats for prayer under the assumption that there will be at least two days each week that do not fit into this rhythm. However, if you are fortunate enough to have a sixth or seventh time, you can simply choose to repeat any of the offered formats.

My hope is that the flexibility of the formats and the opportunity to reflect on the lectionary scriptures will encourage you to be good to yourself and strengthen that connection with God that has drawn you into your faith. God's call in your life was not a mistake, and the church needs your gifts in response to the hunger of God's people. May God strengthen you for the journey that lies ahead.

Five Formats
For
Your Time
Of
Prayer

Praising God

Invocation

I praise the Lord! I praise the name of the Lord; I give praise as one of the servants of the Lord ... I praise the Lord, for the Lord is good; I sing to God's name, for God is gracious. — Adapted from Psalm 135:1, 3

Personal Prayer

Spend ten minutes offering praise to God for the way in which God has called you, nurtured you, strengthened you, and worked miracles in your life.

Nurtured By The Word

Read the Hebrew scripture for the week.

Spend some time asking how God might be speaking to you through this lesson.

Read the meditation on the first lesson for the week.

If thoughts come to your mind as you muse on this passage, jot them down.

Closing Prayer

Either sing or pray the doxology:

Praise God from whom all blessings flow.
Praise God all creatures here below.
Praise God above you heavenly hosts.
Praise Father, Son, and Holy Ghost.

Confession And Forgiveness

Invocation

You desire truth in the inward being; therefore teach me wisdom in my secret heart ... Hide your face from my sins, and blot out all my iniquities. — Psalm 51:3, 9

Personal Prayer

Take about ten minutes to confess to God those personal and relational sins that burden your soul. Also lay before God the feelings of anger, hurt, and disillusionment that are part of your life.

Assurance Of Forgiveness

Who is in a position to condemn? Only Christ, and Christ died for us, Christ rose for us, Christ reigns in power for us, and Christ prays for us. I claim the good news of the gospel for myself. In Jesus Christ, I am forgiven.

Nurtured By The Word

Read the psalm for the week.

Spend some time asking how God might be speaking to you through this lesson.

Read the meditation on that psalm.

If thoughts come to mind as you muse on this passage, write them down.

Closing Prayer

O Lord, open my lips, and my mouth will declare your praise ... [Help me to recognize that] the sacrifice acceptable to God is a broken spirit; a broken and contrite heart, O God, you will not despise. — Psalm 51:15, 17

Offering Thanksgiving

Invocation

The heavens are telling the glory of God; and the firmament proclaims his handiwork ... There is no speech, nor are there words; their voice is not heard; yet their voice goes out through all the earth and their words to the end of the world. — Psalm 19:1, 3-4a

Personal Prayer

Take about ten minutes to thank God for the many blessings in your life. Thank God for the ways God has been present in your life. Thank God for how God has been present to you since birth.

Nurtured By The Word

Read the gospel lesson for the week.

Spend some time asking how God might be speaking to you through this lesson.

Read the meditation on the gospel lesson.

If any thoughts come to you while you are musing on the gospel, write them down.

Closing Prayer

You prepare a table before me in the presence of my enemies; you anoint my head with oil; my cup overflows. Surely goodness and mercy shall follow me all the days of my life.... — Psalm 23:5-6a

Prayers Of Intercession

Invocation

Give ear to my words, O Lord; give heed to my sighing. Listen to the sound of my cry, my King and my God, for to you I pray. — Psalm 5:1-2

Personal Prayer

Take time to consider and offer in prayer all of the needs of which you are aware within your life. Take note of the spiritual and emotional needs as well as the physical and material needs in your life. Lift up troubled relationships and career challenges as well as family and marital stresses.

Nurtured By The Word

Read the epistle lesson for the week.

Spend some time asking how God might be speaking to you through this lesson.

Read the meditation on this lesson.

If there are thoughts that come to mind as you muse on this scripture, write them down.

Closing Prayer

But let all who take refuge in you rejoice; let them ever sing for joy. Spread your protection over them, so that those who love your name may exult in you. — Psalm 5:11

Benediction

Invocation

As a deer longs for you, O God, my soul thirsts for God, for the living God. When shall I come and behold the face of God? — Psalm 42:1-2

Personal Prayer

Take time to simply rest in the blessings of the Lord in your life. Review times in your life when you have felt the powerful presence of God lifting you up and times when you basked in the sheer joy of the life that God has provided you. Review some high moments in your life and allow them to be signs for you of God's continuing presence calling and guiding you.

Nurtured By The Word

Open the section of meditations at random and choose a particular scripture that is noted. Read it totally free of any agenda for its use.

Spend some time asking how God might be speaking to you through this passage.

Then read the meditation provided.

If there are thoughts that come to you during your musing, write them down.

Closing Prayer

Sing or pray the Gloria Patria:

*Glory be to the Father, and to the Son
and to the Holy Ghost;
as it was in the beginning,
is now, and ever shall be,
world without end.
Amen, amen.*

Lectionary Meditations For Cycle B

Advent 1

Isaiah 64:1-9

> *Yet, O Lord, thou art our Father; we are the clay, thou art our potter, we are the work of thy hand.* — Isaiah 64:8 (RSV)

Advent holds together that tension between a faith that believes God is present to us and a world that raises questions about the absence of God. For many people, faith is based on what others say about the presence of God, and one's personal experience seems more abstract. The faith stories of God's visit on Mount Sinai, when the mountain quaked in God's presence (v. 3), seems to be but a memory for the people in Isaiah's time. They yearn for what seems like a clear sign of God's voice to again be heard among the people. The assumption for many believers is that God's absence in their lives is a sign of their own lack of faith (v. 7). While not diminishing the reality of our own sinfulness, Isaiah boldly reminds God that we are what God has made us to be. "We are all the work of your hands." Our faith lies not in our faithfulness but in God's faithfulness. Advent doesn't speak of the coming of God as a response to our goodness. Advent dares to hope that God will remember that we are all God's people. Advent dares to rest its hope on the goodness of God that can transform our lives and redeem us from our darkness. If God is the potter and we are the clay, then God can shape and reshape us until God's love is pleased with the result.

Psalm 80:1-2, 8-13

Give ear, O Shepherd of Israel, you who lead Joseph like a flock! You who are enthroned upon the cherubim, shine forth. — Psalm 80:1

Psalm 80 is a community lament that ends in waiting for God's response. It begins with a plea using the image of God as a shepherd and Israel as a flock (v. 1). While it clearly comes after Israel has fallen as a nation (v. 12), it uses the early names of the tribes of Benjamin, who was Rachel's last son, and Ephraim and Manasseh who were the sons of Rachel's first son, Joseph (v. 2). In despair as a nation, they cry out to God for help (vv. 2-4). They remind God of Israel's suffering (v. 5) and how they have become a mockery to surrounding nations (v. 6). The psalmist rehearses God's involvement with this people using the image of a vine. God brought them out of Egypt (v. 8) and planted them in a new land (v. 9). There the expansion of the nation under David is described (vv. 10-11) and then the breakup (v. 12) and defeat as a nation (v. 13). It is on the basis of that memory of relationship that the psalmist lays claim to God's saving power (vv. 14-16). Verse 17 could well be seen as a prayer for a Messiah or a prayer that they, collectively, might be restored as a witness to what God intended for humanity. If restored, they vow to again be faithful (v. 18). The final plea is for restoration (v. 19), and then there is only waiting. In the face of despair, it is the memory of God's faithfulness that sustains us while we await God's response.

1 Corinthians 1:3-9

I give thanks ... because of the grace of God that has been given you in Christ Jesus. — 1 Corinthians 1:4

The church at Corinth was hardly a paragon of virtue, as Paul makes clear in this letter. There was immorality, selfishness, greed, fighting, and so forth. Yet Paul gives thanks for the grace of God in their lives. How do we discern grace in a community filled with the normal human foibles? Paul says that the people of Corinth are not lacking in any spiritual gift needed for the revealing of our Lord Jesus Christ. Do we discern God's grace as we recognize surprising signs of the presence of Christ among us? Are those signs discerned because we have first seen them manifested in Jesus' living and now discover them breaking out in our community? It is because we are tempted to greed that a communal decision of generosity touches our soul. It is because we are prone to bickering that an experience of the healing power of love among us is so powerful. When someone offends us in the church, we are given the opportunity to reveal Christ through our forgiveness. Advent is a time of watchfulness for the small signs of God's grace peeking through the ordinary lives of people whom God has gathered together in worship.

Mark 13:24-37

> *But in those days, after that suffering ... Then they will see the son of Man coming in clouds with great power and glory.* — Mark 13:24, 26

Advent is a time of expectation in the midst of a troubled world. It reveals itself in the tension between the suffering caused by evil in this world and our belief that God is working for good. It is in the "dark night of the soul," when it appears that evil has triumphed and we cry out, "My God, my God, why have you forsaken me?" and we experience light in the midst of our darkness that reveals the triumph of God. It is when we have felt overwhelmed by forces beyond our control and recognize that our only hope is God that we recognize the power of God in our lives. Advent becomes a rehearsal of such faith so that we can cling to God in the dark times. We recall the many ways that God has walked with people in their distress and saved them from disaster so that as we experience disaster, we don't lose hope. Advent is a time of expectation, a time when we can realistically hope for the birth of saving grace in our lives.

Advent 2

Isaiah 40:1-11

> *The grass withers, the flower fades; but the word of our God will stand forever.* — Isaiah 40:8

The people of Israel had been taken into exile. Everything that they had held onto as a sign of their special identity — land, temple, king — had been taken away from them. Now the prophet is called to speak words of comfort to a despairing people. "In the wilderness," in the time of exile, they are told "to prepare the way of the Lord." When they are commanded to cry out that the Lord is coming, they respond in despair that "all flesh is like grass" that soon withers under the sun. There is no hope that new leaders will rise up to lead them. Their cynicism is overwhelming. Like today, when people have lost all confidence in politicians and religious leaders and despair that all people are selfish and self-serving, so Israel had lost all hope. The prophet challenges that despair not by denying the weakness of humans but by proclaiming the power of God. The light in the darkness is not some new scheme of reform or some champion of the people but the truth that God cares for us like a shepherd for his flock. As you reflect on your own life, where are the points of despair and where are you looking for help? What does it mean for you to trust that God cares for you in your particular situation?

Psalm 85:1-2, 8-13

> *Steadfast love and faithfulness will meet; righteousness and peace will kiss each other.* — Psalm 85:10

The shalom of God includes both God's initiative and our response. "Faithfulness will spring up from the ground and righteousness will look down from the sky." We are caught in a tension within the church between those who want to pursue righteousness at any cost and those who insist on peace at any price. The thought that "righteousness and peace (must) kiss each other" is hard to grasp. Perhaps part of the problem is that we do not take the other person seriously enough to listen beneath the rhetoric. Those who insist on an ethical stance must hear the fear of those who seek peace, and those who insist on peace must hear the hunger of those who yearn for what is right. Each needs to know that commitment to each other will not allow for separation. "Steadfast love and faithfulness" must meet if there is to be shalom. A community that worships the absence of conflict puts integrity on the altar, but those who are willing to split the community because others will not agree on their issue substitute self-righteousness, for God's righteousness which we only "see through a glass darkly."

2 Peter 3:8-15a

The Lord is not slow about his promise, as some think of slowness, but is patient with you, not wanting any to perish, but all to come to repentance. — 2 Peter 3:9

Context is everything. If it is true, as Paul reminds us, "... that with the Lord one day is like a thousand years and a thousand years are like one day," then a factor in our struggles within the church may be our failure to trust in God's timing. Our own lack of patience causes us to push for decisions within the body before the body has discerned the mind of God. The temptation of churches is to model themselves after political bodies that make decisions by votes that leave winners and losers. Yet God's will is that all will come to an awareness of the mind of God so that "none shall perish."

If the church is a body rather than an organization, it may be that coming to a decision too quickly is like the fingers saying to the arm, "since we are more than you, we win the vote and have no need of you." Discernment of the will of God is the task of the church. Such discernment invites people to study the scriptures, share a variety of opinions within the community, pray a lot, and then have patience. Whether the issue is one of the current ones around the issue of sexuality or one of the previous ones around democracy, slavery, the role of women in the church, the struggle for civil rights, or the response of the church to poverty or war, God is taking the faithful acts of many Christians and slowly working within the church for the salvation of humanity. Consider the power of making your faithful witness but also having patience with your neighbor to await the working of God in his or her heart.

Mark 1:1-8

The voice of one crying in the wilderness: "Prepare the way of the Lord." — Mark 1:3

A member admits to me that he does not like Advent because it tries to make a mystery out of something he already knows. He wants to go right to the celebration and skip the preparation. But what he celebrates is a past event. Mark suggests that the kingdom of God is knocking at this member's door waiting for him to experience the baptism of repentance so that he can be prepared to receive this new thing. Advent is a difficult season for many of us because we want to blur the season into Christmas. The liturgical calendar does not make sense to us because we really are not preparing for a surprise. We think that we already know the end of the story. And more importantly, we do not believe anything different will happen this year. It is hard to prepare the way of the Lord when we do not expect the Lord to come. But what if this year God is about to act decisively, and we miss it altogether because we weren't willing to prepare? What if Advent only rehearses the past event to illuminate how we are to discern the sign of the times? What would take place if Christians prepared for God's coming to us fully expecting that this may happen?

Advent 3

Isaiah 61:1-4, 8-11

They shall repair the ruined cities, the devastation of many generations. — Isaiah 61:4b

Those who had returned from exile in great expectation found the cities of their land in ruin and utter poverty among the peoples. The prophet proclaims that the Spirit of the Lord has anointed him to bring good news to the afflicted. The fruits of the Spirit of the Lord resting on him were the practical ministering to those who had been devastated by conditions in their life. It included not only attending to their personal needs but to the repair of their cities. Jesus would later take this passage as a text that demonstrated that the spirit of the Lord rested on him as well. He healed the sick, fed the hungry, and raised the dead as an expression of God's care for those in need. Later, the early church would also be moved to attend to the practical needs of their neighbors as a sign of the Spirit moving among them. They went out into the street and cared for those who others had abandoned. Today we seek the Spirit in repairing the ruins of our cities devastated by the spiritual poverty of many generations. In what way do you sense the Spirit of God resting on you and urging you in a particular direction of ministry?

Psalm 126

Then our mouth was filled with laughter, and our tongues with shouts of joy. — Psalm 126:2

Psalm 126 is an almost giddy response to the totally unexpected experience of good fortune. Israel had been in exile, and though they yearned for the land of Israel, the political realities made that seem an impossible dream. Then in one of those impossible twists of fate, they were free to go home. It all seemed so unreal — like a dream (v. 1). The only response possible was sort of a giddy laughter and the deep joy of being confirmed in the eyes of the nations (v. 2). The response to God's blessing was joy (v. 3). Like the water in the Negeb, which in a flood seems so out of control and then is returned to the banks that control its flow, so Israel had direction returned to their lives (v. 4). The lesson in life was one of patient trust in God's care. Those who sow in tears but patiently trust in God's faithfulness reap with shouts of joy (v. 5). The agricultural metaphor of the sweat and tears of planting and cultivating with only the silent trust that such effort will bear fruit would later be used by the church to understand the cross and the resurrection (1 Corinthians 15:35 ff). Like the farmer, one has a responsibility to plant the seed, but it is an offering to God. There is an interval between planting and harvest that we do not control (Matthew 13:1-9), but at the harvest we are glad (v. 6).

Luke 1:47-55 (Psalm alternate)

For he has looked with favor on the lowliness of his servant. — Luke 1:48

The song of Mary is a strong reminder of the passionate freedom of God to disrupt history in favor of the disenfranchised. For all the tradition that has been built around Mary, scripture is silent about her pedigree and suggests that she is simply a young virgin who is responsive to the voice of God in her life. She is a woman in a man's society, she is young in a world where age is respected, and she is a virgin in a society that honors a woman's fertility.

Yet out of her anonymity, she experiences God's blessing in the form of her pregnancy. It is this experience of God's blessing in her life that causes her to erupt in song. From her personal blessing, she perceives the pattern of God's intervention in history. Her song quickly moves from praise of God in her life to a praise of God's grace as it continues to be experienced in the world. God blesses the poor and oppressed and hungry, and God is a counterforce to the proud and the powerful. And most of all, this is a God who keeps promises and expresses mercy to the children of Abraham.

Mary's song is a song of hope for all who sense defeat or experience brokenness in this world. It is an advent hope that interrupts darkness and causes each Advent to be a season of expectation in our own lives. It is also a caution for those who might get lost in the celebration and forget that God is most likely to be experienced where we are joining God in responding to the needy in our society.

It is important to note that Mary celebrates God's actions on behalf of the needy in the past tense and not as a future expectation. As you look back on this past year, where can you identify the work of God that you can celebrate in a manner that gives you courage for the future?

1 Thessalonians 5:16-24

Rejoice always, pray constantly, give thanks in all circumstances; for this is the will of God in Christ Jesus for you. — 1 Thessalonians 5:16-18

There is a continual thrust in the Christian faith toward a positive trust in the sovereignty of God. "Rejoice always," Paul says, and we want to respond, "Life is not always good." Paul continues: "Give thanks in all circumstances," and we want to challenge that we are not thankful for everything. But that is why Paul admonishes us to "pray constantly." It is not that life is always rosy or that "positive thinking" conquers all. Rather, it is that God is sovereign and can redeem any circumstance. We are to rejoice in the sovereignty of God in the darkest of circumstances and give thanks for God's redeeming power exactly where we least see it. The only way we can prevent ourselves from being defeated by the tragic in life is to stay in contact with the transcendent. It is precisely because life is not always positive that we need to rejoice and give thanks to God in every circumstance. Call to mind a dark moment in your life that you can now give thanks for because out of that circumstance God worked a good result. Let that memory give you strength for the future.

John 1:6-8, 19-28

I am the voice of one crying out in the wilderness. — John 1:23

The story of John the Baptist is a story of the word of God coming to us from the fringe of our lives. The center of religion in Israel was

Jerusalem, the temple, and the religious leaders. This would have been where people would have expected to hear the word of God proclaimed. But it was in their encounter in the wilderness that they heard God's word proclaimed. Too often, we expect God to come to us at the points of our strength and places where we are in control and comfortable. Yet God's voice is often that which speaks in the desert of our lives. Think of those spaces where we are least in control or the spaces that are empty of the busyness that fills our lives. Advent is an invitation to explore the empty corners of our lives in anticipation that we might hear the Lord. It is in the person or the experience that we do not know that we are likely to discover God addressing us. Advent is a time for listening to our wilderness. Where do you need to listen this Advent?

Advent 4

2 Samuel 7:1-11, 16

Your house and your kingdom shall be made sure forever
before me, and your throne shall be established forever. —
2 Samuel 7:16

This text in 2 Samuel is the source of the messianic expectations in Israel following the fall of Jerusalem in 586 BCE. It is the origin of that hope that finally resulted in the affirmation of Jesus as the Christ, the Son of David. It is a most appropriate text for the final Sunday in Advent.

Because of the ease with which the hope of Christmas is distorted in our society, it is interesting to note that this story describes how a faithful person, David, having consulted the chief spokesman for the faith, Nathan, and with the best of intentions, to honor God, can make decisions that are contrary to the purpose of God. David felt blessed by God in his life. He had prospered, triumphed over his enemies, and was struck by the contrast between the fine cedar house in which he lived and the tent in which the Ark of the Covenant resided. With the best of intentions, he proposed to honor God with a structure equal or better to that in which he lived.

Even when we act with the most sincere intentions and the support of all that we know from our faith, it can be dangerous to presume that we understand what God wants from us. Advent is a time for listening to God's intentions for our lives and a time for experiencing the freedom of God to move in our lives in a totally unexpected manner. David wanted to honor the eternal God with a finite structure and discovered that God chose to make an everlasting promise to the finite David. What is the everlasting promise that God is implanting in your life?

25

Luke 1:47-55

See the meditation for Advent 3.

Psalm 89:1-4, 19-26 (Psalm alternate)

I have made a covenant with my chosen one, I have sworn to my servant David. — Psalm 89:3

Psalm 89 is unique in that it starts with praise and ends with lament. The psalmist sings of God's love and faithfulness (vv. 1-2). He recalls the terms of the covenant God made with David (vv. 3-4). He acknowledges God's unchallengeable power in the heavens (vv. 5-8) and on earth (vv. 9-11). The power of God reaches from the north to the south and is praised by the mighty mountain ranges (v. 12). God's power (v. 13) is built on righteousness, justice, love, and faithfulness (v. 14). Israel finds its joy in worshipping God (vv. 15-16) because by God's strength they need not fear the enemy (vv. 17-18). The psalmist recalls how God took an ordinary person (v. 19) and made him God's personal agent (v. 20). God gave David victory over all his foes from the Mediterranean to the Euphrates (vv. 21-25). Their relationship was as father to son (vv. 26-27), and God established a covenant with him for as long as the heavens endure (vv. 28-29). If David's children sinned, they would be punished; but the family line will always retain the throne (vv. 30-37). It is on the basis of this promise by this powerful God that the psalmist now raises the complaint to God about how Israel has fallen and become a mockery to their neighbors (vv. 38-45). How long, the psalmist cries, shall such contradiction between God's promise and Israel's experience continue? (vv. 46-48). Where now is God's steadfast love that God swore to David?(49). Remember, O Lord, how your servant is taunted (vv. 50-51). The reputation of God awaits God's action.

Romans 16:25-27

Now to God who is able to strengthen you according to my gospel ... to whom be the glory forever! Amen. — Romans 16:25, 27

Paul brings to a close his letter to the Romans with this doxology. Since it is easy to become myopic in our focus on Jesus during this season, it is an important reminder that this is the window into the mystery of God. God's glory is made manifest in the incarnation because here we see the reconciliation that is central to God's eternal purpose. The particular of the birth of a Jewish boy in the small Palestinian community is joined with the cosmic reality of God who transcends all time and space. The wisdom of God is experienced in a crucified Christ, and the hope for Gentiles is discovered in a Jew who explodes the prophetic writings to be a truth for the Gentile, as well as the Jew.

A doxology is meant to be an explosive crescendo of awe in the face of this mystery that, while never fully understood by us, is now available to us. In this life of a single person, all of creation comes together. Even as we are stunned by the power of God, we are humbled by God's willingness to become vulnerable to this world. As you near the end of your Advent preparations, you are invited to simply praise "the only wise God, through Jesus Christ, to whom be the glory forever! Amen."

Luke 1:26-38

The angel Gabriel was sent by God to a town in Galilee called Nazareth. — Luke 1:26b

Given all the important places there are at any given time in the world, it is striking that the announcement of Jesus' birth takes place in such an ordinary village as Nazareth. It confirms again how that which is really important in our world is often revealed in the most ordinary of events. We sometimes overlook the ordinary and pay attention to the spectacular in life and thereby miss the visitation of God. The birth of a baby is both miraculous and common. Babies are born all the time, and yet in each birth lies the potential revelation of God. We eat meals every day, and yet in each meal we see revealed the love of God. A bath or shower may be commonplace for us, and yet in that cleansing is hidden the cleansing power of God. In both young Mary and elderly Elizabeth, we see signs of God's presence. We search the ordinary events of life and listen for the greeting: "Greetings favored one, the Lord is with you." Commit yourself to focusing on the ordinary events of this day and listening in each event for the greeting of God.

Christmas Eve/Christmas Day

Isaiah 62:6-12

You who remind the Lord, take no rest, and give him no rest until he establishes Jerusalem and makes it renowned throughout the earth. — Isaiah 62:6b-7

One of the great questions that should occur during Advent and find its culmination in the celebration of Christmas is what you expect from God. In some ways, the power of Advent is robbed by low expectations from believers. We approach Christmas like a mystery whose final pages we have already read. Is the reason congregations always want to sing Christmas carols early because they assume they already know the end of the story? When we finally arrive at Christmas Day, we celebrate the birth of Jesus way back in history, we go home for the big meal, and we turn to the real mystery — what will I get for Christmas?

What if you really believe that God has promised to intervene in the world's affairs in order to bring justice and reconciliation to a broken and hurting world and that this may be the year? Maybe we are too polite to mention it to God, but perhaps that is the problem of our faith journey. Maybe we live with too low a set of expectations for God. The prophet Isaiah spoke to a disappointed people living in exile, but he was not so reticent. Keep nagging God, he said, and don't give God any rest until he has established Jerusalem and made it renowned throughout the earth.

The prophet is able to be so bold because he believes that God has made a promise and he has a right to expect that God will fulfill his promises. "The Lord has sworn by his right hand and by his mighty arm: I will not again give your grain to be food for your enemies ..." (v. 8). Because the prophet believes in the promises of God, he feels emboldened to cry out to God: "When are you going to fulfill your promise?" Not only that but he is willing to make preparation: "Go through the gates, prepare the way for the people; build up, build up the highway, clear it of stones ..." (v. 10). Now that is Advent preparation. Maybe this year is the year that the Prince of Peace will reign throughout the world. If you believe that this promise is possible, how will you want to live?

Psalm 97

The Lord is king! Let the earth rejoice; let the many coastlands be glad! — Psalm 97:1

That is a startling statement. First, if God is king, why is the earth in the state that it's in? But second, how much rejoicing would there be if it were suddenly realized that God is king and "fire goes before him, and consumes his adversaries on every side"? (v. 3). The psalmist declares that "righteousness and justice are the foundation of his throne" (v. 2). Given the fact that the earth does have huge disparities in wealth, that no one could possibly claim that God approves of the obvious injustices that occur on a daily basis, and that many of us benefit from certain circumstances that are built on conditions resulting in others suffering, how might we have to change our lifestyle if we were to choose to be fully obedient to the God who reigns in our world? Look at Acts 4:32-35 for one example of early Christians that decided to live in radical obedience. Were they foolish or faithful?

When this psalm is read on Christmas Day, we are reminded that the God incarnated in Jesus Christ is our king. The psalmist draws upon the image of Moses on Mount Sinai to describe the awful presence of God on earth. "Clouds and thick darkness are all around him; righteousness and justice are the foundations of his throne. Fire goes before him, and consumes his adversaries on every side. His lightnings light up the world; the earth sees and trembles" (vv. 2-4). When we celebrate the coming of God in Christ, do we tremble? Have we lost a sense of the power of God that is present in this small baby whose birth we celebrate? Consider for a moment how your life might change if you made an absolute commitment to "have the same mind in you that was in Christ Jesus" (Philippians 2:5).

What would it mean to recognize God as revealed to us as the Christ and our Lord? Like for the psalmist, the vision is in front of us and we are dependent on the grace and mercy of God as we seek to move toward that hope. On this day, however, it might be good for us to pause and tremble a little bit for the cost of our discipleship as seen in the life of Jesus.

Titus 3:4-7

But when the goodness and loving kindness of God our Savior appeared, he saved us, not because of any works of righteousness that we had done, but according to his mercy. — Titus 3:4-5a

At its most basic, the Christmas story is a story of God's overpowering grace. The reason for the birth of Christ was not that God looked on humanity and said, "You know, they have been such good people and have really struggled to be faithful. I think that I will try to do something special for them." In fact, God could have repeated the judgment that was reported in Genesis 6:5: "The Lord saw that the wickedness of humankind was great in the earth, and that every inclination of the thoughts of their hearts was only evil continually." Despite that reality, God chose to respond to humanity not according to our merits but according to his mercy. The Christmas event that we celebrate is a celebration that God chose not to respond to humanity according to what they deserved but according to the possibilities contained in his redeeming love.

The passage from Titus is considered to be drawn from an early church baptismal liturgy. This unearned merciful love is most clear in the baptism of infants. Before the infants are able to do anything to merit God's love, God reaches out to receive them. The Christmas story and the world's response to the love Jesus offered is a proclamation that God is not defeated by the sins of humanity. What begins at the dawn of Jesus' life with the killing of the infants (Matthew 2:16) and continues to the end of his life at the cross is a demonstration of the depth of sin in humanity and God's power to transform even such sin into a redemptive possibility. We are reminded each year at this time that "my grace is sufficient for you, for my power is made perfect in weakness" (2 Corinthians 12:9).

Luke 2:(1-7) 8-20

When they saw this, they made known what had been told them about this child; and all who heard it were amazed at what the shepherds told them. — Luke 2:17-18

One of the striking things about the Christmas story is how many people were unaware of what was happening. Of course, the Emperor Augustus and all those who were so busy making the powerful decisions that they assumed shaped the world missed what was happening. They had no idea that anything important was happening in that remote village in a forgotten corner of a third-rate colony of the Roman empire. Perhaps the story of the innkeeper has been romanticized, but clearly if he had known what was happening, would he not have gladly given his own room to make space for the birth of Christ? One does not have to attribute cruelty to his actions but simply a lack of awareness about what was important. Skip the angels for a moment, and think about the other people nearby. The shepherds, Luke tells us, "made known what had been told them about this child; and all who heard it were amazed" (vv. 17-18). We do not know who the all were, but clearly they did not understand the significance of the event before the shepherds spoke. Even the mother of the child, Mary, appeared blissfully unaware: "Mary treasured all these words and pondered them in her heart" (v. 19). It was only because the shepherds had heard words from beyond their world that they had at least a partial understanding of what had taken place.

The Christmas season is a good time to be reminded that God is often at work in the seemingly ordinary moments of life. When you think of the shepherds, do not think of the romantic picture that we have created for shepherds. In the Jewish community of the time, shepherds were not held in high respect. They were the ones who did what others avoided. They stayed out all night, slept on the cold ground, and smelled badly as a result of associating with all those sheep. A comparable person in our society might be the garbage collector or the street sweeper. They were not the people who you first thought of when you wanted to hold a party. Yet, they were the ones to whom God communicated and they were the ones who brought the message to others who would listen.

31

Think of the least important person in a congregation or in your own personal life. Or think of the most mundane task in the ministry of the church. Perhaps it is, like the work of the shepherds, a task that we count on being accomplished but not one that we pay much attention to. In what way might God be trying to speak to you through that which you often overlook? Could it be that the person or task that you often overlook might be the very context through which God can speak of heavenly peace on earth?If we are to hear the word of God in our lives, it is important that we learn how and where to listen.

Christmas 1

Isaiah 61:10—62:3

... as a garden causes what is sown in it to spring up, so the Lord God will cause righteousness and praise to spring up before all the nations. — Isaiah 61:11

It is an ironic but true fact of human nature that the Sunday immediately following the high moment of the birth of our Savior is usually a low Sunday in both mood and attendance at worship rivaled only by the equally low attendance on the Sunday following Easter. From a human standpoint, the excitement climaxes on Christmas, and the following week seems so ordinary. Yet from a spiritual standpoint, the birth is the beginning of a great event. Isaiah uses the analogy of the natural event of growth from a seed planted in a garden to illustrate the natural process by which that which God has planted will grow. The seed that God has planted is righteousness and praise. If God has again planted the seed of righteousness and praise within your congregation this Christmas in the celebration of the birth of Christ, then what new thing should be anticipated in your life and the lives of those near to you? With the growth of this seed, something entirely new can spring up. Isaiah speaks of God giving a new name by which the people shall be called. Within the Hebrew culture, a name contains a person's inner character. What is the inner character of the Christian community of which you are a part that needs to be cultivated so that it will grow and "shine out like the dawn"? A seed planted in a garden can easily have its life snuffed out by weeds or a failure to receive proper water and nourishment of the soil. What might you be able to do that could help cultivate the new thing that God wants to do in your community of faith?

Psalm 148

Let them praise the name of the Lord, for he commanded and they were created. — Psalm 148:5

Psalm 148 is a psalm of praise that incorporates every facet of existence. It is a psalm that belongs at the end of the hymn of creation when God "saw everything he had made and behold it was very good" (Genesis 1:31). Then, on that sabbath rest when God stands back to rejoice in this new creation, the peals of praise echo forth from God's creation. Praise comes from the heavens, the angels, and the hosts (vv. 1-2). It springs forth from the sun, moon, and stars (v. 3) and from the waters that were left above the firmament on the second day of creation (v. 4). This watery chaos, whose bounds were fixed by God, gives testimony to the sovereignty of God over all the forces of chaos (vv. 5-6). That same praise echoes from the mystery of the forces within the created world: sea monsters, deeps, fire and hail, snow and frost, and stormy winds all obey God's commands (vv. 7-8). From mountains to hills, from fruit trees to cedars, and all forms of animal life, all reflect God's praise (vv. 9-10). All classes, sexes, and ages of people from kings to children should join in such praise (vv. 11-12). Praise is at the center of all creation because every facet of the jewel reflects God's continuing glory (v. 13). It is this same God who has chosen to raise the sign for a chosen people as a sign of God's love for all people. The ultimate symbol of God's glory is God's capacity to love a particular people (v. 14). Thus the creator of all can personally care for the few.

As you reflect in this post Christmas glow, look around you and notice all the facets of life that exist and give glory to God. Rest in that praise for a time and know again God's evaluation: "And indeed, it was very good" (Genesis 1:31b).

Galatians 4:4-7

But when the fullness of time had come, God sent his son ... so that we might receive adoption as children. — Galatians 4:4-5

From Paul we hear how the cosmic event of the incarnation has a very personal impact on us as individuals and on all those who are our neighbors. It is easy to lose sight of our own dignity in the eyes of God and consider our lives as an unimportant collection of atoms in a vast and unfeeling universe. If Jesus is affirmed as God's Son, then by adoption we are made the brothers and sisters of Jesus and children of God. By that act, our lives are given a value and a dignity that challenges all that would suggest that we are unimportant. We are invited into the family council by which God discusses how we should best live, and we receive the benefits of being a member of God's family. The daunting challenge, of course, is that how we live reflects on God because we come from God's family.

Families often have quarrels and bicker among themselves, but, in the best of families, they also know how to stick together when an outside force threatens any member of the family. Consider the vast Christian community that is spread across this world and the impact that it could have if as a family it realized that the true threat to all of us comes not from doctrinal disputes within but from the secular pressure that challenges the very truth of God from without. Sometimes important families try to use their power to obtain special favors, but our most famous brother declared that the character of God's family is to be one who serves others. The cosmic challenge of the incarnation of Christ is to accept the dignity of one who calls God "Abba" and to live in a way that reflects the love of God for the whole world.

Luke 2:22-40

She was of a great age, having lived with her husband
seven years after her marriage, then as a widow to the age
of eighty-four. — Luke 2:36b-37a

This passage features two elderly people in the temple, Simeon and Anna, who witness the dedication of Jesus to the Lord by his parents. As we near the celebration of the New Year with its secular symbol of an old man (representing the year past) welcoming the new baby (representing the year to come), it may be appropriate to recognize the witness of these two elderly people. As is common for Luke, he balances the witness of males and females as a testimony to the truth that the enmity between male and female that was the result of sin (Genesis 3:15) has been overcome in Christ. By bringing together the witness of the elderly, the obedience of the much younger parents, and the presence of the baby Jesus, Luke also reconciles the division among the ages. In an era when the aged are often dismissed as irrelevant to the future, this passage is an important reminder of the value of their testimony. It was out of their years of faithfulness that they were able to recognize the presence of God in their midst and offer hope to the future generations.

As you conclude your celebration of the birth of Christ, ask yourself who the elderly are that you need to listen to so that you might draw from the wisdom of their faith and thus see signs of God's presence near you? How might your church community make room to listen to these important witnesses who have lived faithfully for these years and have an important message to all those who "are looking for the redemption of Jerusalem"?

Christmas 2

Jeremiah 31:7-14

He who scattered Israel will gather him, and will keep him as a shepherd a flock. — Jeremiah 31:10b

Even as we celebrate the birth of Jesus, there is a nagging question of whether it really happened in a way that will change the world. Isn't part of the letdown after Christmas due to the fact that we have to return to the ordinary world with all its fractures and divisions? The most shameful part of that world is the multiple divisions of the very body of Christ. Jeremiah, in the midst of the exile, called on his people to celebrate that which had not yet happened. "Sing aloud with gladness for Jacob ... See, I am going to bring them from the land of the north, and gather them from the farthest parts of the earth ..." (v. 8). With the total people of God, both north and south, now defeated and by some estimates, as many as three and a half million people carried off into exile, it would be easy to give in to despair. But Jeremiah commands them to praise the God who will restore them like a shepherd does his flock. Christians have often divided time between the first and the second coming of Christ. Christmas celebrates the first and anticipates the second. Jeremiah envisions the time when God will bring the scattered (and divided) people of God back together as one people. As you survey the state of our society, can you begin to celebrate the time when God will reconcile the world "not counting their trespasses against them" and in light of that celebration can you see yourself rededicating yourself to the ministry of reconciliation? (2 Corinthians 5:19). Can you even dare to hope, with Paul, that such reconciliation will include Christians and Jews? (Romans 9-11).

Psalm 147:12-20

He has not dealt thus with any other nation ... Praise the Lord. — Psalm 147:20

Psalm 147 is a prayer of praise that seems to oscillate between the human and the cosmic. Those whom God has appointed as part of the community of faith, both Jew and Christian, have a particular obligation to make visible the praise of God. Those whom God has gathered as a witness should praise him (v. 12) because this God protects them outside and inside (v. 13) and provides peace and provisions (v. 14). By God's command the earth also receives its peace and provisions (vv. 15-18). This cosmic God who cares for the entire universe is the same God who has instructed Israel about what he wants. All other nations in the world depend upon Israel to declare what God has revealed. Even Christians must remember that God revealed the divine will through the Jewish people and a Jewish person (v. 20). We are to praise this God and no other.

As you reflect on the last half of this psalm, you may want to look at your own life and consider how the movements of your life can reflect your praise of the God who has provided not only you but also the whole world with that which is necessary for life.

Ephesians 1:3-14

... he chose us in Christ before the foundation of the world to be holy and blameless before him in love. — Ephesians 1:4

Ephesians is speaking about the church and making a claim for it that even the most optimistic of Christians would have difficulty in making. How can the author claim that the church was chosen before the foundation of the world to be holy and blameless before God? Paul makes very clear, especially in his letters to the church of Corinth, that the church is full of problems and hardly blameless in its behavior. Yet, Paul says that the church has been blessed with every spiritual blessing in heavenly places.

When people condemn the church for its failures, they are obviously viewing the church from a worldly perspective. From that perspective, there is no cause to be arrogant. We can only hang our heads in shame at our behavior. But is there a spiritual perspective from which we can also look at the church? Do we see in the church, frail as it is, a reflection of the love of God by which we are made blameless? Can we see God's power made perfect in the weakness of the church in a way that allows God's glory to shine all the more?

Take some time to consider how your particular church, despite its sometimes obvious frailties, is still a reflection of God's love for the world. Perhaps in that reflection you will sense how the people of God experience their salvation not through their moral heroism but how "we have redemption through his blood, the forgiveness of our trespasses, according to the riches of his grace that he lavished on us" (vv. 7-8). Here is the true miracle of what God has done for us.

John 1:(1-9) 10-18

In the beginning was the Word and the Word was with God.... — John 1:1

In an obvious imitation of the creation story in the book of Genesis, John begins his gospel with the phrase, "In the beginning...." There is also an association with Proverbs 8 in which the wisdom of God is said to have been with God at the beginning of creation, but in this case wisdom is pictured as the first act of God's creation (Proverbs 8:22). For John, the Christ is not some being that was created by God, as was the rest of creation. Rather, John asserts, this is the very expression or Word of God that was part of God from the beginning.

It is the story of Jesus, but Jesus is more than a man: He is the Christ of God. The astounding truth of the gospel is that the very Word of God took on flesh and dwelt among us. The eternal God entered time and lived as one who was constrained by time to a past and a future. But the story gets even more incredible because even though "the world came into being through him; yet the world did not know him. He came to what was his own, and his own people did not accept him" (vv. 10-11). It is very easy for us to reduce the miracle of Jesus' life to the life of a very good man and to overlook the unbelievable assertion that in the person of Jesus we are encountering God in the flesh of a human being.

As you begin this new year, take a moment to reflect on the meaning of the fact that the God who created the whole universe chose to become flesh and blood and live on this planet in order to convey God's love for us. How does knowing this affect how you live your life and pursue your profession?

The Epiphany Of Our Lord

Isaiah 60:1-6

Lift up your eyes and look around; they all gather together, they come to you; your sons shall come from far away, and your daughters shall be carried on their nurses' arms. — Isaiah 60:4

There is a continual theme in scripture of the scattering and the gathering. Cain is driven from his home after killing Abel. The people are divided and scattered at the Tower of Babel. Later, the Israelites will be carried off into exile. The prodigal son leaves his family home. The early followers of Jesus are driven from Jerusalem and Paul finds a hearing only among the scattered in Gentile lands. But there is also the countertheme of the gathering together of that which was once scattered. Whether we refer to the scattered as the prodigal Israel gathered in from exile or the Pentecostal experience of the multilingual people once again hearing the common, healing, reconciling message of God, the prodigal does come home.

The gathering will be not only of the faithful remnant but of the whole world. "Nations shall come to your light and kings to the brightness of your dawn" (v. 3). This third person to write under the name of Isaiah wrote after the people had returned from exile. When they returned, they found a land of poverty and they lived on the edge of despair. That is also the darkness of deprivation that so many people experience. But in the gathering of the future, the wealth of the nations shall serve the glory of God: "... because the abundance of the sea shall be brought to you, the wealth of the nations shall come to you" (v. 5).

Whatever your present darkness or scattering, you are also claimed by the God who promises the gathering. As did the Israelites, so we are given courage by the vision of what God yet will do. Our faithfulness

41

over our little area of the world is not pointless but a part of God's great gathering. "Arise, shine, for your light has come, and the glory of the Lord has risen upon you" (v. 1).

Psalm 72:1-7, 10-14

Give the king your justice, O God, and your righteousness to a king's son. — Psalm 72:1

For Christians, this psalm becomes a prayer on behalf of Jesus. You can almost hear the wise men from Matthew 2:1-12 praying this prayer before the baby Jesus as they kneel before him. Could we ever hope for more than a leader who would "judge your people with righteousness, and your poor with justice"? (v. 2). Yet for Christians, as for the rest of the world, though our ideal would be a day when righteousness would flourish and peace abound, it is still a prayer for which we await fulfillment. All people struggle with a sense of justice in light of whatever oppression they experience and they pray for a leader who will bring about a world of peace and justice.

As we prepare to celebrate Epiphany, we recount the visit of the wise men from the East as the first sign of the world coming to acknowledge the wisdom of God as reflected in the birth of Christ. Epiphany is a time to recognize again that our hope rests in God. We have reason to hope that a day will come when "he delivers the needy when they call, the poor and those who have no helper" (v. 12). The predominant image of the ministry of Jesus was in his reaching out to the helpless and rejected and drawing them into the circle of God's love and healing acceptance.

As you prepare to celebrate Epiphany, reflect again on how you might discover signs of God's activity in bringing about peace and justice in this world.

Ephesians 3:1-12

For surely you have heard of the commission of God's grace that was given me for you, and how the mystery was made known to me by revelation.... — Ephesians 3:2-3

Either in Paul's words or the words of a close disciple of Paul, we are hearing about a mystery that shatters normal world perceptions and commissions the church with an onerous responsibility. It is appropriate that this passage be read on Epiphany Sunday because we are dealing with a revelation of truth that includes both Gentiles and Jews. As a cautionary tale for those of us in the church, it is significant that Matthew records that the first to submit to Jesus as the Christ were not members of the believing community but pagan astrologers from the Parthian empire in the East. Sometimes it is those outside of the community of faith who instruct us as to the truth of our own faith.

In Ephesians, Paul (or the Pauline school) speaks of the mystery revealed in Christ that the grace of God was for all equally and without reference to national, racial, or social identity (see Galatians 3:28). He made this clear in Ephesians 1:9-10: "He has made known to us the mystery of his will, according to his good pleasure that he set forth in Christ, as a plan for the fullness of time, to gather up all things in him, things in heaven and things on earth." In our passage, Paul speaks of the major division within the community of faith. "The Gentiles have become fellow heirs, members of the same body, and sharers in the promise in Christ Jesus through the gospel" (Ephesians 3:6).

Because most of us come from the Gentile side of that equation, it is easy for us to get too comfortable with this conclusion. If you consider other dimensions of the divisions within our world, the message becomes more of a challenge. If God's purpose is to reconcile all things to him, then the bearer of that revelation, the church, has a significant responsibility to demonstrate provisionally such reconciliation between peoples and between humankind and the natural creation. Paul makes the extent of our responsibility clear: "So through the church the wisdom of God in its rich variety might now be made known to the rulers and authorities in the heavenly places" (v. 10). Our responsibility is not contained within the boundaries of the faith community.

On Epiphany Sunday we are confronted again with the scandal of the divisions within the Christian community and the radical plan of God to reconcile all the divisions that we have come to accept in our world. Our responsibility as Christians to demonstrate this radical grace is made even more explicitly in Corinthians: "All this is from God, who reconciled us to himself through Christ, and has given us the ministry of reconciliation; that is, in Christ, God was reconciling the world to himself, not counting their trespasses against them, and entrusting the message of reconciliation to us" (2 Corinthians 5:18-19).

Matthew 2:1-12

When King Herod heard this, he was frightened, and all Jerusalem with him. — Matthew 2:3

There is a haunting reality to this story that exposes the shadow side of humanity even while it offers a glimpse of God's way of salvation. The setting is in the holiest city of the entire world where God's chosen people have built the temple and where God is worshiped daily. Where else would you go if you wanted to understand what God was doing in this world? The pagan wise men followed a star, but even they knew that finally you had to inquire in Jerusalem where the priests were the keepers of the faith if you wanted to know where truth was to be found. Yet, when they suggest that what the faithful community had continuously prayed about had actually happened, the reaction was one of fear. We may pray that God would visit us with a clear sign of his presence and make his will known, but what would our reaction be if that actually took place?

Even the religious of this world seek to have a measure of control over their lives. If God made his way clearly known, then we would no longer have any excuse but to obey. Further, and perhaps more frightening, we would no longer be in control but would have to trust this mystery that never fully discloses the future but keeps inviting us to trust in a God that we cannot control. The story of the visit of the wise men suggests that the secular wisdom of the world often recognizes what we resist in acknowledging. How often have developments in the secular world led Christians to recognize God's truth rather than the other way around? What might the society be trying to show the church in our era that the church is too frightened to recognize? Are we willing to encourage our church to accept what God is demonstrating to us in the larger world?

The Baptism Of The Lord
Epiphany 1
Ordinary Time 1

Genesis 1:1-5

> *Then God said, "Let there be light"; and there was light.*
> — Genesis 1:3

If you have ever experienced total darkness, you know how disorienting it can be. We depend on light, even a little light, to give us a sense of direction. In the midst of chaos, God seems to merely speak a word and light splits the darkness. Later, in the gospel of John, the author imitates this hymn by starting his gospel with the words, "In the beginning" and then goes on to speak of the Word of God as the light that "was the light of all people. The light shines in darkness, and the darkness did not overcome it" (John 1:4-5). Again a word split the darkness. There are many people who live in the darkness. They seem to be disoriented, and their lives appear to be utter chaos. There are moments in our own lives when we feel the same way.

In response to moments of chaos in his life, Luther is reported to have repeated over and over to himself, "I am baptized." It reminded him that he was claimed by God and therefore a person of dignity and worth. As you think about the baptism of Jesus in this season, consider how God's claiming you, as God did Jesus at his baptism, makes you worthy to be called a child of God (John 1:12). If by grace you are a child of God, then how does that alter your response to the experiences of darkness in your life? Consider also how such a belief would be a great gift to those who hunger after direction in their own lives. Baptism is an impetus to sharing the good news with others.

Psalm 29

> *Ascribe to the Lord the glory of his name.* — Psalm 29:2a

Psalm 29 could well be a reflection on the doxology, "For thine is the kingdom, the power and the glory." The imagery in the psalm is that of a powerful storm that sweeps over land and water. The thunder (v. 3) and lightning (v. 4) and driving winds (v. 5) evoke a response of awe and humility. Witnessing such a storm reminds one of the awesome power of God that makes the oft-used symbols of power — the cedars of Lebanon (v. 6) and the great oaks (v. 9) — seem like mere playthings. This exhibition of power evokes a response from both the heavenly beings (v. 1) and those in the temple (v. 9). Cry glory. To glorify God is to acknowledge the incomparable contrast between our earthly symbols of power and the reality of God. The storm is but a metaphor that reminds us that we have not begun to probe the dimensions of God's majesty. The flood is a symbol of chaos, yet God sits enthroned over it (v. 10). There are no limits to God's kingdom, power, and glory (v. 10). Recognizing that, all we can do is petition God for strength and peace (v. 11) knowing that in the end our strength and peace come from the one who holds all power, glory, and majesty in his hand.

Pause to reflect on the awesome power of God hat makes all other powers in this world seem like mere playthings.

Acts 19:1-7

Did you receive the Holy Spirit when you became believers?
—Acts 19:2

This question by Paul has taken on a contemporary meaning with the rise of the Pentecostal movement. Many mainline Christians are immediately put on the defensive when someone asks if they have been baptized with the Holy Spirit. This is especially true for those who were baptized as infants and have no memory of the event. It is important to follow the sequence of events in this story. Paul discovered twelve believers in Ephesus and asked them this question. John's baptism, as he made clear, was a baptism of repentance. The baptism of repentance was a moral decision to turn from one way of life and to start off in a new direction. It was necessary preparation in order to "believe in the one who was to come after him, that is, in Jesus" (v. 4).

Yet there is more to the faith than a decision to repent. You must also be open to God's Spirit that can open you to God's renewal in your life. Preparation comes first but then comes surrender to the guidance of the Spirit in your life. The problem with assuming that an ethical decision to change your way of living is sufficient is that it leaves you open to the temptation of self-righteously judging others who have not done what you did. To be baptized in Jesus' name is to receive the Spirit of Christ who came to proclaim God's forgiveness and release people from judgment.

At Pentecost, the believers spoke in tongues that enabled them to overcome the divisions of the world and be reconciled in Jesus' name. It is an appropriate time to ask yourself whether your life is guided by guilt or grace. Judgment separates, but grace reconciles.

Mark 1:4-11

John the baptizer appeared in the wilderness, proclaiming a baptism of repentance for the forgiveness of sins. — Mark 1:4

In the dark moments of our lives, it is easy to grow bitter at the misfortunes that have befallen us. In our pain we become the center of the universe by which all reality is judged. If an event or situation affects us positively, then it is good. If it affects us negatively, then it is bad. Sin is a rebellion against God based on our self-centeredness. Repentance is a turning from such self-centeredness and opening ourselves to the creative Spirit of God. Instead of nurturing our wounds in the darkness, repentance is allowing God's light to illumine our darkness. Repentance is shifting focus from self to God. John was a prophet who preached a baptism of repentance for the forgiveness of sins. Jesus was a man who opened himself to the Spirit of God and therefore allowed God to be the center of his life. When he did so by presenting himself for a baptism of repentance, God responded by saying, "You are my Son, the Beloved; with you I am well pleased" (v. 11).

As you reflect on the baptism of Jesus and recognize the humility of not regarding "... equality with God as something to be exploited, but emptied himself ..." (Philippians 2:6b-7a), consider how it might shape your day if you considered each action in light of God's purpose rather than how it affected you. It is a radical act to shift the center of the universe from your ego to that of God's will.

Epiphany 2
Ordinary Time 2

1 Samuel 3:1-10 (11-20)

Go, lie down; and if he calls you, you shall say, "Speak, Lord, for your servant is listening." — 1 Samuel 3:9b

The call of Samuel and the necessary preparation for his ministry is reflective of the call and nurture of Jesus in preparation for his ministry. At the same time, it illustrates a state of religion that creates a caution for all of us. "The word of the Lord was rare in those days; visions were not widespread" (v. 1). When our community of faith falls into a routine in the practice of our faith, it results in little expectation that God will speak through our lives at all. When that is the condition, even when God does speak, most people, like Samuel and Eli, will fail to recognize it as the voice of God. Samuel assumed it was Eli that was calling him, and Eli assumed it was just the precocious act of a child. Neither was prepared to recognize the call as a divine voice. It is a credit to Eli that once he recognized that it was God speaking, he insisted on hearing the message even when it was a message of judgment.

While it is easy to become cynical about the state of the church and suggest that it is unable to hear God's voice when it is spoken, it is important to recognize that the community of faith is still where God chose to speak. God was persistent in this scripture and spoke on four different occasions, and it was Eli, the keeper of the faith, who finally recognized what was happening. It is a vital question to ask whether God is trying to speak through our church today and no one is listening. It is equally important to recognize that our preparation to hear God speak comes through that same church. Consider what part of the faith you need to examine more deeply so that you might be open to hearing the voice of God.

Psalm 139:1-6, 13-18

O Lord, you have searched me and known me. — Psalm 139:1

Consider the possibility that your life, with all its experiences, has been a continual experience of the presence of God nurturing and guiding you. Reflect back on some of the significant moments in your life and notice the impact of now seeing them as moments when God was nurturing or challenging you. You may recall the story in Genesis 12 where Abram was asked to leave behind all that gave his life security and was familiar to accompany God to a land that God would show him. Abram had to trust that God knew him better than he knew himself and could be trusted to assist him in facing an unfamiliar future.

It is often only upon reflection of our own lives that we can notice that our lives have been a series of "leaving behind that which was familiar" events in order to discover again and again that God is our true companion. How often in your life did you think it was going in one direction only to discover a sharp turn in the road that led you into a totally new experience that only later would you discover to be an urge to be true to the person God wanted you to be? What are the decisions that you are now trying to make in your life? Are you tempted to stick with the familiar and resist exploring new territory? If God is inviting you to leave the familiar behind and go in a new direction, what part of your character is God aware of that now needs to be developed? Can you trust that God will be your faithful companion as you pursue this new direction in your journey?

1 Corinthians 6:12-20

Or do you not know that your body is a temple of the Holy Spirit within you, which you have from God, and that you are not your own? — 1 Corinthians 6:19

Paul uses the vivid image of sexual relations with a prostitute to illustrate a truth that is increasingly foreign to our modern age. The truth is that we are not our own. That is, we are accountable to a reality outside of ourselves. For most people, if they were loaned a very expensive car to drive or invited to wear a very expensive piece of jewelry, while they might be excited, they would also be a little nervous because what they had was not their own. They would likely take extra care that nothing happened that would damage the gift. What would be the effect of taking that same attitude toward your own body? There are some basic truths about taking care of your body. Your body can be damaged by continuous lack of sleep, improper diet, lack of proper exercise, or a regimen of stress that does not recognize the need for a proper rhythm of rest and recreation to be part of your routine.

While there may be some health issues that are still in dispute, these are almost universally accepted. If your body is a precious jewel that is on loan to you by God, are you treating this gift with the proper respect that honors the one who loaned it to you? It is a very practical and concrete issue of the faith that is worthy of more consideration.

John 1:43-51

Nathaniel said to him, "Can anything good come out of Nazareth?" — John 1:46

Because we are reading scripture, Nathaniel's question jars us. Upon reflection, we can recognize that we are accustomed to making initial judgments about people based on their place of origin, residence, family, education, and status in society. It would be natural to assume that the Messiah would come from Jerusalem and be a person of religious prominence. People do not just come out of nowhere but develop in a recognizable fashion; except the Bible keeps bringing people onto the scene without any preamble as to their background. We are never told why Jesus chose who he did as disciples or why God chose Abraham to be the father of his people.

God's mysterious way of making choices in our world forces us to stop and listen to everyone so that we do not overlook the one through whom God is speaking. It is also noteworthy that Philip's response to Nathaniel's question was not to try to convince him through argument but to ask him to "come and see" (v. 46). The Christian faith is rarely conveyed through argument and most powerfully is conveyed through experience. One of the most powerful means of witnessing to the faith is to live a life that reflects the love and grace of Christ and trust that God will enable people to experience Christ through you. Consider how the next person you meet will know Christ through you. What will their impression be? Consider, as well, that you might meet Christ through them.

Epiphany 3
Ordinary Time 3

Jonah 3:1-5, 10

Now the people of Nineveh believed God; they proclaimed a fast, and everyone, great and small, put on sackcloth. — Jonah 3:5

Despite all the programs developed to alter people's behavior, there is still a mystery as to why people suddenly change. The setting for this tale of the infinite expanse of God's grace and mercy is the sudden change of heart among the Ninevites. The tale confronts believers with a challenge to their normal assumptions. Nothing is said about a conversion of the Ninevites that took place. All that is suggested is that the Ninevites believed that God would punish them if they did not repent and therefore they repented. While there is much to be said for faith-based programs to change people's lives, this tale suggests that change might come about in the lives of people who have not decided to join the community of faith. It also suggests that God is responsive to behavioral change and shows mercy to nonbelievers who want to turn their lives around.

While the scripture is clear that we are saved by faith and not by works, there is still a hint that God is responsive to pure behavior. The Ninevites are very pragmatic in their decision. "Who knows? God may relent and change his mind ... so that we do not perish" (v. 9). Are we too quick to demand that people must conform to our way of believing before God will help them? Perhaps God is more complex than that.

Psalm 62:5-12

For God alone my soul waits in silence, for my hope is from him. — Psalm 62:5

In our noisy world, too often we overlook the power of silence. It is almost impossible to find a place in which we can experience absolute silence. If we are to discover the depth of silence, we are going to have to practice coming to silence within ourselves. We are going to have to move beyond words, even words formed in our thought patterns, and reach for God beyond all images, thoughts, and noise. There is a powerful healing that can take place when we set aside all attempts to form words or listen to sounds and simply rest in the mystery that is totally beyond our comprehension. Here, outside of any thought pattern, is the God who is our rock and our refuge. After all the doctrinal disputes are done, all the arguments about ethics have grown stale, and even the worship patterns have grown cold, there is still God who is there for us. This is the God that we can go to in all honesty and vulnerability. "Trust in him at all times, O people; pour out your heart before him; God is a refuge for us" (v. 8). That may be the hardest promise to trust of all.

1 Corinthians 7:29-31

For the present form of this world is passing away. — 1 Corinthians 7:31b

This is a strange set of verses that seem to be based on Paul's assumption that the end of the age is very near. What is about to happen is so critical and contrary to the ordinary that it calls for a whole new response. We get some understanding of this if we think about how we respond to a crisis. Say you had a set of appointments and responsibilities laid out for the day and then suddenly a member of your family was in a serious accident. Immediately what is important and how you order your time is drastically changed. This does not devalue what you originally had planned, and you will likely return to it eventually. But for the moment, there is a different set of priorities.

With the impending coming of Christ, our domestic priorities and our personal feelings no longer dominate, and our commercial and economic activities are viewed from an entirely new perspective. And later, when we do return to those other activities, we view them differently. We recognize that what we may have given top priority before is really of useful but only secondary importance.

In a mild way, you might get some feeling for this by reflecting on what you have been focusing on as vitally important for the past year and then asking yourself, "If I knew that Christ was coming tomorrow, how would I view these concerns differently?" From that perspective, you may get a better sense of what God wants you to consider as of primary importance. The rest can still be enjoyed but must be seen as secondary.

Mark 1:14-20

And Jesus said to them, "Follow me and I will make you fish for people." — Mark 1:17

While we normally read Jesus' calling his disciples as a change in their vocation, there may be a sense that the real change was in the perspective with which they engaged in their vocation. It would be possible to continue to fish after you became a disciple of Jesus, but the purpose of your fishing would be altered. Before, you may have been fishing to see how many fish you could catch and, therefore, how much money you could receive for them. Now the purpose of your fishing is to feed people.

As will be clear as we continue to read about the ministry of Jesus, the focus of the life that he offered was never to secure wealth, security, or status.

It was always about reaching out to others, especially those who may have felt excluded, and healing their wounds. Our vocation or calling might cause us to be engaged in any number of ways to exercise the gifts that we have been given. Yet the true measuring stick is not what we do but how other people are affected by what we do. As we go throughout the day or as we reflect on the accomplishments of our work, are people's lives being enhanced? Are people discovering that they, too, are children of a loving God and therefore of value in the unfolding of God's story in this universe? Jesus' call shapes how we do what we do, and we all discover that we are called to "full-time ministry."

Epiphany 4
Ordinary Time 4

Deuteronomy 18:15-20

The Lord your God will raise up for you a prophet like me from among your own people.... — Deuteronomy 18:15

In this final speech of Moses before the people cross over to the promised land, Moses is addressing a primary anxiety among the people. For two generations Moses has led them. He spoke to them on behalf of God and to God on their behalf, and he makes the critical promise that God will not leave them alone after he is gone.

We use the label of prophet easily in our society to speak of people who challenge our society, particularly in an ethical sense. The Bible, however, had a very specific role in mind for the prophet. A prophet was a person who stood between God and the people and spoke to each on behalf of the other. When speaking to the people, the prophet speaks with the authority of one who has been given the words by God. Because the prophet is speaking God's judgment, the words may be harsh at times, but they are always spoken toward God's ultimate purpose of redemption.

Later, the New Testament would find this promise fulfilled in the person of Jesus who spoke with authority bringing the presence of God to bear on the people's lives and being an advocate to God on behalf of the people. As is evident in our own society, this passage recognizes that there will always be those who presume to bring a prophetic message, but their words will be from their own ego and not words that God has placed in their mouths. The validity of the prophetic message, however disturbing it is to our way of life, is whether it brings the presence of God to bear on how we are living. Since God promises to always raise up a prophet among us, it is important to ask where the prophetic voice is in our lives at this moment.

Psalm 111

Praise the Lord! I will give thanks to the Lord with my whole heart.... — Psalm 111:1

Psalm 111 focuses the praise of God in recalling within the company of believers what God has done (vv. 1-2). Memory and corporate worship become the two legs of praise. It is by recalling what God does in the company of other believers that we are struck with awe at the nature of God (v. 3). God is the one who causes us to remember what God has done that reflects grace and mercy (v. 11). God provides the food, manna, to his people (v. 5) and with great signs and wonders leads them to a promised land (v. 6). God provides them laws that can guide them and that are the mirror image of God's own faithfulness and justice (vv. 7-8).

God's whole relationship with this people is one of redemption because God will not give up on his covenant (v. 9). It is in recalling this constant faithfulness, most clearly visible in that first exodus, that we begin to experience the awe of the Lord that is the beginning of wisdom. As we begin to respond to such faithfulness with our faithfulness, we deepen our understanding of God, which again evokes our praise (v. 10). It is the corporate rehearsing of the nature of God as seen in what God has done that fills our mouths with praise. To reflect on what God has done in your own life to bring you to this moment in time is a good preparation for worship.

1 Corinthians 8:1-13

But take care that this liberty of yours does not somehow become a stumbling block to the weak. — 1 Corinthians 8:9

As a church — the body of Christ — we exist through Christ. Our reason for existence is Christ. "While we still were sinners, Christ died for us" (Romans 5:8). God, through Christ, took note of us in our weakness. Jesus often stepped beyond the boundaries of the community to draw one who had been excluded back into the community of God's love. To know that we are saved through Christ is not the end but the beginning of our journey. Now we are to take note of and be responsive to our neighbor who is weak. Paul uses the example of eating meat that has been sacrificed to idols. It was not the eating of this meat that was wrong but the possibility that a neighbor who is weak in the faith would see us doing so and be tempted to participate in idol worship.

In a contemporary setting, we must ask what we do that might drive people away from the very community that could nurture them in the faith. The church, in an attempt to reach out to those outside the faith, will often stretch the comfort zone of their own members. In doing so, they are assuming that the one who should be most flexible in the faith is not the one who is outside but the one who is already part of the community. Sensitivity to those outside the church would suggest that, while we are free in Christ, we must be careful that the exercise of that freedom does not mislead a person who is still struggling to understand the faith. People will see Christ through what they see the church doing. The question is: Will they be welcomed or discouraged by what they see?

Mark 1:21-28

What have you to do with us, Jesus of Nazareth? — Mark 1:24

It was a shocking, bizarre, disruptive, offensive incident that took place in the midst of our worship in the synagogue. We were listening to a quite wonderful sermon about the nearness of God in our lives when we heard it. This man suddenly stood up and screamed, "That is a bunch of bull. I have people clawing at me all day long like a pack of wild dogs, demanding this, asking that, until my head is about to explode. I can't stand it anymore. You come here talking about the nearness of God. I say bull. God isn't near. The demons are in control. Get out of here, Jesus of Nazareth. Your holiness is useless. Leave me alone. I don't want your holiness crap."

He was crazy, of course, but as I looked around at your faces, as I felt deep in my heart, I could hear the silent scream of many of us joining like a chorus. "What have you to do with us, Jesus of Nazareth? We know who you are, the holy one of God, but what has that to do with us?" There are days when we want to scream as well. It is as if the pressures of life have crowded out any possibility of hearing the holy in our lives.

That day, Jesus listened unafraid to the demons that screamed from deep within that man. Then he spoke with a quiet intensity that I had never heard before. "Be quiet, come out of him," and the man was suddenly convulsed on the floor as the demons spewed forth. Then he was calm as if his life had been cleansed of all the horror that had possessed him. I want to hear that voice again speaking to me, quieting the demons in me. Yet, I am afraid. I don't want to be convulsed. I want to experience that deep peace that wards off the pressures, but I am afraid of the holy. What is this voice of Christ? What is this authority that can command the evil spirits, and they will obey? I see the craziness around me, and I am afraid; but I am also afraid of this Jesus.

Epiphany 5
Ordinary Time 5

Isaiah 40:21-31

> *... those who wait upon the Lord shall renew their strength, they shall mount up with wings like eagles, they shall run and not be weary, they shall walk and not faint.* — Isaiah 40:31

The prophet speaks to the people who are living in exile and accuses them of myopia. They are so nearsighted that they cannot see that God is really in charge. The prophet's words are like a hymn to the transcendent majesty of God who is so far above the earth that the inhabitants are like grasshoppers and their rulers are nothing. This is the God who "stretches out the heavens like a curtain" and "brings out their host and numbers them, calling them all by name ..." (vv. 22, 26). The prophet was challenging the people to believe, despite all the evidence, that God was the only real authority that they needed to obey and that they could trust this God to bring them home from exile.

Given the fact that the nation had been completely destroyed, the temple torn down, and the people carried off and transplanted in foreign lands at the whim of the emperor, it was a hard truth to believe. Often we are overwhelmed by the immediate circumstances and join the Israelites in saying, "my way is hidden from the Lord, and my right is disregarded by my God" (v. 27). We can grow weary in our efforts to be faithful and in our attempts to witness to the justice and mercy of God. At such times we need to hear the prophet's call to "wait for the Lord" who "shall renew (our) strength." We are not alone in our efforts, and the transcendent God will be faithful.

Psalm 147:1-11, 20c

> *But the Lord takes pleasure in those who fear him, in those who hope in this steadfast love.* — Psalm 147:11

59

Psalm 147 is a prayer of praise that seems to oscillate between the human and the cosmic. As is befitting full praise, which includes physical acts and emotional expression as well as words, we are urged to sing our praise (v. 1). We are reminded that God's work on behalf of the needy (vv. 2-3) is the same power that orders the cosmos (vv. 4-5). It is this all-powerful God who enters the battle between the oppressed and the oppressor (v. 6). We are urged to express our thanksgiving musically (v. 7) to God who feeds the earth with water (v. 8) and animals their food (v. 9). Such a God is not impressed with demonstrations of power (v. 10) but does respond to those who trust in God's love (v. 11). Those whom God has gathered as a witness should praise him (v. 12) because this God protects them outside and inside (v. 13) and provides peace and provisions (v. 14).

By God's command the earth also receives its peace and provisions (vv. 15-18). This cosmic God who cares for the entire universe is the same God who has instructed Israel about what God wants. All other nations in the world depend upon Israel to declare what God has revealed. Even Christians must remember that God revealed the divine will through the Jewish people and a Jewish person (v. 20). We are to praise this God and no other.

Far too often in the contemporary Christian community, we have reduced praise to thanksgiving, and the focus of our worship is on our own response and not the God whom we worship. The psalmist offers us a strong reminder that the focus of our worship is the praise of God.

1 Corinthians 9:16-23

I have become all things to all people, that I might by all means save some. — 1 Corinthians 9:22b

Paul, having described his own freedom, speaks of voluntarily limiting his freedom in order to accommodate himself to the needs of the particular group before him. It is an instructive passage in light of the variety of strategies that many in the Christian community have adopted to reach out to the various groups within our society. How far should we go in accommodating our message to the various segments of our society? Paul's accommodations could have resulted in his violating certain behavior that others would have seen as essential to the faith. In recent years, styles of worship have been the source of great controversy as the church reaches out to the unchurched. Other controversies have been raised over the ability of the church to accommodate various sexual ethics. Still other debates have centered around the church's voice in societal issues.

Can the church be so well grounded in Christ that it has the freedom to accept the variety of accommodations made on behalf of Christ so that more will be reached by the faith? Where are the lines that you have drawn beyond which the church should not go in reaching out to others? When do those lines become small idols that have replaced the freedom of Christ?

Mark 1:29-39

He came and took her by the hand and lifted her up. Then the fever left her, and she began to serve them. — Mark 1:31

This little incident with respect to Peter's mother-in-law is packed with meaning. Women had very little means of supporting themselves apart from their relationship with their family. When two people were married, the woman left her home and joined the man's home. It was the relatives of the man's family who would have responsibility to support her if anything happened to her husband. So why was the mother of Peter's wife living with them? It would seem as if her husband must be dead and there were no relatives who would be willing to accept the responsibility. Not only was she living with them, but also she was ill and, therefore, increasing the burden on the family. Jesus, by healing her, not only released her from the illness but also restored her sense of dignity. Now she, too, was free to bring her talents to bear on serving the needs of those within the community.

In doing so, Jesus broke with the narrow definition of family and testified to the expanded definition of family within the new community of faith. Later, he would declare "whoever does the will of God is my brother and sister and mother" (Mark 3:35). Christian family values were not the values of the nuclear family or even the bloodline but were the values that mandate that we care for all members of the community of faith as members of our God-given family.

Epiphany 6
Ordinary Time 6

2 Kings 5:1-14

If the prophet had demanded of you that you do something difficult, would you not have done it? — 2 Kings 5:3b

We live in a world in which we insist on the dramatic and the extraordinary. It creates a situation in which we often overlook the miraculous in the ordinary. Perhaps it is reflective of our ego that we assume that our problems can only be resolved in dramatic fashion. This intriguing little story of the healing of Naaman challenges these preconceptions. When Naaman wanted to be healed, even though a lowly servant girl told him that it was the prophet that would heal him, he went to the king. Important people only deal with important people. When he was finally convinced to go to the prophet, he assumed that the prophet would do something dramatic in executing his healing. And he certainly assumed that his prominence was worthy of a personal audience with the prophet and perhaps participation in some mysterious incantations. He was furious when a mere servant of the prophet gave him the message to simply go and wash in a nearby river.

Again, it was a servant who understood the truth of the message and reasoned with him that he should follow the prophet's instructions. In a world that creates a hierarchy of what and who is important, we are confronted with the fact that God works through the ordinary and speaks through the "least of these" the healing message of God. For Christians this is boldly exemplified each time we take ordinary bread and wine and recognize that through these ordinary basics of life we are directed to the extraordinary truth of God's love for us.

Psalm 30

You have turned my mourning into dancing; you have taken off my sackcloth and clothed me with joy.... — Psalm 30:11

Psalm 30 can be reflected on in the context of Peter's denial. You can imagine Peter, having denied his Lord three times, rushing out into the night weeping, and later finding himself reconciled to his risen Lord, praying this prayer: "I will extol you, O Lord, for those you have drawn me up." He knows that his enemies did not finally triumph (v. 1). His weeping at his own betrayal became a cry to God for help that was heard (v. 2). The betrayal which left him in the despair of death had been broken (v. 3), and he was ready to witness to his own salvation among the saints (v. 4). He knew for certain that the anger of God was a judgment for salvation (v. 5). He knew that he had once bragged of his ability to stick by Jesus no matter what (v. 6) and only later realized that his courage was also a gift of God (v. 7). Yet even in despair, he discovered God had not abandoned him (v. 8), and Peter chose life rescued by forgiveness rather than some abstract of judgment that could only result in death (v. 9).

Therefore, for Peter, his Lord was also his helper (v. 10). Out of Peter's experience of denial and reconciliation, he could pray, "thou hast turned for me my mourning into dancing. Thou hast loosed my sackcloth and girded me with gladness" (v. 2). The result was that his life had been released for praise (v. 12). Peter's prayer becomes our prayer when we become overwhelmed by our own betrayal and wonder at the forgiving grace of God. For those who are captured by their own sense of guilt, it is worth asking whether their sins could be any worse than the total denial of Jesus at the time of his need. If God can forgive Peter and make him a leader in the church, then what is possible for any of us?

1 Corinthians 9:24-27

Athletes exercise self-control in all things; they do it to receive a perishable wreath, but we an imperishable one.
— 1 Corinthians 9:25

It is such a simple image, and one with which anyone who follows sports can identify. Who has not watched an Olympic athlete and wondered at the dedication that could produce such superb results? If someone should say to us that he or she wants to win an Olympic gold medal but that they do not want to practice or train, we would call them utterly foolish. Now Paul turns this simple image on us and our practice of the faith. Compare the medal or ribbon that an athlete will train so hard for to the goal of the Christian faith.

How many Christians want the easy path to faith, which may include an emotional conversion experience? They resist, however, the need to train themselves in the faith through the practice of a strong discipline of prayer, worship, scriptural study, and works of compassion. When we compare our society's insistence on immediate answers and easy rewards with the dedication of an athlete who will train for years with the dream of the Olympic medal, we are stunned by the dedication displayed. What are the disciplines of faith that could cultivate the ground in which God's gift of faith could grow in your life? If you had faith so as to move mountains, would that be a worthy pursuit?

Mark 1:40-45

See that you say nothing to anyone but go show yourself to the priest. — Mark 1:44a

Moved with pity, Jesus cleansed the leper and then warned him not to say anything to anyone but to go directly to the priests and make a testimony to them. It is a strange moment in which Jesus' healing touch is responded to by the man's refusal to keep quiet. Jesus was apparently trying to avoid the pressures of a spreading fame by restricting displays of healing. Yet he was so moved by the leper's condition that he went against his own desires and healed him. The very thing that Jesus did not want began to happen. Why would Jesus warn him to say nothing about this miraculous cleansing? Was the leper, in going out and proclaiming it freely, making a show of his healing? There would be many who had not experienced healing. By proclaiming his healing, was he trying to make himself special as if God had particularly favored him above others?

Can our testimony of what God has done in our lives become our own ego-trip that only seemingly gives credit to God? Jesus told the leper to go show himself to the priest and make a specified offering to God. By quietly following the ritual of thanksgiving, he was thanking God but not making himself the center of attention. When does our witness draw too much attention to ourselves and thereby distort the truth of God working in us? Can a church or an individual be too showy in their faith and thereby hinder the work of Christ?

Epiphany 7
Ordinary Time 7

Isaiah 43:18-25

I, I am he who blots out your transgressions for my own sake, and I will not remember your sins. — Isaiah 43:25

As second Isaiah speaks to the people living in exile, they are confronted with two equally unpalatable conclusions. Either their God was incapable of defending this chosen people in the face of the onslaught of pagan outsiders or God was allowing them to suffer exile as punishment for their sinful behavior. If it was the former, then, in contemporary terms, secularism is victorious and victory belongs to the powerful. On the other hand, if God was still in charge, as all the prophets declared, then God must have finally given up hope of redeeming them and left them to suffer the consequences of their sins. In either case, they had little reason to have hope for the future.

In the face of this, God declared through the prophet, "Do not remember the former things, or consider the things of old. I am about to do a new thing ..." (vv. 18-19). The sins of previous generations, or even their own sins, did not determine their fate. God, not their behavior, was what shaped the future. Once before, when they were hopeless, powerless slaves in Egypt, God effected a miracle that opened up for them an entirely new possibility. God was about to bring about a new exodus. Why was God going to do this? It was certainly not because they had earned God's favor through their good behavior. God would blot out their transgressions and remember their sins no more because that is who God is. God's nature is one who redeems. Here in Isaiah, we hear this powerful gospel that we are saved by grace not by works so that no one can boast (Ephesians 2:8-9).

Psalm 41

> *Happy are those who consider the poor; the Lord delivers them in the day of trouble.* — Psalm 41:1

Psalm 41 contrasts the one who is compassionate toward a needy person with those who take advantage of a person in need. The person is blessed, protected, and sustained who is considerate of the poor (vv. 1-3). A person who is needy, even though he has sinned against God (v. 4), has a right to appeal to God for help against those who wish him ill (v. 5). The enemy may well be one who pretends to be a friend and visits him in time of need (v. 6), yet grows impatient with his neediness (vv. 7-8), and yearns for this claim of friendship to be over (v. 9). At such times, our only source of help is God (v. 10).

Our faith is reaffirmed by the very fact that such betrayal does not triumph over us and utterly destroy us (v. 11), and our integrity as an individual is reaffirmed because, unlike a fickle friend, we are able to count on the eternal presence of God (v. 12). The reason why one is blessed who is considerate of the poor or weak (v. 1) is now made clear. In her compassion, she reflects the image of God who is present in times of need (v. 12). Thus, even as we pray *deliver us from evil*, we are commanded to deliver from evil by being steadfast to others in their time of need.

2 Corinthians 1:18-22

> *For the Son of God, Jesus Christ, whom we proclaimed among you ... in him it is always "Yes."* — 2 Corinthians 1:19

Paul is responding to criticism of his ministry. Some said that you could not depend on Paul because he was always responding to whatever situation in which he found himself and therefore was not always consistent. Scholars have long held that the letters of Paul must be understood in light of the particular church or situation that he is addressing. Paul, they suggest, is not making universal pronouncements for everyone everywhere but rather seeking to apply the gospel to specific situations. "I became all things to all people ..." (1 Corinthians 9:22).

Pastors often find themselves adapting the faith to fit the particular pastoral situation, which at times may make them appear inconsistent. Paul's defense is that he is applying Christ to each situation and that Christ is God's "Yes," which is consistently applied to the redemption of humanity. While, on the surface, it may appear that Paul's behavior bends with the wind of circumstances, the underlying core of his actions is determined by the way in which God fulfills his promise to humanity through Christ. What appears to be abrupt changes in decisions find their consistency in the overall reconciling ministry of Christ that clearly demonstrates God's affirmation of humanity. When you need to make a decision, ask yourself what the action is that most clearly demonstrates God's reconciling love and affirmation of humanity? (2 Corinthians 5:18-20).

Mark 2:1-12

And when Jesus saw their faith, he said to the paralytic, "My son, your sins are forgiven." — Mark 2:5

There are two striking things about this sentence. First, it was on the basis of the faith of his friends, not that of the paralytic, that Jesus acted. Our faith has an effect on our neighbor. The Christian faith does not suggest that each of us stands alone before God. Rather we stand together before God. We are not even told whether the paralytic had any faith. When my faith is weak, I can lean on my neighbor's faith, and I have the privilege of offering my faith on behalf of my neighbor. The second thing that stands out is that Jesus offers forgiveness of sins rather than physical healing. We might think that Jesus had the order backward. The friends brought him because he was physically paralyzed. But Jesus' response was based on a deeper reality.

Sin is what separates us from God and neighbor. If we are in deep communion with God and neighbor, even a physical disability can be redemptive, but if our lives are lived in a state of alienation, even perfect health is not enough. All through life, we have to learn to live with physical limitations, but our redemption is discovering that such conditions do not separate us from God or neighbor.

Epiphany 8
Ordinary Time 8
Proper 3

Hosea 2:14-20

Therefore, I will now allure her, and bring her into the wilderness, and speak tenderly to her. — Hosea 2:14

Whether it be in war-torn and continually threatened Judah or the fractured and divided Christian church, there is a longing for a renewed intimacy with God in which the promises of faith will be fulfilled. Hosea speaks of the step toward that promise being a withdrawal to the wilderness where God can once again speak tenderly to the people's hearts. The imagery is one of courtship leading to the intimacy of marriage. This is not a hierarchical marriage where the wife is subservient but a marriage of intimacy and equality. "On that day, says the Lord, you will call me, 'My husband,' and no longer will you call me, 'My Baal' " (v. 16), which means "my master."

Later Jesus would speak of this same transition of relationship (John 15:15). There will be an ecological peace with nature and a political peace with neighbor (v. 18) and a new intimacy with God. "I will take you for my wife in faithfulness; and you shall know the Lord" (v. 20). It may be instructive for all Christians who yearn for that day to recognize that the peace for which we long begins by a withdrawal from the daily battles and a renewed courtship with God. While God takes the initiative, we still are responsible for responding to the invitation to come aside into the wilderness. It is possible that the noise of our lives is shutting God out and causing us to overlook what God invites us to recognize.

Psalm 103:1-13, 22

Bless the Lord, O my soul, and all that is within me, bless his holy name. — Psalm 103:1

Psalm 103 is a call to praise based on God's faithfulness to forgive, heal, redeem, and benefit you with a constant love and mercy (vv. 1-5). The focus of the psalm is on how God redeems us from our own condition. Because of what God did through Moses for the people of Israel, we know God works to save the oppressed (vv. 6-7). God's very character is revealed as one slow to anger and abounding in steadfast love (v. 8). By God's patience with Israel as he redeemed them in the wilderness, we know how God responds to our transgressions and understands our limitations (vv. 9-11).

The entire psalm calls us to an act of memory. The reason why we continually read scripture in worship and recall the stories of Israel and the acts of God through Jesus' life is to provide us a language of remembrance so that we can recognize God's redemptive activity in our own lives. We are called to recall how God has acted in the past and use that memory to reinforce our trust in the faithfulness of God to redeem us in our present condition. God's sovereignty is reflected in how even God's response to our sins demonstrates God's purpose (v. 22).

2 Corinthians 3:1-6

> *You yourselves are our letter, written on our hearts, to be known and read by all; and you show that you are a letter of Christ, prepared by us.* — 2 Corinthians 3:2-3a

It was customary for people visiting a new community to bring a letter of recommendation from a trusted figure in another community in order to establish the visitor's credentials. Paul suggests that the Christian community is his letter of recommendation. Further, he claims that the Christian community is a "letter of Christ." It is humbling to suggest that a minister's reputation rests on the congregation with which he or she works and further that the reputation of Christ rests upon how they represent Christ through their lives.

Yet, whether we like it or not, is that not the way that the outer world reads us? When a minister is considering another call, what the inquiring church wants to know is what happened in the previous church. When a nonbeliever is considering the possibility of accepting Christ, is it not the impact of the faith on the people's lives in the inviting congregation that has the major impact? Paul is quick to state that the real result is not based on his skills but on the power of God working through him (vv. 5-6). He trusts that the Spirit of God is working through him and through the Corinthian church to send the message of Christ to others. If what Paul says is true for our churches as well, it may be that we need to expend more energy in recognizing the way that Christ is at work among us. If, according to Paul, the letter is written, then our task may be to read what is written of Christ in our own congregation.

Mark 2:13-22

As he was walking along, he saw Levi son of Alphaeus sitting at the tax booth, and he said to him, "Follow me." And he got up and followed him. — Mark 2:14

The gospels are frustratingly sparse in their details with respect to the call of the twelve disciples. We get almost no back-ground on them in order to know why Jesus called them. They seem to respond instantly, and we never know why. In Levi's case, what background we are given would seem to suggest that he was an unlikely candidate. As a tax collector, he would have been considered a traitor to his people. His work was on behalf of the Romans, and his income was normally considered to be from charging an additional sum to the tax that the Romans required. Jesus calls this unlikely candidate, and he, in turn, gives up a lucrative career in order to follow an itinerant preacher.

The mystery of faith is like that. How can you explain why certain very good people are never attracted to the faith or why others will suddenly make dramatic shifts in their life and become very active Christians? What is it that happened in your life that caused you to respond as you did? Sometimes when we continue in our journey of faith, we forget how much of a gift we have been given and begin to assume that somehow it was all due to our morally superior willpower. Since the call is not just a one-time event but can be reshaped by the further working of the Spirit in our lives, it is worth reflecting on the dramatic change in Levi's life. All the evidence would suggest that Levi was not the type of person to expect God's call, but the Spirit of God evoked in him a completely unexpected response. What might the Spirit be doing in your life at this time?

Epiphany 9
Ordinary Time 9
Proper 4

Deuteronomy 5:12-15

Observe the sabbath day and keep it holy, as the Lord your God commanded you. — Deuteronomy 5:12

It is interesting to note that the sabbath commandment requires more explanation than any of the other commandments and that it is the only one to receive different explanations in the giving of the commandment in Exodus 20 and here in Deuteronomy 5. In Exodus, the reason for the commandment is based on the creation story. This suggests that the reason for the commandment is that this rhythm of life was built into the very structure of the universe. Living creatures, including livestock, were not meant to work continuously but by their very nature require a rhythm of rest and work. In the Deuteronomy passage, the reason given for the sabbath is based on God's act of freeing them from slavery in Egypt. Here it may be interpreted that the sabbath was meant to enable people to preserve their freedom. God commands us to step back from incessant productivity in order to reflect on who we are and to pay attention to our relationships with God and each other. Failure to do that will result in our becoming slaves and losing our full humanity. The sabbath commandment deserves further reflection in light of the pressures of our current society. It may again be the gift of God that protects our humanity and freedom.

Psalm 81:1-10

Sing aloud to God our strength; shout for joy to the God of Jacob. — Psalm 81:1

Psalm 81 is a call to praise by the entire worshiping community. The people are called to shout (v. 1), the Levites to use their instruments (v. 2), and the priests to blow the shofar to begin the celebration (v. 3).

Such worship constitutes the identity of Israel (v. 4) from the time that God revealed himself to Joseph's ancestors who were slaves in Egypt (v. 5a). God had not been revealed as a "saving" God until he began to rescue the Hebrews through the plagues in Egypt (v. 5b). God lifted the burden of oppression (v. 6) in response to their cry for help (v. 7a), even though they doubted God's ability to save when they were thirsty in the wilderness (v. 7b). Worship is Israel's opportunity to listen to the God who has claimed them (v. 8). It is in worship that they (we) are confronted with the tendency to bow down to other gods (v. 9) and forget that our existence depends on none other but God (v. 10).

Worship becomes the context in which we reaffirm our central identity. It is when we reaffirm our allegiance to God who has called us forth as a people (vv. 1-4). We do that in worship by remembering how God has revealed God's self to us by responding to our cry for help in the past (vv. 5-7a). We also remember how God stayed with us even when we resisted God (v. 7b). It is in worship that we hear God appealing to us afresh (v. 8) and reminding us of the misplaced priorities that have become gods for us (v. 9). In remembering how God has been faithful in the past, we are encouraged to again trust him for our future (v. 10). Without regular worship, which remembers us with God and each other, we quickly forget and succumb to a world that resists God.

2 Corinthians 4:5-12

But we have this treasure in clay jars, so that it may be made clear that this extraordinary power belongs to God and does not come from us. — 2 Corinthians 4:7

It is easy to become discouraged by the frailty of the church and its failure to exemplify the very gospel that it proclaims. It is important to recognize that this is not a recent issue but one that has been part of the faith community from the beginning. From Abraham to the disciples and the early church, there is ample evidence of the failure of the community of faith to live out their faith. Paul is fully aware of that and describes many of the weaknesses in his letters to the Corinthians. Has God failed again in creating a church that shows no more ability than previous communities had to be faithful to God? Paul believes that there is a message of hope in this very reality.

The church is like a clay jar whose flaws are clearly visible precisely so that as the grace of God is made visible in our lives we will be fully aware that it is not our accomplishment but God's. The temptation to self-righteousness is especially strong among religious peoples. Most of the bloodiest wars have had a religious impulse behind them. The recent deluge of "how to create a growing church" books reflects the temptation to believe that success in churches is a matter of technique rather than God's work. Paul's response suggests a more realistic view of the church as like a clay jar whose imperfections are obvious. When you begin with that viewpoint, you are more open to the amazing things that God is doing among us and less tempted to think that we have achieved a formula for success.

Mark 2:23—3:6

Look, why are they doing what is not lawful on the sabbath?
— Mark 2:24b

The sabbath commandment has proved to be one of the most perplexing commandments of the faith. In Jesus' day the controversy was over whether he or his disciples had acted in a way that violated the sabbath. There were many areas of life over which the Jewish people had little control, and there were many temptations for them to abandon the faith and blend in with the larger world. Yet throughout the exile and during the time of their occupation, each week they stepped aside from the demands of living and reconnected with the divine through their worship. Once a week, despite all that had happened during the week, they experienced again who they were as a people of God. Some believe that their identity throughout their history rested more on the sabbath than any other reality in their lives.

Ironically, in our time, the opposite challenge has arisen. In the West, the culture around us once supported our faith by providing time for a sabbath; now that passive support has been removed from us, and that time is challenged by many competing activities. Christians, in the meantime, have grown lax about their practice of the sabbath, and the result is that for many they have lost their sense of identity. Jesus' famous saying, "The sabbath was made for humankind, and not humankind for the sabbath" (v. 27), has often been used to liberate people's conscience from oppressive legalisms with respect to the sabbath. Today, however, we may need to remember again that the sabbath was established in order to protect our humanity and that its neglect may cost us both our connection with the divine and our own freedom as humans.

The Transfiguration Of Our Lord
(Last Sunday After Epiphany)

2 Kings 2:1-12

Please let me inherit a double share of your spirit. — 2
Kings 2:9b

As we approach the Sunday when we reflect on the transfiguration
of Jesus, we read about the ascension of Elijah, who later would be
one of the figures who would consult with Jesus on the mountaintop at
the time of Jesus' transfiguration. Elijah was one of two people in the
Hebrew scriptures who did not die. (The other was Enoch in Genesis
5:24.) Because scripture reported that Elijah did not die, the tradition
developed that Elijah would return to prepare the way for the coming
of God's Messiah. Therefore we have the debate in the gospels as to
whether John the Baptist was Elijah returned.

At the time that Elijah was about to be taken up in the chariot
of fire, his protégé, Elisha, asked that he might receive double the
share of Elijah's spirit. The story will have a haunting echo for Jesus'
disciples because, unlike Elisha, the disciples will abandon Jesus as
he goes on his final journey. Yet Elijah's response will also play an
important role in Jesus' disciples' journey. Elijah says, "If you see me
as I am being taken from you, it will be granted to you; if not, it will
not" (v. 19). In the story of the transfiguration, there is evidence that
the three disciples that accompany Jesus wish to stay close to him,
as did Elisha with Elijah. Yet later they will abandon him at a critical
stage of his crucifixion. It is only later, at his ascension (Acts 1:8), that
the disciples will see Jesus' departure and receive the promise of the
Holy Spirit.

In both stories, the reception of the Spirit is less dependent on the
one who will receive it than it is on God. God determines if and when
we will receive the Spirit that enables us to do God's bidding. We are
not in charge. We can only wait and trust in the wisdom of God.

Psalm 50:1-6

Out of Zion, the perfection of beauty, God shines forth. —
Psalm 50:2

This portion of Psalm 50 reminds us that the presence of God is an awesome experience. Like God's presence on Mount Sinai (Exodus 19:16-19) and later at the transfiguration, God's coming is accompanied by signs that time cannot be visited by eternity without clear signals that the natural has been disrupted. "Our God comes and does not keep silence, before him is a devouring fire, and a mighty tempest all around him" (v. 3). When faith is considered a natural routine that fits comfortably into the other events of our life, we are not prepared for God's presence in our life. To pray that God might be present to us is to pray that our life might be disrupted in a life-changing experience. The psalmist also reminds us that God's coming is more than a personal event. When God speaks, God "summons the earth from the rising of the sun to its setting" (v. 1). Faith experiences of the divine that remain private events are experiences of a God that is far too small. When God, who is timeless, reaches into time to express a divine word, "the heavens declare his righteousness, for God himself is judge" (v. 6). This portion of the psalm is a call to worship. As we prepare ourselves to worship the eternal God, our world is measured against "the perfection of beauty," and we all must stand in awe. Allow yourself to be bathed in the awe of God and be humbled.

2 Corinthians 4:3-6

For it is the God who said, "Let light shine out of darkness," who has shone in our hearts to give the light of the knowledge of the glory of God in the face of Jesus Christ. — 2 Corinthians 4:6

Paul suggests "... the god of this world has blinded the minds of the unbelievers, to keep them from seeing the light of the gospel of the glory of Christ, who is the image of God" (v. 4). There is an echo in this statement of the Genesis statement that we were created in the "image of God" (Genesis 1:27). In that sense, Jesus is what we should have been. The image of God in each of us has been defaced because

76

we have been blinded by the god of this world. It is not hard to identify the various manifestations of the worldly loyalties that "blind" us to what in Christ we could be. Our own transfiguration, in which we can once more shine forth in the beauty that God originally intended for us, can only take place as we submit ourselves like "slaves for Jesus' sake" (v. 5).

The very idea of submitting ourselves to anyone is contrary to our prideful independence. Yet the irony of faith is that we are asked to risk our independence by submitting ourselves like a slave to the very one who has chosen to be our slave. "The light of the knowledge of the glory of God (is seen) in the face of Jesus Christ." Such an approach may give fresh meaning to that much distorted passage in Ephesians 5:21-33 where husbands and wives are asked to enter into a mutual submission in the same way as we do to the Lord who has committed himself totally to us.

Mark 9:2-9

And he was transfigured before them, and his clothes became dazzling white, such as no one on earth could bleach them. — Mark 9:2b-3

This is a story rich with symbolism that deepens our understanding. It begins with the phrase, "six days later." Is this simply chronology or is there an echo of the creation story and a suggestion that we are marking a sabbath that both brings to an end and indicates the beginning of a new creation? The disciples are led "up a high mountain apart" (v. 2). It is common to believe that you can experience closeness to God on a high mountain that is apart from the bustle of civilization. The presence of God is marked by a transformation that cannot be explained by earthly events. "And his clothes became dazzling white, such as no one on earth could bleach them." White also speaks of a purity that cannot be equaled. The confirmation of this revelation is made manifest by the presence of the two premier figures through which God has spoken. There is Moses, the bearer of the law, and Elijah, symbolizing all the prophets who recalled people to obedience.

Peter, representing all disciples, speaks out of the terror that anyone would experience in the presence of the holy. Most interpreters suggest that he wanted to freeze the experience by making three booths there on top of the mountain. If that is correct, it is certainly a warning to those who cling to a profound religious experience and seem never to be able to move beyond repeating the story over and over again. God is not dissuaded by their terror but overshadows them with a cloud. The message is clear: " 'This is my Son, the Beloved, listen to him!' Suddenly when they looked around, they saw no one with them anymore, but only Jesus" (vv. 7-8).

The entire interpretation of God's revelation from law to prophecy was now seen in Jesus. The response expected was not to stay frozen in terror but to listen to the one who has overcome our fears and opens for us the manifestation of God in our lives. We are invited to be part of God's new creation.

Lent 1

Genesis 9:8-17

This is the sign of the covenant that I make between me and you and every living creature that is with you, for all generations. — Genesis 9:12

It is a rainbow coalition that we experience on earth. There is no race or individual that does not belong to God's covenant. This is not a colorblind society, but a society that is rich in its diversity and together creates the beauty that reminds us of God's love for us. It is a peculiar thing about rainbows. They are created by the combination of the sunlight shining through the prism of a raindrop that releases an array of colors. Too much sunlight and we die. Too much water and we die. Life is only possible through a combination, either part of which by itself means our death, but together not only allows life but also releases the full, diverse beauty of life. God makes a promise to preserve that balance. The covenant is not a dependent promise. Even though God makes demands upon humans to make life sacred, God's keeping of the covenant to prevent the destruction of the world is not dependent on human obedience.

Despite our continual rebellion, the hand of God has held us back and provided us the opportunity to discover the fullness of life. As was established in the story of Adam and Eve and is so in this story of second birth, we are reminded that we are all of one stock and equally covenanted with God. Also, we are reminded that God's love extends to the creatures of the earth that God also preserves. If we disdain a creature or a human, we disdain God who is bound to us all.

Psalm 25:1-10

Do not remember the sins of my youth or my transgressions; according to your steadfast love remember me, for your goodness' sake, O Lord! — Psalm 25:7

While arrogance and pride are certainly a destructive feature of humanity, guilt is an equally paralyzing characteristic for many humans. While we can casually say that we are saved by grace and not by works, we still have a hard time understanding why God would want to forgive us. Many people, while theoretically believing in the forgiveness of God, harbor the dark conviction that their sins are too great to have been forgiven. The sad part of such a conclusion is that it is a judgment on the limitations of God rather than the depth of human sin.

In Psalm 25, the psalmist prays to overcome such limitations. "O my God, in you I trust; do not let me be put to shame" (v. 2). His dependence is on God, not on his own goodness. He pleads with God to "Lead me in your truth, and teach me, for you are the God of my salvation; for you I wait all day long" (v. 5). Then the psalmist makes an astounding case for God's forgiveness. It is not based on the sinner's efforts nor is it based on some offsetting series of good qualities. Rather, he calls on God to remember who God is. "Be mindful of your mercy, O Lord, and of your steadfast love ..." (v. 6). He then urges God to shift focus from the transgressions of his psalmist to the steadfast love.

The reason that God forgives us is not because of our efforts or any mitigating circumstances that explain our errors. The reason that God is urged to forgive us is because it is consistent with his goodness. In redeeming the sinner, it is God, not the sinner, who is honored. As we enter the season of Lent, it is important to remember the character of the church. When Peter is named the rock upon which the church is built, the foundation is not Peter's goodness but his trust that it is in the goodness of the Lord that he has found the source of God's redemption.

1 Peter 3:18-22

For Christ also suffered for sins once for all, the righteous for the unrighteous, in order to bring you to God. — 1 Peter 3:18a

Historically, Lent has been a season of reflecting on the suffering of Christ, which was entered into symbolically through one's own season of sacrifice. This passage from 1 Peter makes the helpful reminder that the value of the sacrifice was that it was the sacrifice for the sake of others. This is not an invitation to suffering for suffering's sake. The value of Christ's sacrifice was that it was for the sake of others. Therefore, our imitation of Christ would be better represented in Lent through making a significant sacrifice for the betterment of someone else.

It is also important to note that in Christ's sacrifice, it was "the righteous for the unrighteous." Too often people are only willing to make an effort on behalf of the needy that are deserving. Yet Christ's example is precisely being willing to suffer for the undeserving. If you sacrifice for someone who has demonstrated by his or her efforts that they deserve a helping hand, then the message is that they have earned what you offer. If you offer help to someone who has not demonstrated worthiness, then you have demonstrated God's love. Jesus did this in order to put the focus on God rather than either the giver or the one who receives. How might you reach out to someone and demonstrate the love of God during this Lenten season?

Mark 1:9-15

And the Spirit immediately drove him out into the wilderness. He was in the wilderness forty days, tempted by Satan. — Mark 1:12-13a

This is the moment of divine affirmation. Jesus is baptized by John in the Jordan, and in that moment God pronounces his affirmation. Mark is spare in telling the story of the gospel. We have none of the birth stories or early childhood events. There is an urgency to Mark's narrative that the gospel must be proclaimed. From Mark's story, we know nothing about where Jesus came from or even who he was. The only thing that is important is that God had prepared the way through John, and now God confirms that this is indeed his beloved Son.

Having received that affirmation, Jesus must begin his ministry immediately — well, not quite immediately. Notice that this temptation in the wilderness is not a delay in the ministry but an integral part of Jesus' preparation for ministry. It is the Spirit, not the devil, which drives Jesus into the wilderness to be tempted. To receive God's call to ministry is critical to our life's journey. The danger of such a call is that we assume that what we do in response to the call is godly work. History is replete with examples of people who have used their call to ministry in destructive manners.

To experience God calling you is a heady experience that can easily lead to arrogance. While Mark does not describe the specific temptations, as Matthew and Luke do, he makes clear that responding to God's call in your life begins a struggle "with the wild beasts" and requires us to seek the counsel of "the angels" (v. 13). Lent is a good time to reflect on our vocation or calling by God and to wrestle with where we have allowed our own ego to distort our response.

Lent 2

Genesis 17:1-7, 15-16

You shall be the ancestor of a multitude of nations. —
Genesis 17:4b

It was an incredible promise to a man who was almost 100 years old and to his wife who, at ninety years of age, had yet to bear a child. Abram had heard God before in his life, but each time was like the beginning of a new chapter. When does our life begin? Is it each time we feel like we have reached a dead end and then we hear a call to a new beginning? A major barrier for many is the ability to trust God in the face of a hopeless situation. When all common sense invites you to despair, to trust God at such times seems absurd. In one passage Abram is described as falling down on his face and breaking out in laughter at the incredulous promise. Faith invited Abram to recognize that there are no age requirements that preclude new beginnings. For Abram to hear God at 99 was to hear God at a time when biology and common sense said life was about over, and yet God was speaking of new beginnings.

Paul speaks of this as trusting in grace rather than the law. Whether it be the law of nature or the law of ethical behavior, we know the measure of reality. But grace explodes our calculations of the possible and introduces something new that could not have been foreseen. When you have analyzed all the reasonable alternatives and have reached a dead end, faith asks, "What does God want?" Faith believes God can give birth to something new where common sense says there is only barrenness. We accept certain limits of reality — economics, social, physical, and the like — but God is not bound by our sense of reality. Grace is the boundless God acting in our time.

Psalm 22:23-31

You who fear the Lord, praise him! — Psalm 22:23a

Praise is at the center of all faith. Life can be seen as a continuum from lament to praise. The earlier part of this psalm contains the very famous lament of Jesus from the cross. It reflects the reality of the suffering and our protest against it. But faith enables us to transform lament into praise. It is in our praise that we lay claim to the one who continues to redeem even our worst of circumstances. And our praise frequently consists of a retelling of how God has done just that. "For he did not despise or abhor the afflictions of the afflicted; he did not hide his face from me, but heard when I cried to him" (v. 24). It is this continual remembering and proclaiming what God has done in the past that gives us courage to face the uncertainty of the future.

Our praise does not stop with words but results in a transformed life in which we become instruments of God's saving grace. "From you comes my praise in the great congregation; my vows I will pay before those who fear him. The poor shall eat and be satisfied; those who seek him shall praise the Lord" (vv. 25-26). Our acts of praise that result in others being lifted out of their despair provides memory for others to recount until "all the ends of the earth shall remember and turn to the Lord" (v. 27). Such sentiment would seem hopelessly idealistic unless one believes in God who continues to effect saving throughout the world. "For dominion belongs to the Lord, and he rules over the nations" (v. 28). Lent provides us an opportunity to not only give voice to praise but to renew our commitment to live it out in our lives.

Romans 4:13-25

Who gives life to the dead and calls into existence the things that do not exist. — Romans 4:17b

One of the distinctive characteristics of both Jewish and early Christian faith was their perception that all of life was sacramental. A sacrament made use of ordinary moments in life to point to an extraordinary truth about God. Paul saw in the fact that Abraham received the promise of many descendents from God before there were Ten Commandments to obey as a sign that God gave him a "right" relationship with God by grace rather than the law. He was not saved or reconciled to God by being obedient to a set of standards since this happened before those standards or commandments had been revealed. Abraham trusted that God could do what the law of nature and the law of merit said could not happen. He trusted that Sarah could bear a child after she had passed through menopause.

For Paul, this revealed that God's grace was given to us not as we earn it but as we respond to it. We still have trouble accepting the radical suggestion that we are not saved by what we do. We have been measured in our society all our lives by what we do, and it seems inconceivable that God does not work by the same law of merit. The economy of God's grace says we are not judged by what we do but by our faith in God who is able to do what we assume is impossible. The thief on the cross had not led an exemplary life. He was saved because he trusted in the God he saw in Jesus.

Mark 8:31-38

> *Get behind me, Satan! For you are setting your mind not on divine things but on human things.* — Mark 8:33b

Jesus' sharp rebuke is directed at Peter. This comes almost immediately after Peter's confession that Jesus is the Christ. There is an echo of the wilderness experience where Jesus faced the temptation of Satan immediately following the high moment of God's affirmation at his baptism. Mark seems to be driving home the point that "mountaintop" experiences of the faith are fraught with temptation. Soon, Jesus will demonstrate great compassion for people who struggle with honest doubt (Mark 9:24). The danger seems to be most prevalent precisely where we have experienced faith. Peter has just proclaimed his belief in Jesus as the Christ. Jesus makes his first prediction of his coming suffering. Peter's response is to rebuke Jesus. It seems apparent that Peter cannot reconcile his understanding of Jesus as Christ or Messiah and the possibility of his suffering and being killed.

From a human perspective, we try to act in ways that result in praise and success. Jesus counters that being obedient to God, in a world that is engaged in rebelling against God, will naturally lead to suffering. Lest there be any misunderstanding that this message was meant only for the disciples, Mark records Jesus calling the crowd to him and giving them the same message. Here is a gospel that runs counter to the wisdom of the world. "For those who want to save their life will lose it, and those who lose their life for my sake, and for the sake of the gospel, will save it" (v. 35). It is a hard word for churches to hear when the pressure is to behave in ways that help to insure institutional survival. It is a worthy passage for reflection during Lent.

Lent 3

Exodus 20:1-17

I am the Lord your God, who brought you out of the land of Egypt, out of the house of slavery; you shall have no other gods before me. — Exodus 20:2-3

This is the beginning of the Ten Commandments. It leaves no doubt that the saving grace of God comes first. Before the commandments were given or obeyed, God reached out to save the people. Having acted, God provides a framework in which the people can respond to what they have already been given. We act in obedience to God's commandments not in order to win God's favor but in order to thank God for what has already been done for us. Obeying the commandments is an act of thanksgiving that recognizes the profound gift God has given us.

When Jesus would later suggest that all of the law and the prophets could be summed up in loving God and loving neighbor, he was echoing the framework of the commandments. The first three commandments directly concern our relationship to God. The fourth blends a response to God and to neighbor. The last six frame our relationship with others. It has often been noted that with the exception of the fourth commandment, the others are expressed in the negative. The result is that we are given outer parameters but within that framework we have a great deal of freedom to make our own decisions. God's laws are provided for us in order to protect our freedom.

Psalm 19

The heavens are telling the glory of God; and the firmament proclaims his handiwork. — Psalm 19:1

Psalm 19 could serve as a foundation for Paul's declaration in Romans 1:19-20: "Ever since the creation of the world ... his eternal power and deity, has been clearly perceived in the things that have been made." The psalmist, too, believes that the heavens and the firmament declare the glory of God to the ends of the earth (vv. 1-4). As an example, he gives the strong and steady course of the sun which evokes awe in the observer (vv. 5-6). The experience of awe evoked by nature leads to a desire to respond. The law of the Lord is God's gift that informs us, in a way that nature cannot, of how we can respond to this mysterious power that orders the universe. The law revives the soul, makes the simple wise, rejoices the heart, and other such actions (vv. 7-10). It enables life to have direction and purpose in relation to one's creator. Yet, the law also makes us aware of our inadequacies and makes us even more aware of how dependent we are on God to liberate us from sin (vv. 11-13). This, too, is Paul's message in Romans 1. Only with Christ as our rock and redeemer can the words of our mouth and the meditations of our heart be found acceptable to God (v. 14).

1 Corinthians 1:18-25

For God's foolishness is wiser than human wisdom, and God's weakness is stronger than human strength. — 1 Corinthians 1:25

Judaism is based on a rehearsal of the involvement of God in the lives of the Jews. Their liturgy is filled with recounting the signs of God's saving presence. God is not an abstract set of concepts that form a philosophy, but rather this mysterious power that keeps interrupting their lives. Greeks, on the other hand, were fond of the abstract. They loved philosophy and mathematical theory. Paul, in bringing the gospel to the Gentiles, tried to blend Jewish and Greek worldviews. He also believed that in Christ he had experienced an alternative to a dependence on signs or theories of wisdom. The core of his faith was the cross that raised significant challenges to both Jew and Greek.

The Jews believed in a saving God who acted on behalf of his people. If Jesus were truly the Messiah, why would God have let him die? The Greeks thought it would be illogical to claim victory in what was clearly a defeat. If the way of life Jesus proclaimed was true, it should have resulted in a successful philosophy and not have ended in his cruel death having been abandoned by his closest followers. Paul countered with the cross as evidence that God had allowed Jesus to face the worst that the world could do to him and in the resurrection had demonstrated God's victory over death. The simplest of individuals could understand how to respond in faith to one who had already proved his faithfulness to them. It was the God of life, not the fear of death, which would shape their lives.

John 2:13-22

Stop making my father's house a marketplace! — John 2:16b

What begins as a helpful service can easily begin to dominate. At the Passover, Jews came from all over the world in a pilgrimage to Jerusalem. They came from far away, and it was impractical for them to bring the appropriate animals from their own flock for sacrifice. Also, the coins of the realm were Roman coins that had an image of Caesar on them that made such coins inappropriate for worship. A service of exchange and a provision of animals for sale had emerged as a response to this genuine need. Yet over time the service began to be a major commercial enterprise in support of the temple.

Jesus was offended by this commercialization of the house of worship. He responded in anger and drove the merchants from the temple. Was this a human or a divine response or both? In today's church, many people talk of "shopping for a church." They seek out a church that has programs that will meet their needs. Churches want members to support their programs, so they develop programs that will attract the most people. The question arises as to when this pragmatic approach begins to distort the central focus of the church? Worship is that moment when we step aside from the pragmatic issues that dominate our life and focus on God who has made our life possible. We need to continually ask whether Jesus would be pleased with the balance we have struck between the marketing of our faith and the praise of God.

Lent 4

Numbers 21:4-9

Make a poisonous serpent, and set it on a pole; and everyone who is bitten shall look at it and live. — Numbers 21:8b

Anyone who has responded in despair to the constant complaining and bickering in churches will readily identify with Moses' having to endure the constant groaning and grumbling of the children of Israel as they crossed the wilderness. Normally, in response to their grumbling, Moses intercedes, and God graciously responds to their need for food, water, or security. This time, however, the people are visited by a plague of poisonous snakes that cause death within the camp.

One of the first signs that Moses performed as a sign that he was sent from God was to transform his staff into a snake (Exodus 4:1-5). The serpent is a sign of God's displeasure, and once again the Hebrews turn to Moses as their liberator only this time it is from the anger of God. When Moses prays to God on their behalf, God tells Moses to make a bronze image of a poisonous serpent and put it on a pole. The people have to look into the face of their fear in order to be healed. This is the last of their reported grumbling, so perhaps the continual reminder of the consequence of their complaining has its effect. It is not clear what could be a parallel reminder today for people within the community of faith. It is clear that their bickering has the effect of poisoning the body.

Psalm 107:1-3, 17-22

Let the redeemed of the Lord say so, those he redeemed from trouble and gathered in from the lands, from the east and from the west, from the north and from the south. — Psalm 107:2-3

This passage lifts up two continuing themes of scripture. The most obvious one is that God is a saving God. The whole psalm is a litany of thanksgiving recalling the various ways in which God has reached out and saved different peoples. The second theme is that God is a gathering God. God calls people together. God not only hears the cry of those who suffer but he also seeks them out. Suffering is an isolating phenomenon, and God is a God of community. If sin is a rebellion against the will of God that results in alienation from God and neighbor, then God's reconciling purpose is accomplished by gathering those who have experienced isolation. In the opening chapters of Genesis, the whole world is spoken of as a single family. Later in the call of Abram, the call is described as having a positive result for every nation on earth (Genesis 12:3). The psalmist describes the various ways that God continues to gather people and redeem them, and then the psalmist invites people to respond with a song of joy. "And let them offer thanksgiving sacrifices, and tell of his deeds with songs of joy" (v. 22).

Ephesians 2:1-10

For by grace you have been saved through faith, and this is not your own doing; it is the gift of God — not the result of works, so that no one may boast. — Ephesians 2:8-9

What if it is really true that we have nothing to boast about in the fact that we are Christians? What if the fact that we are Christians has absolutely nothing to do with our character, morals, will power, or insight? If it is a fact that our faith is totally an undeserved gift from God, does it cause us to look differently at both ourselves and those who do not believe? Paul is pretty blunt about this. "All of us once lived among them in the passions of our flesh, following the desires of flesh and senses, and we were by nature children of wrath, like everyone else" (v. 3).

Most people want to dilute that message. They may say that generally they were also sinners; but then they made the decision for Christ, and now they are a cut above nonbelievers. However, Paul will not let us boast even about making the decision for Christ. For reasons that only God can understand, God has chosen to shower "the immeasurable riches of his grace in kindness toward us in Christ

Jesus" (v. 7). All we can do is stand in awe that we have been so blessed. "For we are what he has made us, created in Christ Jesus for good works, which God prepared before hand to be our way of life" (v. 10). It also suggests that our attitude toward nonbelievers should be one of respect because they are no different from the rest of us by nature. We are to reach out to them with good works because that is what God has done for us. If God chooses to use our good works to bring others to belief, that, too, is a reason for thanksgiving. But that is a decision left to God. We are to love our neighbor, believer or nonbeliever, anyway.

John 3:14-21

Just as Moses lifted up the serpent in the wilderness. —
John 3:14a

The serpent has a peculiar journey in scripture. When most people think about the serpent in the Bible, they think of the Garden of Eden and the temptation of Eve that led to death. Later, when the children of Israel were given freedom and were traveling in the wilderness, the hardships of life became too much. They complained that their God and Moses had let them down. When they complained, the serpent again enters the story; only this time it is a poisonous serpent that kills those it bites. But when the Hebrews once again turn to Moses and God in crisis, the serpent, which was sent as a judgment for their complaining, was transformed by God into an instrument of life. It has a strong similarity to the medical symbol that reflects the thirst for healing.

In John, this symbol of a serpent is used to interpret the meaning of the cross. The cross is meant as a judgment by the state against those who violate its laws. It can also be seen as a judgment against humanity who rejects God's Son. Yet, like the serpent, God transforms the cross into a means of salvation. Now the symbol of Satan is transformed into the Savior of the world. The serpent that the Israelites thought was a condemnation for their disobedience is lifted up by God, not to condemn the world, but so that the world might be saved through him. Darkness is made as light of day (Psalm 139:12). Our hope is discovered by staring evil in the face and trusting God to enable us to overcome it. Salvation is not found in escaping the evil in us but in allowing it to be transformed for good.

Lent 5

Jeremiah 31:31-34

No longer shall they teach one another, or say to each other, "Know the Lord," for they shall all know me, from the least of them to the greatest, says the Lord; for I will forgive their iniquity, and remember their sin no more. — Jeremiah 31:34

Many Christians see this promise of a new covenant being fulfilled in Christ. This is why we consider the second part of the Bible to be the New Testament or New Covenant. We need to be cautious, however, to recognize that this promise was made to the Jewish people. As Paul would say in Romans 11:28b: "But as regards election they are beloved, for the sake of their ancestors; for the gifts and the calling of God are irrevocable." Jeremiah was convinced that the defeat and exile of the people of Israel was God's punishment for their sins. Yet Jeremiah recognized, as Paul would later proclaim, that the people were incapable of saving themselves. If God's people were to be truly saved from this or any future disaster, it was not going to be because they had finally understood the law and had learned to obey it. If it were to come about, it would be because God had taken a new initiative to reformulate their character.

The new community that God would develop would have obedience to God as part of its inner nature. They would not need to be taught what God wanted because it would be second nature to them. Only God could do this, and God will do it through forgiveness. Later, Christians would see the first fruits of this promise fulfilled in Jesus who sought to reformulate the community through his proclamation of the grace and forgiveness of God. For Jews, as well as Christians who through Christ have been grafted into the people of God, the invitation is to trust that in God all things are made possible.

93

Psalm 51:1-12

Against you, you alone, have I sinned ... wash me, and I will be whiter than snow. — Psalm 51:4a, 7b

Guilt is the great paralyzer of humanity. We were born to sin, not in the sense of having evil intent, but in the sense of being totally self-centered and self-absorbed. If you think about an infant, there is no one who is more self-absorbed. If he or she is dry, warm, and full, then the universe is all right. But if any of these are missing, the infant is not interested in considering your needs but only his or her needs of the moment. As we mature, we begin to include others in our world and consider their needs as well as ours.

Still, even at our best, our behavior is tainted by self-interest. Tradition attributes this psalm to David in response to the prophet Nathan's exposing his sin with Bathsheba. When we recognize that God accepted this prayer on behalf of one who had committed adultery and murder, it provides us with plenty of space for us to see ourselves and our sins within those parameters. It also illustrates the step we must take in shifting our focus from ourselves to the one who is capable of cleansing us. Most of us allow our guilt to be the focus of our energy and the shaper of our response. The psalmist, and perhaps David, shifts his attention to God who is more powerful than his sin. It is this God who can cleanse him and us. It is this God who can create in us a clean heart and put a right spirit within us.

Hebrews 5:5-10

Although he was a Son, he learned obedience through what he suffered. — Hebrews 5:8

The letter to the Hebrews develops its understanding of Christ through emphasizing the humanity of Jesus. As was emphasized in Philippians 2:6, so Hebrews emphasizes that "Christ did not glorify himself" (v. 5). Rather he made identification with the struggle of humanity. God appointed him our high priest. The task of the high priest was to mediate between God and humanity. Jesus was able to be our mediator because he was willing to suffer what we suffered and therefore knew from experience what he lifted up to God on our behalf. "Jesus offered up prayers and supplications, with loud cries and tears, to the one who was able to save him from death" (v. 7). While one might expect the Son of God to deliver us through the exercise of divine power, Hebrews emphasizes that he completed his mission through suffering.

In this last Sunday of Lent, the emphasis is on the suffering of Jesus for our sake. As Jesus identified with us through suffering, so we are invited to identify with Jesus as the one who was for us. The church, as the body of Christ, must not try to glorify itself but must represent Christ in willingly suffering for the sake of humanity. As the church risks itself for the sake of others, it reveals the Christ who reconciles the world to God.

John 12:20-33

Now my soul is troubled. And what should I say — "Father, save me from this hour"? No it is for this reason that I have come to this hour. — John 12:27

We have grown confused as to what gives life meaning and purpose. We have confused "self-fulfillment" with "self-aggrandizement." To be true to oneself is not always to pleasure oneself or even to protect oneself. When some Greeks came to Philip and said, "Sir, we wish to see Jesus" (v. 21). Jesus begins to talk about the sacrifice that the faith requires. He speaks of a grain of wheat that must die before it bears fruit and that "those who hate their life in this world will keep it for eternal life" (v. 25). When Jesus faced the possibility of suffering and death, he chose not to escape it. He recognized that to do so would violate the very meaning of his life. It is a mistake to focus our energies on either pleasure or security, even though both are pleasant blessings in life. There is within us a self to which we must be true even when that requires much sacrifice. Sometimes life faces us with hard choices that include the risk of pain and suffering. We may cry out to God for help in such times and discover that he responds to the true center in us. God may permit us to suffer so that we may discover how much we have built a false shell that hides the true self. When Jesus cried out to God to glorify himself, he was praying that the image of God within him might be revealed.

Passion/Palm Sunday

Isaiah 50:4-9a

> *I gave my back to those who struck me, and my cheeks to those who pulled out the beard; I did not hide my face from insult and spitting.* — Isaiah 50:6

While the Christian will immediately see the suffering of Jesus at the hands of the soldiers in this passage, it is instructive to recall that the words were first uttered on behalf of the Judean exiles near the end of the Babylonian exile. Approximately fifty years earlier, they and their descendents had been taken off into exile bereft of their country and their way of life. The prophet personalizes his people's suffering and recognizes their suffering. At the same time, he sees a hope in God that transcends their situation. "Therefore I have set my face like flint, and I know that I shall not be put to shame; he who vindicates me is near" (vv. 7-8a).

In the midst of this suffering, the prophet recognizes the call of God: "The Lord God has given me the tongue of a teacher, that I may know how to sustain the weary with a word" (v. 4). He sees his vindication coming from God and therefore feels sustained even in the midst of his suffering: "Who will contend with me? Let us stand up together. Who are my adversaries? Let them confront me. It is the Lord God who helps me; who will declare me guilty?" (vv. 8-9). Such a passage must have surely strengthened Jesus as he faced the insults and suffering leading to the cross. Both the witness of Isaiah and that of Jesus provide strength to those who suffer injustice in our world. Their hope is derived not from the strength of humanity but from their faith in God.

Psalm 31:9-16

My times are in your hand; deliver me from the hand of my enemies and persecutors. — Psalm 31:15

There are times of stress and suffering in every person's life. The psalmist captures our own feelings at such times. The pain of those moments can be long lasting, emotionally draining, and physically wasting: "... my eyes waste away from grief, my soul and my body also" (v. 9). At such times, our sense of time is compressed, and we feel as if it has been forever: "For my life is spent with sorrow, and my years with sighing; my strength fails because of my misery, and my bones waste away" (v. 10). If the pain or stress is severe enough, it often isolates us. We shut ourselves off while at the same time we feel abandoned by our friends and family: "I am the scorn of all my adversaries, a horror to my neighbors, and object of dread to my acquaintances; those who see me in the street flee from me" (v. 11).

Faith is the path to breaking out of such isolation and reconnecting with the one who can give us relief. Having given voice to his stress and his feeling of isolation, the psalmist reaches out to God: "But I trust in you, O Lord; I say, 'You are my God.' My times are in your hand; deliver me from the hand of my enemies and persecutors" (vv. 14-15). On the cross, Jesus spoke an earlier verse from this psalm, verse 5: "Into your hand I commit my spirit" (Luke 23:46). The journey of faith is often difficult. At times it may feel as if all those you have counted on have abandoned you and that your pain is overwhelming. At such times, this psalm and Jesus' use of it can remind us of the sustaining love of God.

Philippians 2:5-11

Let the same mind be in you that was in Christ Jesus.... — Philippians 2:5

This famous hymn in Philippians summarizes the ministry of Christ as it was understood by the early church. It is the pattern of Christ's life that is offered as a model for Christian living. The church is always tempted by what some have called the theology of glory. This is the belief that some special privilege should come to those who have chosen to be Christians because they possess the truth of God.

The hymn reminds us that Christ chose the opposite path. "Though he was in the form of God, [he] did not regard equality with God as something to be exploited" (v. 6). Picture the church being asked to empty itself of all special privileges and choosing to simply be the slave of the society around it. It would give up all tax benefits, zoning privileges, societal respect, and special allowances. Like a slave, bereft of all power, it would be at the beck and call of those in need. The church would be willing to risk even its own survival in an effort to be obedient to God who sent it to serve the world that God loves.

This is a radical picture that continues to challenge the fear that shapes the church. It would mean that we would have to place our complete trust in God in the same way that Jesus did, even as his behavior led to the cross. Upon reflection, does this not make Jesus' life all the more incredible? Yet the church proclaims that God "gave him the name that is above every name, so that at the name of Jesus every knee should bend ..." (vv. 9-10). It would be easy to treat the life of Jesus as a divine impossibility, but then we return to the beginning of the hymn where it says, "Let the same mind be in you that was in Christ Jesus." If we are to be the Body of Christ, then we are to allow Christ to be the head of our body.

Mark 14:1—15:47

> *He said, "Abba, Father, for you all things are possible; remove this cup from me; yet, not what I want, but what you want." — Mark 14:36*

If there is any single characteristic of death that most strikes fear into our hearts, it is that in death we totally lose control. Whatever occurs at death, we are no longer in charge. Through the major part of the gospel of Mark, we are told about what Jesus did or taught. Jesus is the initiator of the action. Now, in these final stages leading to Jesus' death, the main feature of the narrative is what others did to Jesus. There is a plot to kill Jesus. Then a woman anoints Jesus' body as if to prepare it for burial. Judas agrees to betray Jesus. Peter denies Jesus. Jesus is arrested and taken before the council. Jesus is tried before Pilate, mocked by the soldiers, and led out to the cross. On the way, a stranger helps him carry the cross. He is crucified and buried. People are acting on Jesus more than the reverse.

We now know that Jesus understands our very human experience of panic when we sense that life is getting out of control. All our lives we strive to gain competence so that we can be in charge of our own destiny. Yet in the end, we have to give all control over to something we cannot fully comprehend. Jesus' cry from the cross in which he expressed his feeling of abandonment gives voice to our greatest fear. Despite all of our strivings, in the end we have to give ourselves over to a mystery that we cannot fully comprehend. We can identify with Jesus' prayer that the cup pass from him, but it is hardest to join him in the final part of that prayer: "Not what I want but what you want." This is the final act of trust, which rests not on our decisions or actions but only on the grace of God.

Easter Day

Acts 10:34-43

> *... but God raised him on the third day and allowed him to appear, not to all people but to us who were chosen by God as witnesses.* — Acts 10:40-41a

While Easter has not been as thoroughly secularized as society's handling of Christmas, there is still an attempt to revert back to the celebration of spring and the budding of new life all around us. This passage is a helpful reminder of what we, as Christians, are celebrating on Easter Sunday. There are several important points that are highlighted by this passage. First, it is God who is in charge of events. This is not an indestructible Jesus or even the immortal soul of Jesus, but a dead Jesus whom God raised. Jesus was not in control nor was it inevitable that he would live again apart from the will of God.

Second, having been raised from the dead, it is God who allows Jesus to appear to others. It is not an inevitable consequence that having been raised, people would be able to see Jesus. If we are raised from the dead, it does not necessarily follow that others can see us. We are dealing with a different dimension of reality here. The appearances of Jesus were not a natural consequence of his resurrection, but rather they were for a special purpose.

Third, Jesus does not appear to everyone but only to a select group. Jesus appeared to those God had selected for the specific purpose of providing a witness to God's sovereignty over life and death. It is God who is in charge of all that happens, and God anointed Jesus as judge of the living and the dead. Jesus' witness during his life had been to the power of God's grace to triumph over sin. By his resurrection, his message is verified. To believe in him is to receive forgiveness.

Psalm 118:1-2, 14-24

Open to me the gates of righteousness, that I may enter
through and give thanks to the Lord. — Psalm 118:19

Our journey of faith is a search for the gate of righteousness that will put us in a right relationship with God. The very path is counterintuitive. "The stone that the builders rejected has become the chief cornerstone" (v. 22). We know that Christ leads us on a path that includes a journey of suffering. Yet, we are invited to rejoice. "This is the day that the Lord has made, let us rejoice and be glad in it" (v. 24). This is a retrospective affirmation for the psalmist. The psalmist has been through a difficult journey in which he nearly died (v. 18) and in which those who normally control one's destiny had given up on him (v. 22). But in ways that never could have been predicted, God has brought him through his trials and put him in a right relationship with himself.

Looking back, the psalmist now can say that this day was shaped by God and despite all its trials now can be celebrated. We are asked to come in the name of the Lord seeking a blessing from the house of the Lord because it is in doing so that we will find meaning in the suffering that has been part of our journey. Our righteousness or right relationship is opened to us when we can be centered in the light God has provided us and not be swayed by the shadows. The suffering of Jesus that was part of his journey was given new meaning because it was seen in the light of the journey that God had laid out for him. Easter casts a new light on our journey as well.

1 Corinthians 15:1-11

I persecuted the church of God. But by the grace of God
I am what I am, and his grace toward me has not been in
vain. — 1 Corinthians 15:9b-10a

The Easter celebration of Christ's resurrection was for Paul a release into the universe of the transforming love of God. He was living proof of the spread of that transforming love. God took an archenemy of the church, one that not only did not accept Jesus as the Christ but also actively sought to eliminate those who did. Without Paul having taken any initiative of asking for God's help and long

101

before Paul had acknowledged Jesus as Lord and Savior, God reached into Paul's life and turned him around. Where Paul's life was headed for death and destruction, God did what Paul could not do for himself. He transformed him and raised him to a new life. As that transforming love spreads through the generations up until now, it offers radical freedom for the future.

No condition, attitude, or direction is so fixed in our life that God cannot fill us with a new hopeful possibility. There is a power greater than us that can help us when we cannot help ourselves. While this power may help us despite ourselves, as it did Paul, by the resurrection of Jesus we are invited to submit ourselves to that transforming love and greet our future with expectation.

Mark 16:1-8

So they went out and fled from the tomb, for terror and amazement had seized them; and they said nothing to anyone, for they were afraid. — Mark 16:8

This is the strangest ending of any of the gospels. It is so strange that apparently later Christians could not accept it and decided to add a new ending that was more satisfying. If we did not have the other gospels, we would have none of the stories of Jesus' resurrection appearances. All we would have is the story of a young man dressed in a white robe telling the women not to be afraid and instructing them to tell the disciples to go to Galilee, and there they would see Jesus. It is not even an angel that tells the women about Jesus. The young man would appear to be the same young man who ran off naked when Jesus was arrested (Mark 14:51).

While we can profit from the witness of the other gospels, it is important for us to also hear a message from Mark. The good news of Christ is not a sure thing but depends upon the women overcoming their fear and the disciples' obedience. If the women let fear triumph over their amazement, the news of Jesus' resurrection may not be told. If the disciples do not go to Galilee, they will not encounter the risen Christ. On Easter Sunday, we hear the amazing story of Jesus' being raised from the dead. Then comes the decision following the worship service. Will we let it affect our lives, or will we let our natural fears overwhelm us? Are we willing to go where Christ directs us in our world so that we can meet the living Christ and not just repeat a story from history? The story of the tomb is important, but the risen Christ is available to us in Galilee if we are willing to make the journey.

Easter 2

Acts 4:32-35

No one claimed private ownership of any possessions, but everything they owned was held in common. — Acts 4:32b

The very fact that this passage is so disturbing to many is evidence of the powerful hold our possessions have on us. We have been so educated to believe in private ownership and possession of wealth that to suggest that what we have is not ours is almost unbelievable. Most of us understand the effect of greed, envy, and covetousness is to create distrust, suspicion, and protectiveness. When we look at the Ten Commandments, 20% deal with overcoming our desire for what our neighbor has. "You shall not steal" and "You shall not covet" (Exodus 20:15, 17). Acts claims that the power of the resurrection can be seen in its ability to break the power of things and possessions in our life. Consider the impact of only loosely holding on to our possessions. Such a move requires an act of trust. Note that the distribution was through the apostles (or church leadership), so the first risk you have to take is whether you trust the body of Christ as it is manifested in the church.

In this passage, such an act of trust results in their lives becoming centered on God rather than themselves. It also lessens interpersonal rivalry because they become focused on the good of all. Because Jesus commanded us to hold love of neighbor as a primary command and defined our neighbor as anyone in need, so now the power of the resurrected Christ enables a Christian community to say, "There was not a needy person among them" (v. 34). By the power of the resurrection, these believers knew that things could not ultimately harm them and that life was discovered in meeting the needs of others. It begins with trusting God who has proved his love for us.

Psalm 133

How very good and pleasant it is when kindred live together in unity! — Psalm 133:1

Psalm 133 is a celebration of the blessing of community. In Genesis there is a statement of God's conclusion that it is not good for a human to be alone (Genesis 2:18). In the dry climate of the Middle East, it was a sign of hospitality to anoint a guest's head with olive oil that could refresh the skin dried by the weather. Human community (v. 1) is refreshing like the generous oil put on Aaron's head (v. 2). Aaron, Moses' brother, became the head of the priesthood in Israel and Moses' interpreter for God's word. God's will was for a generous hospitality among God's people. The dew of Hermon was the life-giving water that enabled the plants to bloom. Life together is like that precious water that enables life to flower (v. 3). It flowers in Zion, the place where God has chosen to make his presence visible.

God's presence becomes visible and productive where people dwell together enriching and refreshing each other under God's guidance. All attempts to demonstrate our goodness that results in division of community are a failure to discover the blessing of God that produces the fullness of life (v. 3b). We cannot love God and hate our neighbor. To hate our neighbor becomes a failure to receive God's precious gift of community.

1 John 1:1—2:2

He is the atoning sacrifice for our sins and not for ours only but also for the sins of the whole world. — 1 John 2:2

Try to conceive of the implications of Christ's having atoned for the sins of the whole world. We are not talking about a conditional atonement, which will come about once people in the world have confessed their sins. This is a much more radical claim for Christ than the fact that in Christ Christians can find forgiveness. This atonement also severely affects how we relate to others in the world. If Christ atones for the sins of the world, what becomes of our power to judge others? If I am angry and I condemn another for what that person has done, I am condemning a person for whom Christ has already atoned. If sin is any act, attitude, or failure to act that rebels against God's

105

purpose that we love one another and atonement is God's effort to reconcile that which has been separated, then in my judging another I am judging one who has been reconciled to God.

By Christ's atonement, we are set free of the necessity to look for darkness in a person's life. Now we are asked to look for light because God is light. "If we walk in the light as he himself is in the light, we have fellowship with one another" (1:7). The unity of the human family, or even the body of Christ, is not based on our strength of character but rather on our discovery of a reflection of God in each of us. Our task is to become reflectors of that light so that the world might discover the truth about itself. The truth is that the world also is in the light.

John 20:19-31

If you forgive the sins of any, they are forgiven them; if you retain the sins of any, they are retained. — John 20:23

If one is to take this statement as a statement of truth about the church, it suggests that we have a frightening responsibility. You may recall the story in Mark 2 where a paralytic is brought to Jesus and Jesus tells the young man, "Son, your sins are forgiven." The reaction of some of the scribes was to accuse him of blasphemy because forgiveness of sins can only be done by God alone. How comfortable would you be in accepting your responsibility as part of the church to forgive people's sins? Could you accept God saying to you, "The responsibility is yours? If you do not forgive a person's sins, then his or her sins are not forgiven. He remains paralyzed by his sins." Would you consider it bordering on blasphemy, and certainly self-righteousness, for the church to withhold forgiveness?

Yet this is what Jesus declares to his disciples. Jesus, who was sent by God to proclaim God's forgiveness, turns to the disciples and says, "As the Father has sent me, so I send you" (v. 21). When he had said this, he breathed on them and said to them, "Receive the Holy Spirit" (v. 22). Protestants have been quick to criticize the Roman Catholic church for assuming the power to forgive sins. But all of us must consider the other side of this question. What if the reason that the world is so mired in guilt and the bizarre actions that result from that guilt is because as a church we have not been willing to proclaim the forgiveness that they need? What if the world awaits the church's accepting Christ's mandate for the world, and we have been too frightened to engage in the task?

Easter 3

Acts 3:12-19

> *And the faith that is through Jesus has given him this perfect health in the presence of all of you.* — Acts 3:16b

Peter and John have invoked the name of Jesus to restore a crippled person to health. In an age when we have become so dependent on science, we are of divided minds over such a story. On the one hand, we have been educated to believe that all events that take place in the universe have to have a rational explanation according to the physical laws of the universe. Therefore we look for a rational explanation for such an event. We almost want to explain away the miracle so that the universe will keep operating according to the laws that we have discovered. This keeps everything orderly and gives us a measure of control over our lives. On the other hand, the story evokes hope in us that there may be a power beyond our universe that we can call upon to assist us. When we are confronted by the limits of our knowledge or are confronted by an impossible situation, we want to believe that God's healing power is accessible to us. Can the name of Jesus restore us to perfect health? In our insatiable drive to be in control, we seek to find ways to invoke this healing power at our command.

If we could just learn the right religious formula, then we could be healers as well. Peter points to this temptation when the people come running up to him after the healing. "You Israelites, why do you wonder at this, or why do you stare at us, as though by our own power or piety we had made him walk?" (v. 12). Peter rejects this temptation and points to God as the source of healing. We do not have such power at our beck and call. It only comes by faith in Christ's name. Peter's action in healing the man becomes a means by which Peter calls us to repentance "so that your sins may be wiped out" (v. 19). We have divorced sin from our pursuit of health. Yet Peter sees the two together.

108

Our access to the source of healing in the name of Jesus comes not through some religious formula or pious act but through a repentance of our sins.

Psalm 4

When you are disturbed, do not sin; ponder it on your beds, and be silent. — Psalm 4:4

One of the reasons for continual prayer is that we live in a world that constantly disturbs us. The events that surround us as well as people's behavior become a challenge to our well-being. When we are disturbed by events, we are tempted to sin or act in a way that distances us from God and neighbor. We so easily forget that God is at the center of our lives and is the source of our well-being. When we lie down to sleep, we are putting ourselves in a vulnerable position. In sleep, all our defenses are let down. Prayer reminds us of the one true source of safety that is available to us when we sleep. Prayer also reminds us of the true source of our gladness. Continual prayer becomes a defense against that which disturbs and threatens to shame us. In the end, it is not the lies and vain words of others that we need fear. Rather, it is the loss of contact with God who is the center of our dignity.

1 John 3:1-7

Beloved, we are God's children now; what we will be has not yet been revealed. — 1 John 3:2a

There is a present and an impending tension in this passage that most Christians know in their own lives. When we observe other very admirable people who do not claim the faith, we recognize that the fact that we are Christians is not due to any moral or intellectual superiority. Faith is a gift from God. "See what love the Father has given us, that we should be called children of God" (v. 1). We can only stand in awe that God has stirred within our hearts a yearning for faith and has fed that yearning with the grace of Christ. But even as we are grateful for what God has provided us, we are equally aware that our lives have failed to meet even our own expectations of what the life of a Christian should be. John is very blunt when he says, "No one who abides in him sins; no one who sins has either seen him or known him" (v. 6).

Faith is received as a gift, but having received this gift, there is an ethical urgency to our lives. A child is born into a family in a manner that is beyond his or her choice. But growing up in the family is full of choices of whether the child's living reflects positively or negatively on the family name. Jesus "was revealed to take away sins, and in him there is no sin" (v. 5). Yet, having been invited into God's family by the grace of God, we are engaged in an effort to live our lives in a way that reflects positively on the name of Christ that we bear. "And all who have this hope in him purify themselves, just as he is pure." Such purification, however, is not just an internal effort but a social effort at social righteousness. "Everyone who does what is right is righteous, just as he is righteous" (v. 7). As is made clear throughout the scriptures, righteousness is composed of right relationships. As 1 John 4:21 puts it, "The commandment we have from him is this: those who love God must love their brothers and sisters also."

Luke 24:36b-48

While in their joy they were disbelieving and still wondering. — Luke 24:41a

The experience of the risen Christ brought great joy but still left room for questioning and doubt. This stands in contrast to those who claim a religious experience that has removed all doubt from their lives. Those who actually experienced the risen Christ did not have all their doubts wiped away. A life of faith includes some doubt and questioning. This is part of the growing edge of our journey of faith. Our joy is in the experience of God's presence and not in a life in which we have all the answers.

The Easter resurrection did not solve all the riddles of life for the first disciples or for us. Rather, it demonstrated the faithfulness of God who was more powerful than death. The report of Jesus eating the fish was to demonstrate that he was physically alive and not just a vision or a spirit. Our faith in the faithfulness of God cannot be just an abstraction but must be experienced in the physical realities of life. It is in eating and drinking and in working and playing that the resurrection of faith must be experienced.

The complexity of our life, filled with both doubt and wonder, is the context in which Jesus continues to meet us as the living Christ. It is as we take those questions seriously, not as a challenge to our faithfulness, but as an arena for our advance in faith, that we can be open to the joy of faith. As we join in the struggle with the issues of life that often cause people confusion, then repentance and forgiveness of sins become a message that can be heard in all nations.

Easter 4

Acts 4:5-12

There is salvation in no one else, for there is no other name under heaven given among mortals by which we must be saved. — Acts 4:12

This verse along with John 14:6b, "No one comes to the Father except through me," is the basis for a triumphalist attitude of the Christian church toward other faiths. Unfortunately, the attitude derived from this absolutist claim has resulted in events such as the crusades and the holocaust. While such a conclusion is in complete contrast to Jesus who demonstrated openness to outsiders and who tried to heal rather than exclude, such behavior has been justified by these verses. The context of this verse is important. Peter and John have just healed a lame beggar and told the crowd that the power to heal him had come from their God who had also raised Jesus from the dead. Then Peter addressed the Sanhedrin who had been the authority that rejected Jesus and turned him over to the Romans to be crucified.

When Peter declares that "there is no other name under heaven," we have to decide whether he is speaking of Jesus as the revelation of the word or truth of God or whether he is speaking of Jesus as the exclusive instrument of God. If it is the latter, then Jesus can be possessed by others, but the unbelievers must come to Christians to receive God's blessing. If it is the former, then in Jesus we have seen the servant ministry of Christ as the way of salvation. In our increasingly pluralistic world, where we have met people of other faiths that demonstrate what to us is a "Christlike life," can we trust in the mercy of God for them as well?

Could this be what Jesus was referring to when he said, "I have other sheep that do not belong to this fold, I must bring them also..."? (John 10:16). Does this also raise a caution about those who claim Jesus' name but act in ways that betray that very name through arrogance and cruelty? Was Peter contrasting the faith of the Sanhedrin who had permitted the crucifixion of an innocent person with his faith in the one who had willingly given his life that others might live? Perhaps it was less a statement about people of other faiths and more a challenge to the authenticity of our own faith.

Psalm 23

You prepare a table before me in the presence of my enemies; you anoint my head with oil; my cup overflows.
— Psalm 23:5

There is perhaps no more well-known passage in the book of Psalms than Psalm 23. The lectionary usually chooses a psalm to be read as a response to the previous lesson. If we think of this psalm in relation to Peter and John being dragged before the Sanhedrin, certain phrases take on new meaning for us.

In the gospels, Jesus predicts that the faithful will be hauled before councils and governments to give an account of their faith. At such time they were told that they need not worry about what to say because the Holy Spirit would provide them with the right words. So Peter, filled with the Spirit, has the right words to speak to his accusers.

Whether it is the turmoil of the world or the tension within a given congregation, there are times when we feel surrounded by our enemies. It is not only the Sanhedrin who challenges us to tell them by what authority that we do what we do. The psalm reminds us that even in the midst of the challenges of our life, we have a Lord who does provide us with everything that we truly need. By relying on God as our shepherd, we find restoration for our soul and the right path to follow.

God sometimes chastises us as a shepherd does with a rod and sometimes rescues us as a shepherd does with the crook of the staff. There are respites of goodness and mercy that sustain us even in the midst of our enemies. This is not a faith of arrogance that ignores the challenges of those who accuse us. Rather it is a faith of humility that recognizes that even accusations can be an opportunity for us to testify to our faith. This is what Peter discovered, and this same faith is available to us.

1 John 3:16-24

Little children, let us love, not in word or speech, but in truth and action. — 1 John 3:18

John is a pastor of his flock. He has heard the words of faith and then watched people treat each other with a lack of love. Jesus said that all of the law and the prophets were summed up in the twin commandments of love of God and neighbor, and John urges his congregation to demonstrate that love. He uses the very actions of Jesus to demonstrate the true meaning of love. This is not a feeling we have that attracts us to another. This is an action we take on behalf of another. Love is a verb and not an abstract feeling. "We know love by this, that he laid down his life for us — and we ought to lay down our lives for one another" (v. 16).

Any pastor or active member of a church has sometimes been discouraged to see members who loudly proclaim their faith in Christ turn and take actions or make decisions for the church that reflect a cruel indifference to the needs of some other person or group. Historians suggest that the dramatic attraction of the early church to nonbelievers was that they saw these Christians risking their own safety and comfort to respond to the neediest of their society.

The powerful effect of Mother Teresa on the world was not based on her wealth, power, or even intellect. It was due to her almost single-minded devotion to serving the most needy of the streets in India. An individual or a church begins their renewal of faith when they shift their focus from themselves and begin to search out someone or some group that is clearly in need. When they respond without asking anything in return, they discover Christ waiting for them there.

John 10:11-18

I have other sheep that do not belong to this fold, I must bring them also, and they will listen to my voice. — John 10:16a

It is difficult to be sure of whom Jesus is speaking. On one level he is surely speaking of including the Gentiles as the church reaches beyond Judaism. But as the living Christ who continues to speak to the church in her ever-changing context, could he also be speaking to

114

us as we become increasingly familiar with our pluralistic world? Can Jesus now be speaking to us with respect to people of other faiths as well? Jesus speaks of them listening to his voice and his needing to respond to them. The vision that he offers is that of one flock and one shepherd.

People have often dreamed of one world religion, and yet we often divide and even engage in religious wars over the particulars. It is important to note that Jesus speaks of others hearing his voice because he lays down his life for them. If the church is the extension of Christ on earth, then our voice speaks to those outside of the church when we voluntarily sacrifice on their behalf. Can you imagine the different outcome of the crusades or the holocaust if Christians had voluntarily risked their lives on behalf of the Muslims or the Jews? A faith that includes everyone is not a faith that overwhelms others but a faith that serves others.

The Korean church has designed an approach to evangelism that approaches another person at their point of need. Only when they have addressed that person's need and the person's inquires, do they proceed to tell the story of their faith. The good news of the gospel is that each person has a story to tell and that his or her life has meaning because it is part of a much larger story. When we address their need, we declare that their story is important. When they understand that their story is part of a much larger story of the unfolding of the universe, then their life has meaning. When we join their story with our story, we rediscover the meaning of our lives as well.

Easter 5

Acts 8:26-40

Then the Spirit said to Philip, "Go over to this chariot and join it." — Acts 8:29

The Spirit of the Lord continues to guide the church in reaching out to those who are beyond the faith community. As Gentiles, who are now the beneficiaries of this exploding grace of God, it is hard for us to appreciate how radical an act that was. To understand, we would have to picture in our minds some people whose lives seem beyond the pale of acceptability and who clearly, based on scripture, seem to have been excluded from the blessings of God. Here was an Ethiopian eunuch — an outsider from a racial, national, and sexual perspective. Yet he had been sufficiently attracted to the faith to make the journey to Jerusalem to worship and sought to understand by reading the scriptures.

Philip was led, not by his understanding of faith or scripture but by the Holy Spirit, to approach him. When he does, he discovers the eunuch reading from Isaiah. Philip takes the opportunity to show the eunuch how this scripture finds its meaning in Jesus. It is interesting to note that though the Spirit leads Philip, it is the eunuch who guides the action. It is his question about the prophet Isaiah that provides the direction for the conversation. Later, it is his initiative in asking, "What is to prevent me from being baptized?" (v. 37). that moves the action along. Philip responds to the leading of the eunuch and joins him in the water, offering him baptism.

The human mind tends to seek order and therefore is often constrained by the wisdom of the past. This is the reason that religion is often a very conservative process. The Spirit of God demonstrates a freedom to lead us into a new understanding of the future that God opens for us. To respond to the Spirit is to trust that the God who gave order to the chaos at creation has the capacity to give meaning to the uncertainty of the future. Since we do not know what will happen, we will have to continually learn to trust God and respond to the leading of the Spirit.

Psalm 22:25-31

The poor shall eat and be satisfied; those who seek him shall praise the Lord. — Psalm 22:26a

From utter despair to complete confidence, this psalm moves across the entire spectrum of human emotions. Prior to this passage, the psalm begins with the now famous words that Jesus is quoted as saying on the cross, "My God, my God, why have you forsaken me?" (v. 1). But now the psalmist expresses his confidence in the all-encompassing dominion of God. God's dominion includes the poor and afflicted with whom he is continually concerned. God's rule is open to all who seek him. Because God is creator of the entire universe, none can be excluded from his concern. "All the ends of the earth shall remember and turn to the Lord" (v. 27). Bridging those human-made distinctions that determine nations is too small a thing for God.

God comes from eternity and will not be contained by the limits of time. The dead are also included. "To him, indeed, shall all who sleep in the earth bow down" (v. 29). However even this is not enough to express the full dominion of God. "Posterity will serve him; future generations will be told about the Lord, and proclaim his deliverance to a people yet unborn" (vv. 30-31). God's concern is for the poor and the wealthy, those who have already died, those who have not yet been born, and all people of all nations.

The psalmist, having experienced complete isolation in the abandonment of God, now experiences the fullness of the community of God that includes all dimensions of time and space. When we find ourselves becoming mired down in the trivia of our life, it is good to recall the universality of God.

1 John 4:7-21

In this is love, not that we loved God but that he loved us and sent his Son to be the atoning sacrifice for our sins. — 1 John 4:10

The issue of atonement is how God overcomes the gap that exists between God and the created world. This is often illustrated by breaking the word into three separate words: "at one ment." The word we use to describe the alienation or separation that exists between the world and God and that is exhibited between humans and creation as well as between fellow humans is sin. It not only describes a rebellion against God but also the state of separation in all our relationships that violates his intention. This is why Jesus could summarize all the law and the prophets in the commandment of love of God and love of neighbor. John first makes clear that the initiative for overcoming this gap is not left on the shoulders of humanity but is taken up by God. God does this, not in response to some noble or heroic act on our part but simply because he loves us.

The action taken by God was to send Jesus as an atoning sacrifice for our sins. Because we are so aware of child abuse, this image of God sending Jesus as a sacrifice strikes many ears as an act of abuse. A human parent that would cause his child to suffer for the parent's agenda would be said to be engaging in child abuse. An alternative interpretation is that God's love for humanity and all creation was so great that God would send the best, his Son, to reflect his love and therefore win them back. Jesus makes clear in the gospel of John that this is a voluntary act on his part. The cross becomes the price Jesus is willing to pay rather than the price God demands. In an age in which people use scripture to justify sinful behavior, it is a distinction that is important to make.

John 15:1-8

I am the true vine, and my Father is the vinegrower. — John 15:1

Israel is symbolized as the vineyard that God has planted (Isaiah 5:7). The prophets criticized Israel for not bearing the fruit that God intended (Isaiah 5:2). Now Jesus is seen as a midrash or commentary on the life of Israel. If Israel was alternately obedient and disobedient to God, what would it have been like if Israel had been obedient?

Like Israel, Jesus is seen as God's firstborn Son (Exodus 4:22). It is said of Israel that God took a "no" people and made them into God's people. Jesus does not come from the natural process but comes

118

from that which is freshly created, the virgin birth. Jesus has his own wilderness experience where he is tempted by his own needs and is led out of his own bondage to Satan. In a way similar to God's providing the Ten Commandments that marked Israel as special, so at Jesus' baptism, he is marked as special and becomes a light to the nations.

The vine has branches (the disciples) who themselves must bear fruit. While being a disciple does not protect you against evil, the suffering you experience can be like a pruning, even as Israel was pruned during the period of the judges. Jesus is not a new vine that replaces Israel but is the embodiment of Israel as obedient child. Through Jesus we can be grafted on to the vine even though, as Gentiles, we were not the original branches. All branches must bear fruit. The test of the true Israel, be they Jew or Gentile, is whether they bear fruit. "Those who abide in me and I in them bear much fruit ... Whoever does not abide in me is thrown away like a branch and withers ..." (vv. 5-6).

Easter 6

Acts 10:44-48

Can anyone withhold the water for baptizing these people who have received the Holy Spirit just as we have? — Acts 10:47

Acts relentlessly pushes the boundaries of the community of faith by telling in rapid succession how those who previously were considered unacceptable have received the Holy Spirit. Following the Pentecost experience of the Spirit drawing the people of all nations together and filling the disciples with boldness, this same Spirit gets out ahead of the disciples. The Holy Spirit sees the unacceptable as acceptable. First there was the man with physical deformities, which excluded him from the temple and forced him to be a beggar outside the gate. Then there was the Ethiopian eunuch whose sexual orientation made him unacceptable. Now there is a group of Gentiles who are filled with the Spirit. In the first case, Peter saw faith in one banned from the temple. In the second, Philip discovered a faith already growing in one who either by nature or environment had been in a lifestyle that was unacceptable. Now the Spirit bursts the bonds that exclude Gentiles.

The conclusion begins to emerge that the Holy Spirit does not understand religious propriety. It is so obvious that only the most hard of heart could deny that God was doing a new thing. In Christ, the unacceptable was being made acceptable and the outsider was being made the insider. "The circumcised believers who had come with Peter were astounded that the gift of the Holy Spirit had been poured out even on the Gentiles ..." (v. 45).

Why is it, after all this time, that even we, the Gentiles who are received into this community of faith against all tradition and understanding of scripture, still resist the movement of the Spirit in the lives of those who tradition have found unacceptable?

Psalm 98

Let the floods clap their hands; let the hills sing together for joy at the presence of the Lord, for he is coming to judge the earth. — Psalm 98:8-9a

This picture of nature joining the entire human race in singing praises to God reflects the intricate web of relationships within God's creation. As humans, we sometimes think that the rest of the world, both animate and inanimate, is simply the neutral stage on which we operate. In our arrogance, we assume that we are both the only victims of sin and the ones that God cares about. We forget the words of Paul in Romans 8:19: "For the creation waits with eager longing for the revealing of the children of God; for the creation was subjected to futility, not of its own will but by the will of the one who subjected it, in hope that the creation itself will be set free from its bondage to decay and will obtain the freedom of the glory of the children of God."

With poetic grace we see in the psalmist's words the victory celebration of God over all that has frustrated God's purpose. The intimacy of the Garden of Eden is again reestablished and the liberated creation joins humanity in singing God's victory song. The ecological crisis that now faces our world is as much a reflection of the sin of the world as the wars and violence that threaten the relationship that God intends for all people. "He will judge the world with righteousness and the peoples with equity" (v. 9). For those who seek to discern signs of the in-breaking of the kingdom of God, they will need a new humility and a new appreciation of the importance of all of nature to the fulfilling of God's purpose. We are all part of an intricate web of God's creation. If any part of that creation is touched by sin, the whole web reacts.

1 John 5:1-6

This is the one who came by water and blood, Jesus Christ, not with the water only but with the water and the blood. — 1 John 5:6a

While these words may seem strange at first, they carry a curious relevance to our modern age. The early Christians were locked in a theological battle with the gnostics. The gnostics thought that the material world was evil and that the key to salvation was to escape the world. Christian gnostics saw Jesus as the Savior from this evil world; but since the material world was evil, the Savior could not be part of this evil world. They, therefore, believed that the Spirit of Christ had entered into the body of Jesus but the Spirit was in fact separate from his material body. In a sense, Christ was masquerading as a human but in fact was purely spirit according to the gnostics. John insists that Jesus came not only by water, which was indicated by his baptism, but also by blood, which was indicated by his physical birth. To believe that Jesus was the Son of God was to believe in both his spiritual and physical dimensions.

We have a strange sort of gnosticism in our own time. There are multitudes of people who proclaim that they accept Jesus Christ as their Lord and Savior; but like the gnostics of old, they want nothing to do with the physical manifestation of Christ in the body of Christ or the church. They want to accept the Spirit of Christ because that seems to be a safe abstraction. The physical reality of the church seems to be too filled with "evil" to be found acceptable to them. John would not let the church off so easily. "Everyone who believes that Jesus is the Christ has been born of God, and everyone who loves the parent loves the child" (v. 1). But lest we become too abstract in that love, John continues, "By this we know that we love the children of God, when we love God and obey his commandments" (v. 2).

To love the child of God is to love the children of God. Jesus' disciples, with full recognition of all their weaknesses and short comings, became the foundation of the church. The commandments of God, as 1 John makes clear, cannot be obeyed in the abstract while ignoring the concrete realities of the human species. The church, as reflected in the first disciples but continued with the rest of us, is a necessary physical reality of living our response to Christ as Lord and Savior.

John 15:9-17

I have said these things that my joy may be in you, and that your joy may be complete. — John 15:11

Notice the contrast between this phrase and the attitude of our frightened, lonely, loveless society. We yearn for relationships and view them in sexual terms. Underneath our behavior is nearly a mirror-opposite of Jesus' statement. Our desire is to dress right or drive the right car so that "your joy may be in me and that my joy may be complete." We too often view relationships in terms of conquest and possession. Our insecurity and loneliness cause us to seek relationships to fill our void. Jesus said, "As the Father has loved me, so I have loved you; abide in my love" (v. 9). Jesus does not act from a position of starvation for love. Rather, his void was filled by God's love, so he did not need to fill his void by conquering another. Since he was already filled with God's love, he was free to seek to fill others. His love for others was made visible in his ability to sacrifice on their behalf.

Imagine the freedom that we would have as people if we had no need to protect our image or worry about whether we were attractive to others. "I do not call you servants ... but I have called you friends ..." (v. 15). One can obey one's master out of fear or even self-interest. To do something for a friend requires a different attitude. Jesus asks us to love one another as friend to friend. You ask a friend to do something because you believe they will benefit from it. Jesus finds a deep inner joy in loving us and wants us to experience that joy, as well. Your joy is experienced as you see your freely given love enabling others to be healed of their woundedness and share out of their overflowing love with still others.

The Ascension Of Our Lord

Acts 1:1-11

> *As they were watching, he was lifted up, and a cloud took him out of their sight.* — Acts 1:9b

As we celebrate the ascension, we are witnessing the movement from Jesus the particular person to the universal Christ. Here was Jesus who had walked this earth with his disciples. He was a person who could be seen, touched, and held on to. Yet if he remained that person, he would have become an idol. He would have been the revelation of God frozen into a particular time and place on earth. But now he was "lifted up and a cloud took him" (v. 9). From the exodus, where a cloud led the people by day, to the mount of transfiguration, where God spoke to the disciples out of a cloud, the cloud has been a symbol of God's presence.

The cloud both hides and reveals — now this cloud takes Jesus. God takes Jesus back to himself. No longer is Jesus only in one place at a time. Now where God is, Jesus is. The Christ is now sent to be among the people in a universal way. Christ is now among us as one who is high and lifted up. Like these first disciples, the church cannot possess Christ even though Christ is among them. The task of the church is to discern the presence of Christ both among them and in the larger world that God seeks to redeem. The scriptures become our guidebook, and the first major clue is that Christ is always out ahead of us. We are informed by the traditions of the past, but we are invited to meet Christ in the future.

Psalm 47

> *God is king over the nations; God sits on his holy throne.* — Psalm 47:8

This psalm is normally referred to as an enthronement psalm. The assumption is that it was used in the yearly enthronement liturgy in which the ark, which symbolized God's presence, was carried out of the temple, the temple was cleansed, and then the ark was carried back into the temple indicating God's renewed rule over all the earth. "For God is king of all the earth; sing praises with a psalm" (v. 7). The church uses this psalm on the Sunday that we recognize the ascension of Jesus because as Jesus was lifted up, he transcended the particular moment in time and assumed his rightful place as Lord of creation. For individual Christians and churches, it becomes a time in which we recognize again that Christ is Lord of our lives.

In the same way that "God has gone up with a shout, the Lord with the sound of a trumpet" (v. 5), so Christ has been lifted up in our lives and deserves our acclamation. In an age when the name of Jesus Christ is mostly used as an exclamation with little significance, it might be very powerful for the church to engage in a liturgy in which Christ reenters the church, and we are reminded again of the sacredness of the name above all names. To reexamine the meaning of acclaiming Jesus as Lord of our life and recommitting ourselves to obedience in his name could become an important preparation for the Pentecost experience in which the Spirit of God again infuses the church with power. To recognize that Jesus is not only our Lord but Lord "of all the earth" and "over the nations" (v. 8), might give a new perspective to how we live our lives.

Ephesians 1:15-23

And he has put all things under his feet and has made him the head over all things for the church, which is his body, the fullness of him who fills all in all. — Ephesians 1:22-23

The challenge for Christian believers in celebrating the ascension of Christ is to find our place in the acknowledged reign of Christ. Paul is clear that God has granted Christ the power that is "far above all rule and authority and power and dominion, and above every name that is named, not only in this age but also in the age to come" (1:3). Paul is equally clear that God "has made him the head over all things for the church, which is his body, the fullness of him who fills all in all" (vv. 22-23). The historical challenge is that the church has often become arrogant when it tried to exercise dominion over other authorities and powers on the earth.

Perhaps in reaction to this misuse of power, or perhaps just in rebellion against acknowledging any authority in our life, vast numbers of self-proclaimed Christians have attempted to divorce themselves from what Paul refers to as the body of Christ on earth. If we acknowledge Christ as Lord of the earth and our Lord, what is our relationship to the church, "which is his body, the fullness of him who fills all in all"? (v. 23). Has the present divided and often quarrelsome state of the church become the Christian wilderness that we must pass through before we can fully understand what it means to trust Christ as Lord? In Deuteronomy, the people are told that the wilderness experience was a time of preparation. "Remember the long way that the Lord your God has led you these forty years in the wilderness, in order to humble you, testing you to know what was in your heart, whether or not you would keep his commandments" (Deuteronomy 8:2).

It is clear that many Christians are starving for spiritual food and, like in the days of Moses, are in a rebellious mood. They leave the church, become eclectic in their religious potluck, and fail to understand that "he humbled you by letting you hunger, then by feeding you with manna, with which neither you nor your ancestors were acquainted, in order to make you understand that one does not live by bread alone, but by every word that comes from the mouth of the Lord" (Deuteronomy 8:3). Perhaps we must relearn that the church best serves by being a servant like its Lord and that in acknowledging Christ as Lord, we are recommitting ourselves to the one truth that gives us unity.

Luke 24:44-53

> *So stay here in the city until you have been clothed with power from on high.* — Luke 24:49b

The disciples have just experienced two major life-changing experiences. First, the risen Jesus "opened their minds to understand the scriptures" (v. 45), and then they saw him being "carried up into heaven" (v. 51). Given the impatient activism of our society, the natural tendency when we have come to a new insight is to want to act

126

on our new understanding. These disciples were commanded to wait until God filled them with power. They were told to hurry up and wait. Having patience to wait upon God is not natural to us. Some of the conflict among churches is an exhibition of impatience.

Our society is falling apart, and we fight among ourselves over what actions we should take. Everybody is certain they know which issues should be acted upon. Perhaps we need to exercise more patience, waiting for the Lord to fill us with power. The disciples spent their waiting time "continually in the temple blessing God" (v. 53). They had their marching orders. "... Repentance and forgiveness of sins is to be proclaimed in his name to all nations, beginning from Jerusalem" (v. 47). For us who have been granted a moveable Jerusalem in the church, perhaps we would have less in-fighting and a stronger testimony for the nations if we were willing to proclaim repentance and forgiveness to each other and then have the patience to wait upon the Lord to understand how we are to proclaim the same message to the larger world.

Easter 7

Acts 1:15-17, 21-26

Friends, the scripture had to be fulfilled, which the Holy Spirit through David foretold concerning Judas, who became a guide for those who arrested Jesus — for he was numbered among us and was allotted his share in this ministry. — Acts 1:16-17

While this passage is primarily about the procedure by which the early church went about replacing Judas with a twelfth apostle, it is important to pause and reflect on Peter's affirmation here. The scriptures have mixed messages about the person of Judas. On the one hand, his betrayal was clearly a matter of his choice. He was responsible for his actions. On the other hand, God used Judas and his betrayal in the unfolding of God's purpose. While the early community was scandalized by Judas' betrayal, they searched the scriptures to understand God's hand in these events. Evil is evil, but it is not beyond the scope of God's shaping hand. Such an understanding allowed the early church to search the scriptures confident that even the most horrible of events could reveal more of God's truth to those who remained faithful.

There is always the danger of religious self-righteousness that expends enormous energy in condemning evil, especially evil among us, but fails to turn to the scriptures and ask what God may be saying to us through such events. While Judas' betrayal led to the death of Jesus and could have destroyed this fledgling community, the church instead tried to hear God speaking through the event and then moved on to respond to God's future. That future asked them to heal the wound of the church by restoring a twelfth apostle to their leadership. They did this by first establishing the criteria of the next apostle.

The new apostle must be one who had been with them during the time when they had been with Jesus and must have been a witness to the resurrection. Then they prayed to God that God might indicate the appropriate one. Finally they cast lots. Casting lots was a means of taking the choice out of human hands. It may seem like a strange procedure in a community that is accustomed to the democratic vote that presumably lets the people make the choice. Still, given the chaotic nature of most church elections, it just may be a more obvious procedure for letting God make the choice. Whatever the procedure, it was important that the church not let evil consume it and that its wounds be healed so that they could proceed with the primary mission of the church. Those might be worthy aims for the contemporary church, as well.

Psalm 1

They are like trees planted by streams of water, which yield their fruit in its season and their leaves do not wither. — Psalm 1:3a

This psalm was chosen by the lectionary to be read in response to the passage in Acts in which the wound in the body of Christ, created by the betrayal and death of Judas, was healed by the choice of a new apostle to join the remaining eleven. This first psalm introduced the whole book of Psalms. In the face of much wickedness and skepticism, the psalm affirmed that those who were intent on living a life in obedience to God would continually find refreshment in their lives. Such people would be like a healthy tree that is continually fed by a stream of water and, therefore, produces good fruit. It is helpful to hear this psalm while reflecting on the results of Judas' betrayal. By doing so, one can hear that "the wicked will not stand in the judgment nor sinners in the congregation of the righteous" (v. 5). This is an important affirmation for the contemporary church that frequently looks with fearful eyes on its own frailty.

There is much literature examining the failure of the church in our age and predicting its demise. The church's condition seems to invite the wrathful judgment of both the liberal and the conservative commentators. Some even suggest that the church is the victim of a massive betrayal. For the Christian, such wisdom of the experts may be very frightening. In the face of the advice of those who "sit in the seat of scoffers" (v. 1), it is an important reminder that God is still in charge. The one who could use the betrayal of Judas for redemption will not be defeated by betrayal in whatever form. The task of the Christian is to focus on what it is that God desires of us and to draw from the stream of living water that enables us to continue to bear rich fruit and not allow our leaves to wither.

1 John 5:9-13

And this is the testimony; God gave us eternal life, and this life is in his Son. — 1 John 5:11

The faith of Easter centers on the resurrection of Jesus from the dead. Against the gnostics, it was important to make clear that Jesus was really dead. Against the romantics of our age, it is important to declare that death is what happens to biological life. When we die, like Jesus, we are truly dead. We do not possess some immortal, indestructible soul that simply climbs out of our bodies and continues on its way. God is eternal and therefore is not constrained by the limitations of time. People who are trapped by the constraints of time live as if death has the last word. When 1 John says that "God gave us eternal life, and this life is in his Son," he is not telling us that we will never experience biological death. Rather, he is saying that in the Son of God we have experienced eternity within time. Now, through Christ, we have eternal life.

That is, we can experience the eternal of life now and not just when we die. We can live our lives in a way that transcends death. "Whoever has the Son has life; whoever does not have the Son of God does not have life." Through Christ we have a window onto eternity and now know that obedience to God, while it often entails sacrifice and occasionally death, is the pathway to discovering the true value and meaning to our life. Many people live their life to survive or to grab a little fleeting pleasure from it. In the end, such a life is void of meaning. For our life to have meaning that transcends any of the sacrifices that may be required of us, we need to be committed to a larger purpose that cannot be defeated by the vagaries of life. Jesus' life was committed to the way of God. His death could have called into question whether that which opposes God was not more powerful.

But, by his resurrection, God affirmed Christ and verified the meaning of his life. Now through Christ we can discover the meaning of our life as well.

John 17:6-19

Holy Father protect them in your name that you have given me, so that they may be one, as we are one. — John 17:11b

In what has become known as the high priestly prayer, Jesus prayed earnestly for his disciples. He knew that his physical time with them was limited. From what we know about the disciples, we know that the unity of their community was frequently at risk because of the human arguments about who was the greatest and by their misunderstanding of Jesus' mission. Yet Jesus had held them together. Now they were going to be without Jesus' forceful presence. The church, without the presence of Christ, is subject to the disunity of all human communities. Later in this same prayer, Jesus noted that their very unity will testify to the truth of their faith (John 17:23). As Jesus demonstrated throughout his ministry, this is not a peace that is purchased by watering down the faith until it offends no one. Rather this is a peace that comes from recognizing that they are unified by their common faith in Christ that transcends all of their causes and arguments.

The scandal of church disunity and division continues to convince the world that we are but one religion among many. It also robs us of the joy of Christ that Jesus prayed might be made complete in us (v. 13). In this week when we reflect on the wounds caused by Judas' betrayal and the necessity for the church to recognize that the betrayal came from within the church community, it is an important time to meditate on the cause of our disunity. It is also important, for those who grow impatient with God's failure to answer their prayers in other situations, to remember that Jesus' prayer for our unity awaits fulfillment. The most perfect prayer by the most perfect person still needs to wait upon God's timing for a response.

The Day Of Pentecost

Acts 2:1-21

All of them were filled with the Holy Spirit and began to speak in other languages, as the Spirit gave them ability. — Acts 2:4

Here is the reverse of the Tower of Babel in Genesis 11 where the arrogance of humanity caused them to want to invade God's heavens and the result was the confusion of languages and the scattering of the people across the face of the earth. At Pentecost, with the power of the Holy Spirit, that which was scattered is gathered together. People from nations all over the world were gathered together in Jerusalem. In a time when we are struggling with the meaning of diversity, it is important to note that these people were not asked to give up their individuality in order to discover this new unity. "... Each one heard them speaking in the native language of each" (v. 6). We discover the meaning of unity in diversity.

The power of God, symbolized by the tongues of fire, enabled the disciples to communicate the good news of Christ in a manner that both transcended the barriers and respected the differences among them. "... In our own languages we hear them speaking about God's deeds of power" (v. 11). Pentecost was the Jewish festival of the renewal of God's covenant. As these Jewish Christians came together to renew their covenant with God, they experienced the power of God enabling them to renew their covenant with all humanity. Pentecost is the time when we open ourselves to the power of God working within us to reconcile all people to him.

Psalm 104:24-34, 35b

When you take away their breath, they die and return to their dust. When you send forth your (breath) they are created. — Psalm 104:29b-30a

This entire psalm is a hymn of creation that shows many parallels with the story in Genesis 2:4b-91. In both places, emphasis is given to the breath of God. The same word can be interchangeably used to refer to either breath or spirit, and it is this play on words that is evoked in both places. All of creation is dependent on the Spirit or breath of God. In Genesis we are told that God formed Adam out of the dust of the ground (Genesis 2:7), but Adam did not become a living being until God breathed his Spirit into him. So the psalmist also declares, "when you take away their breath, they die...." At Pentecost, we hear of the essential presence of the Spirit of God if the church is to live. In connection with this psalm, we recognize that the church is part of the whole creation that also depends on the Spirit of God for its existence.

The major difference is that the church is given the task of proclaiming that essential connection to a world that often forgets it. "These all look to you to give them their food in due season ... when you hide your face, they are dismayed; when you take away their breath, they die and return to their dust" (vv. 27, 29). In contrast to the gnostics who counted the material world as evil to be escaped from, the church celebrates the physical world as part of God's good creation. At the same time, the church recognizes that unless it stays connected with the Spirit of God, it will simply be part of the dust of the universe.

Romans 8:22-27

We know that the whole creation has been groaning in labor pains until now.... — Romans 8:22

Given Paul's reputation as being antifeminist, it is intriguing how often he uses female images for God. Here, as he speaks of the contrast between the future he anticipates and the present frustration he is living, he pictures God as experiencing labor pains. He concludes that it is not only we who suffer the consequences of trying to live our faith, but also the whole creation that experiences this frustration of not having arrived where God intended. This, however, is not because God is too weak to complete the creation or that evil is too powerful. Rather, what we are going through is a necessary process to complete God's creation. While it is painful at the moment, it will all be worthwhile. "I consider that the sufferings of this present time are not worth comparing with the glory about to be revealed to us," Paul states in 8:17. We will look back on these trials like a woman who holds her beautiful newborn looks on the labor pains that guided her delivery. The new creation of God will not come about with some magical wave of a divine wand but will be the patient result of God's working among us. "For in hope we were saved. Now hope that is seen is not hope. For who hopes for what is seen? But if we hope for what we do not see, we wait for it with patience" (vv. 24-25).

John 15:26-27; 16:4b-15

I still have many things to say to you, but you cannot bear them now. When the Spirit of truth comes, he will guide you into all the truth. — John 16:12-13a

There is a freedom within the Christian community that continually warns against making even the words of Jesus into an idol. While Jesus lived at a definite point in the history of our world, we proclaim him to be a living Christ who continues to dwell among us. By his own words, we are informed that there is more truth to be realized than he was able to communicate to his disciples while he was with them. One does not have to read much in the history of the church's interpretation of scripture to realize that people have often misinterpreted scripture in ways that reinforced their fears and bigotries. It is the Spirit of God that continually breaks through the barriers of our understandings and provides us with fresh insight. It is this same Spirit that testifies to the truth of Christ that transcends all of our cultural understandings.

The church often finds itself in trouble when it has used scripture in a woodenly literal fashion that has denied the winds of the Spirit that are blowing through the church. Jesus taught his disciples as much as they could understand while he was with them but then sent the Spirit to open them to even greater truths as they were ready. As a church, we learn from scripture, but it must be scripture as it is interpreted through the Spirit of Christ that is continually opening us to new truths.

134

The Holy Trinity

Isaiah 6:1-8

*Then I heard the voice of the Lord saying, "Whom shall
I send, and who will go for us?" and I said, "Here am I;
send me!"* — Isaiah 6:8

Isaiah lived through a national crisis. The beloved King Uzziah
had died after a long and fruitful reign. The nation felt leaderless.
When we experience the chaos of unexpected transition in our society
or life, we are much more open to the prompting of God. When things
are comfortable, we can become dependent on keeping things as they
are. But in transition, we are more ready for the new. In Isaiah's case,
he had the experience of the presence of God seeking a person to stand
forth in a turbulent time. In experiencing the presence of God, Isaiah
had two responses. First, he felt unworthy. Second, he experienced a
sense of God's call. Isaiah's sense of unworthiness in the presence of
God was cleansed by God. It is God, not we ourselves, that makes us
worthy. Then, having been made worthy by God, God issues a call to
us.

Our vocation is transformed into God's vocation when we allow
God to cleanse us. For some it may be a complete change of direction
in the same profession. Instead of fishing for profit, the purpose for
fishing may be transformed into how it feeds other people. For others
it may be a totally new profession. This does not invalidate what we
have been doing but simply gives our life a totally new direction. In
either case, it begins with the renewed sense of the cleansing presence
of God in our lives.

Psalm 29

*Ascribe to the Lord the glory of his name; worship the
Lord in holy splendor.* — Psalm 29:2

135

Dietrich Bonhoeffer once suggested that each of the psalms could be heard as a development of one of the petitions of the Lord's Prayer. When you think of the petitions of the Lord's Prayer, Psalm 29 could be seen as a reflection on the doxology: "For thine is the kingdom, the power and the glory." The imagery is that of a powerful storm that sweeps over land and water. The thunder (v. 3), lightning (v. 4), and driving winds (v. 5) evoke a response of awe and humility. Witnessing such a storm reminds one of the awesome power of God that makes the frequently used biblical symbols of power — the cedars of Lebanon (v. 6) and the great oaks (v. 9) — seem like mere playthings. This exhibition of power evokes a response from both the heavenly beings (v. 1) and those in the temple (v. 9) — "glory."

To glorify God is to acknowledge the incomparable contrast between our earthly symbols of power and the reality of God. The storm is but a metaphor that reminds us that we have not begun to probe the dimensions of God's majesty. The flood is a symbol of chaos, yet God sits enthroned over it (v. 10). There are no limits to God's kingdom, power, and glory (v. 10). Recognizing that, all we can do is petition God for strength and peace (v. 11) knowing that, in the end, our strength and peace come from the one who holds all power, glory, and majesty in his hand. In an age when we are all too easily mesmerized by human attempts to demonstrate power, it is an important act of worship to contemplate on the absolute power of the one who created and maintains the universe.

Romans 8:12-17

For you did not receive a spirit of slavery to fall back into fear. — Romans 8:15a

We are well aware of the fear of the unknown. People will often stay in abusive relationships or dead-end jobs because of their fear of the unknown. People can be enslaved in a hurtful life because fear is their master. Paul spoke of this as living by the flesh. To live by the flesh is to be directed by the feelings and physical needs that are part of our bodies. If we are hungry, then hunger becomes the center of our existence. If we are envious, then the feeling of envy shapes our actions. The dominant power directing such a life is the fear of death. We can easily become enslaved to our immediate needs and fears.

Paul spoke of the alternative to slavery as living by the Spirit. To live by the Spirit of God is to be adopted into the family of God. Fear rules you like a slave, but God treats you like a family member.

To be a child of God means to be guided in life by one who knows no fear and bids us have courage for the future. To live by the Spirit is to be directed by the pull of God's future rather than be driven by the fear of our insecurities. It is to trust that God's creative Spirit can speak in the midst of our chaos and form a new world out of nothing. It is to allow God's Spirit to shape our spirit so that we move away from fear to hope. It does not mean that we will not suffer, as did Jesus, but that in our own faithfulness, we will be heirs with Christ and glorify God.

John 3:1-17

Very truly, I tell you no one can see the kingdom of God without being born from above. — John 3:3

This whole interchange between Jesus and Nicodemus centered on a play on words. The phrase Jesus used that the NRSV translates "born from above" can either mean that or "born again." When you hear someone use that phrase, you have to decide whether they mean born again or born from above. Nicodemus, and many Christians who have been shaped by the King James Version, mistakenly assumed that Jesus meant born again. Therefore he entered this rather comical interplay with Jesus and asked, "How can anyone be born after having grown old?" (v. 4).

In order to point out the ridiculousness of this, Nicodemus continues, "Can one enter a second time into the mother's womb and be born?" (v. 4). Jesus then corrected Nicodemus' misunderstanding by pointing out that what Jesus was talking about was being born of the Spirit. To be born from above is to open yourself to the Spirit of God rather than the needs of the body and the mind in directing your life. There is a reason why allowing ourselves to be directed by the Spirit of God is difficult. Much of our life is founded on our trying to keep control or at least to be controlled by the predictable in life. The Spirit of God is like the wind: "The wind blows where it chooses, and you hear the sound of it, but you do not know where it comes from or where it goes" (v. 8).

To allow your life to be directed by the Spirit is to be open to the unexpected. The only security in such a life is the security derived from your trust in God who refuses to be controlled.

Proper 4
Pentecost 2
Ordinary Time 9

1 Samuel 3:1-10 (11-20)

*Now Samuel did not yet know the Lord and the word of the
Lord had not been revealed to him.* — 1 Samuel 3:7

When God called Samuel, Samuel did not recognize who it was
that was calling. Before he could fully understand, Eli needed to
instruct him on how to listen and respond to God. Note in the story
this is not because Samuel was inactive. Indeed, he was daily in the
temple and near the Ark, the central symbol of God's presence. Even
for those who are most active in the faith, we still may miss God's
word to us because we have not learned how to listen or respond. The
church has the role of Eli. We are charged with the responsibility of
instructing members how to listen to God. We do that even though
our own eyesight is often dim, and we ourselves too frequently
misunderstand what is taking place. It took Eli several times before he
understood that it might be God who was calling to Samuel. Before
that, he likely thought it was just the action of a precocious child who
was disturbed in his sleep.

Three times Samuel heard the call and thought it was Eli calling.
On the third time, Eli realized what was happening and instructed
Samuel to respond. He told him that the next time it occurred, he
should say, "Speak, Lord, for your servant is listening" (v. 9). From
birth God provides for us. By baptism God calls us. At given points
God addresses us. As a church we are to encourage and instruct our
members on how to listen and to respond. Sometimes, as was true for
Eli, the message that will be heard is not favorable to the church. When
Eli heard the difficult message of God that was spoken to Samuel, he
responded, "It is the Lord; let him do what seems good to him" (v. 18).
It is hard for the church to listen to the judgment of God, but it is an
act of faith to trust God at such times.

138

Psalm 139:1-6, 13-18

O Lord, you have searched me and known me. — Psalm
139:1

We often swing between what theologians call the transcendence
and the immanence of God. On the one hand, we think of God as
an infinite and eternal Spirit who is greater than anything that we
can imagine. On the other, we have often considered God to be our
intimate companion who is concerned with our personal needs. The
psalmist brings the transcendence and immanence of God to bear on
our most intimate moments. It is almost scary to consider that God
is "acquainted with all my ways" (v. 3). Each of us has thoughts,
attitudes, and ways that we would prefer God was not aware of.

When we consider God to be our intimate companion, we want
to consider God to be our confidant and advocate in this crazy world.
Yet there are aspects of our lives that we would be deeply ashamed to
have exposed to God. The psalmist does not even allow our innermost
self to be shielded from God by the constraints of time. He affirms
that God knew us before we were formed (v. 15) and knows our future
before it is lived (v. 16). When we reflect on this, however, there is
also a freedom and a security to such an affirmation. There is nothing
that we need to hide from God because God knows it all. Even when
we have made a disastrous and shameful mistake, God knew it before
it happened, and Christ died for us anyway. Since we cannot hide
from God and we cannot surprise God, we are set free to love the one
who first loved us. We demonstrate that love by living a life that gives
thanks to the God who has already loved us.

2 Corinthians 4:5-12

*But we have this treasure in clay jars, so that it may be
made clear that this extraordinary power belongs to God
and does not come from us.* — 2 Corinthians 4:7

It is extraordinarily hard for the church to take this passage
seriously. In our sociologically fixated age, we are convinced that
we can discover the secret that will make the church a success. We
create program after program designed to grow the church or make
it more effective in its ministry. We are convinced that the light that

comes from the church must be our light and that it can only shine if we discover the secret formula. Paul insists, "We do not proclaim ourselves; we proclaim Jesus Christ, who is the image of God" (vv. 4-5). But what would it mean for a church to recognize that it was just a clay jar with all its imperfections? Could a church relax a little in its strivings and spend more effort on trying to discern where God was at work within it?

The death of Jesus was caused by the sin of the world. Could the church not despair that it, too, carries the death of Jesus in its body "so that the life of Jesus may also be made visible in our bodies"? Paul declares, "For while we live, we are always being given up to death for Jesus' sake, so that the life of Jesus may be made visible in our mortal flesh" (v. 11). Isn't the miracle of the church the fact that God continues to shine through us despite our imperfections? And when that occurs and we can point to how God effectively works through us despite our weaknesses, is not that the good news that the imperfect world needs to hear?

Mark 2:23—3:6

Then he said to them, "The sabbath was made for humankind, and not humankind for the sabbath; so the Son of Man is Lord even of the sabbath." — Mark 2:27

If there is any theological issue that is critical for our time-obsessed society, it is the understanding of the sabbath. It begins with an understanding of the place of the law in the faith. Jesus reminds them of David's actions that broke the law because human need required it. Then, using the law of the sabbath, he reminds them that the whole purpose of the commandments was for the sake of humanity. The law was to serve humans and not the reverse. Jesus' declaration was often used by liberal Christians to oppose oppressive use of blue laws in our society.

Now, however, we need to reflect on the other side of the issue. If the sabbath was made for humanity, what was it meant to provide for humanity that we are now lacking because we pay so little attention to it? The sabbath establishes a rhythm of time that was meant to preserve our humanity. It was also meant to interrupt our focus on our own productivity in order to remind us that God is the real provider of all that we have. For the Israelites who were crossing the wilderness, where every day was a struggle for survival, to interrupt their search for food for 24 hours, was to make themselves vulnerable to the care of God. For clergy to neglect to take a day off is to testify that they, not God, are the Savior of the church. For a professional to insist that he must work round the clock to accomplish his task is to declare that success is dependent on him. For either to interrupt their work with a regular sabbath is to pause and reconnect with the one who is really in charge. Observing the sabbath is to interrupt the tyranny of time and make time the servant of humanity rather than its master.

Proper 5
Pentecost 3
Ordinary Time 10

1 Samuel 8:4-11 (12-15) 16-20 (11:14-15)

> *... and the Lord said to Samuel, "Listen to the voice of the people in all that they say to you; for they have not rejected you, but they have rejected me from being king over them."*
> — 1 Samuel 8:7

Every pastor knows of the experience of having the congregation insist that they be allowed to do something that the pastor knows in his or her heart is displeasing to God. In this case, the people wanted to be like other nations. "They said, 'No! but we are determined to have a king over us, so that we also may be like other nations' ..." (vv. 19-20). More often than not the demand of the people is based on what is happening in their culture. The issue is particularly sensitive when the demand has to do with the people's sense of nationalism. To oppose them at such times appears to be unpatriotic. It is then that this instruction by God to Samuel is very instructive. "Now then, listen to their voice; only — you shall solemnly warn them, and show them the ways of the king who shall reign over them" (v. 9). God is urging Samuel to accommodate to the people's demand. At the same time, he is instructing Samuel to warn them about the danger of their actions.

Whether it be a pastor or the ruling body that is trying to accommodate the demands of the membership, there may well be times when it is wiser to accommodate their demands. However, the responsibility of the leadership is to at least warn the people of the practical and spiritual danger that is facing them. Samuel was to warn the people of the burden that having a king would place on the people. At the same time, God did not insist on a purest stance of opposition from Samuel. It is strange to hear God instructing Samuel to allow the people to rebel against God. It does demonstrate that God recognizes

142

our human limitations and is willing to continue to work through the people of God even when they make a less than faithful response.

Psalm 138

I give you thanks, O Lord, with my whole heart. — Psalm 138:1

Psalm 138 is a personal prayer of thanksgiving that teaches us of the power and importance of shaping our lives by thanksgiving. When we thank God with our whole heart or being, it becomes a witness against all of the other powers or gods that seek to rule our lives (v. 1). Our bowing down in thanksgiving causes us to recall that the true source of our blessing is the steadfast love and faithfulness of God (v. 2).

In our prayers, we recall how God has been faithful to us in the past and sustained us in times of need (v. 3). In addition, our thanksgiving is in anticipation of the time when all the powers on earth will recognize and praise God as the source of blessing (vv. 4-5). There is a confidence that when the nations are aware of the character of God, the rulers of earth will humble themselves because they know God responds to the lowly (v. 6). Even as we engage in such a prayer, we increase our assurance about the future as we rehearse how God responded to us when we were lowly and in need (v. 7). Our thanksgiving is completed when, having acknowledged how often God has been there for us in the past, it suddenly dawns on us that God's faithful activity in our lives suggests that God holds our life as of value. We are the work of God's hands and, therefore, we can pray with confidence: "Do not forsake the work of your hands" (v. 8).

2 Corinthians 4:13—5:1

So we do not lose heart. Even though our outer nature is wasting away, our inner nature is being renewed day by day. — 2 Corinthians 4:16

How often do Christians feel discouraged by the apparent lack of effect on the society that their witness for the faith has? There are times when a member of a church will feel worn down by the bickering and pettiness that is experienced even within the church. At such times, it is good to hear Paul's words. Paul recognized that the church was a very human community that daily reflected the frailty of our humanity. In his own life he suffered rejection, imprisonment, beating, and failure. Yet even as his demanding and not always successful ministry was taking its toll on his physical body, Paul recognized that those very trials were met by God's gift of an inner strength. He was very aware of the constant temptation of human success on our faith.

Paul's life was a commentary on Moses' instructions in Deuteronomy: "He humbled you by letting you hunger, then by feeding you with manna, with which neither you nor your ancestors were acquainted, in order to make you understand that one does not live by bread alone, but by every word that comes from the mouth of the Lord" (Deuteronomy 8:3). Even as he suffered in worldly terms, he was constantly fed by manna from God that renewed his spirit. "For this slight momentary affliction is preparing us for an eternal weight of glory beyond all measure ..." (v. 17). This is not an invitation to seek suffering but an awareness of the constantly nurturing presence of God in one's life. As that is repeatedly experienced, one is enabled to look on even the negative experiences of life as an opportunity to grow closer to God.

Mark 3:20-35

When his family heard it, they went out to restrain him, for people were saying, "He has gone out of his mind." — Mark 3:21

Mark is more explicit about the reason that Jesus' family wanted to take Jesus home than are the other gospels. Jesus' teaching so contrasted with the acceptable norms of society that the word was passed that he was crazy. His mother and brothers came to take him home so that he could "get straightened out." Given the clear commandment that we are to honor our father and our mother, what is Jesus, or any Christian whose family thinks he is carrying his beliefs too far, to do? In a society that is so fearful of families falling apart that they have made the family unit sacred, it is an important question to ponder. Jesus responds by redefining the meaning of family. " 'Who are my mother and my brothers?' And looking at those who sat around him, he said, 'Here are my mother and my brothers! Whoever does the will of God is my brother and sister and mother' " (vv. 33-35).

In our culture, where there are a variety of configurations that seek to be family, this is good news. Now family is not defined by bloodline but by behavior. A single parent, a set of grandparents, adoptive parents, one or more adults who accept the responsibility of parenting and, most importantly, the church become the true definition of family when they practice parental behavior. When we dare to oppose any of these configurations that demonstrate the Spirit of God in their behavior, we find ourselves opposing God. The covenant love that God demonstrates for us is offered as the true criteria for that which makes up the meaning of family. Of course, those who are fixated on legal definitions, be they religious or civil, may think that you are crazy to think this way.

Proper 6
Pentecost 4
Ordinary Time 11

1 Samuel 15:34—16:13

Do not look on his appearance or on the height of his stature, because I have rejected him; for the Lord does not see as mortals see; they look on the outward appearance, but the Lord looks on the heart. — 1 Samuel 16:7

In this story of the anointing of David, we are confronted with the mysterious nature of God's call. First there is the rejection of Saul, which given the later sins of the never rejected David, seems unexplainable. Then comes the rejection of the first seven sons of Jesse even though, from all appearances, they seem to be very attractive candidates. Then, just as we are ready to accept that physical appearances should not be considered, David appears and the scriptures emphasize that "he was ruddy, and had beautiful eyes, and was handsome" (v. 12). When it comes to the call of God in a person's life, we are never going to be able to define ahead of time what the criteria are that God uses. God insists on the absolute freedom to choose whomever God desires to fulfill God's call. Some will be violent, as both Moses and Paul turned out to be. Some will be immoral as David was. Some will appear arrogant as Joseph appeared to his brothers. Still others will be cowardly in times of great stress as were Jesus' disciples.

Finally, we are forced to focus not on our criteria of morality or acceptability but rather on listening for the voice of God. There apparently is no one whose behavior, appearance, or other qualities are so damning that God cannot transform that person into an instrument of God's purpose. It is a humbling exercise for the church to pay attention to God's absolute freedom in choosing people to fulfill God's purpose. In the end, it means that we cannot be assured that anyone can be safely ignored. As a church, when we insist that particular people are unacceptable, we run the danger of being in rebellion against God.

146

Psalm 20

The Lord answer you [the Christ in me] in the day of trouble! — Psalm 20:1

Psalm 20 is a prayer of petition on behalf of the king, God's anointed one. Seen as a prayer for the anointed, for Christians it becomes a prayer for Christ's victory. We pray that God will be responsive to the Christ within us in time of trouble (v. 1). Such a prayer centers in our worship (v. 2). We pray that Christ might triumph in us and his will be fulfilled in us so that we might give witness by our joy and our banners that we erect (vv. 4-5). Verse 6 turns from petition to confidence that God will respond to Christ within us. Such a victory would mean that we can shift our allegiance from trust in the force of arms to trust in God's faithfulness (v. 7).

As Christ did in his earthly life, so we can trust in God and therefore resist the temptation to allow the threats of the world to distort our obedience. Our cry in the face of each new circumstance is "Give victory to the King, O Lord; answer us when we call" (v. 9). For each time, as Christ triumphs in us, we both shout for joy and set up our banners indicating one more area of life conquered for God's purpose.

The full power of this psalm prayer can be felt if in verses 1-5, we substitute "the Christ in me" for "you" and "Christ" for "your." It then becomes a prayer for those who are "in Christ" and seeking to be faithful. Pray it slowly and meditate on what God is saying to you through your prayer.

2 Corinthians 5:6-10 (11-13) 14-17

From now on, therefore, we regard no one from a human point of view; even though we once knew Christ from a human point of view, we know him no longer in that way.
—2 Corinthians 5:16

To regard someone from a human point of view is to focus on the limitations of their time-constrained and physically and psychologically shaped existence. Such a perspective can easily result in a judgment that denies the transforming power of God in a person's life. We may dismiss a person because that person is a psychological misfit or a hopeless case. Paul pointed to the problem that many people had in responding to the physical presence of Jesus. They were so aware of his origin as a carpenter's son that they could not accept that he was from God. For Paul, the resurrection was God's affirmation of Jesus as the Christ, and now one could see the eternal God in him. In the same manner, he believed that we must bring that resurrection perspective to bear on the people around us.

In Christ, the true image of God was restored. We are now to seek that same reflection in others. "For the love of Christ urges us on, because we are convinced that one has died for all; therefore all have died" (v. 14). The grace of God does not deny the past but recognizes that God's creative power is continually bringing light out of every person's darkness. "So if anyone is in Christ, there is a new creation; everything old has passed away; see, everything has become new!" (v. 17). This is the mind-boggling reality that is proclaimed every Sunday when the assurance of forgiveness is declared. The challenge for Christians is to look for that newness in everyone. The power of the church's witness is that strong affirmation that allows anyone that comes among Christians to be healed so that they can again believe in themselves as a freshly born child of God.

Mark 4:26-34

He also said, "The kingdom of God is as if someone would scatter seed on the ground, and would sleep and rise night and day, and the seed would sprout and grow, he does not know how." — Mark 4:26-27

Despite all of the literature on techniques of evangelism, there is a continuing mystery to the development of faith within a person. The kingdom of God, the arena in which God reigns in a person's or a community's life, begins with the planting of seeds. We are not in charge of establishing the kingdom. But we are challenged to plant the seeds that God can cultivate in a manner that evokes a kingdom-like response. The challenge is to plant the seeds and then to let God go to work. We have such an egotistical need to know whether what we are doing is effective. It is worthy to reflect on what type of behavior results in planting seeds in some person's or some community's heart.

Are we truly to be servants of others and demonstrate the grace and love of God to them without asking for any thanks or credit? If so, when we have behaved in a Christlike manner, are we willing to let go and await the work of God? It is only after God has caused the growth of faith that we can enter into the sanctification stage of nurturing them in the faith. The process of sanctification is the harvesting of what God has grown. It need not be dramatic acts on our part. God is capable of taking the smallest of seeds and use it to grow a great shrub that in turn will provide shelter and a resting place for all who come.

Proper 7
Pentecost 5
Ordinary Time 12

1 Samuel 17:(1a, 4-11, 19-23) 32-49

*But David said to the Philistine, "You come to me with
sword and spear and javelin; but I come to you in the name
of the Lord of hosts, the God of the armies of Israel, whom
you have defied."* — 1 Samuel 17:45

Sometimes a biblical story is so familiar that we miss the shocking
challenge present in it. The cultural setting is different, but the
challenge to our mindset from this story is the same. The setting is
that of an overwhelming military machine, in the form of Goliath,
and the most threatening of weapons, in the form of a giant sword
and spear and javelin. How can anyone confront such a military threat
unless they have similar weapons of terror? "Saul clothed David with
his armor; he put a bronze helmet on his head and clothed him with a
coat of mail. David strapped Saul's sword over the armor ..." (vv. 38-
39). Presumably the king had the best armor and weapons of anyone.
If you are going against the threat of the enemy, you go with the best.
Yet sometimes we are weighed down by such conventional thinking.
"Then David said to Saul, 'I cannot walk with these; for I am not used
to them' " (v. 39).

It was not that David chose to go against Goliath unarmed but
that he chose the weapons that God had provided him. "Then he took
his staff in his hand, and chose five smooth stones from the wadi,
and put them in his shepherd's bag, in the pouch; his sling was in his
hand ..." (v. 40). We live in a world in which we have believed that
the one who had the most fearsome weapon would prevail against the
enemy. Recently, we have moved from the rattling of nuclear sabers,
which cost an enormous amount to develop and deploy, to the threat
of terrorists who are able to transform our technology and science
against us at far less expense.

The challenge for believers is to determine what the five stones are that we have been given against such a threat. The traditional "stones" of the church have been worship, education, fellowship, service, and evangelism. They seem so ineffective against the threat of terrorism. Despite the fact that we possess the larger military and economic resources, it is as if the mysterious ranks of terrorism have become the modern day Goliath. "All the Israelites, when they saw the man, fled from him and were very much afraid" (v. 24). David's rebuttal to Goliath was that he would defeat Goliath so "that all this assembly may know that the Lord does not save by sword and spear; for the battle is the Lord's and he will give you into our hand" (v. 47). Christians are challenged to consider again how that which God has provided us might be used to overcome the evil of the world.

Psalm 9:9-20

For he who avenges blood is mindful of them; he does not forget the cry of the afflicted. — Psalm 9:12

It is significant to recall that the very first human communication to God that was not in response to God's initiative was a cry of blood. When Cain killed Abel, we are told, "Your brother's blood is crying out to me from the ground!" (Genesis 4:10). The theme continues throughout the scriptures. In Exodus 3:7, God tells Moses, "I have observed the misery of my people who are in Egypt; I have heard their cry on account of their taskmasters. Indeed, I know their sufferings...." It is this same cry of the afflicted that God responds to when Jesus cries out from the cross, "My God, My God why ..." (Psalm 22:1; Matthew 27:46).

When those who suffer in this world cry out, they are addressing God who "... is a stronghold for the oppressed, a stronghold in times of trouble" (v. 9). The very nature of God who hears the cry of the afflicted is both a comfort to those who suffer and a challenge for those who overlook the suffering of others. It is particularly a challenge for nations who have within their capacity the ability to respond to the needy. In a similar manner to Matthew 25:31-46, the psalmist sees the fate of nations to be dependent on remembering the weak and the suffering.

The fate of the nations is dependent on their remembering who and whose they are. The failure to remember that they are human (v. 20) results in nations believing that their fate is more important than the people they govern. When the needs of the weakest in a nation are considered of secondary importance to the glory of the nation itself, then that nation begins to sink into the pit it has made for itself (v. 15). True patriotism may require us to urge our nation to be responsive to the most vulnerable because by their response they may be determining their destiny.

2 Corinthians 6:1-13

As we work together with him, we urge you also not to accept the grace of God in vain. — 2 Corinthians 6:1

Paul has just declared, "that is, in Christ God was reconciling the world to himself, not counting their trespasses against them, and entrusting the message of reconciliation to us" (2 Corinthians 19). Now he proceeds to illustrate from his own life how the grace of God is to be lived out in ministry. As is true in most of Paul's letters, the key to ministry is seen in the fruits of the Spirit being lived out in times of distress. He reminds them of the multiple stresses that he has endured. "... But as servants of God we have commended ourselves in every way: through great endurance, in afflictions, hardships, calamities, beatings, imprisonments, riots, labors, sleepless nights, hunger ..." (vv. 4-5). Each of what would be considered negative experiences, Paul saw as an opportunity to exhibit the fruits of the Spirit.

Each of these experiences was met with "... purity, knowledge, patience, kindness, holiness of spirit, genuine love, truthful speech, and the power of God; with the weapons of righteousness ..." (vv. 6-7). It may be that some Christians were complaining to Paul that the behavior of members of the Christian community was illustrating anything but the love of Christ as they fought among themselves, disrupted worship with their behavior, and turned the Lord's Supper into a time of gluttony and selfishness. The journey of any Christian within the church is a mixture of encouragement and frustration. It is easy for an individual to convince himself or herself that the faith would be better lived outside of the church. Paul sees the mixed experience in the church as a wilderness experience in which the

152

believer learns to trust in the grace of God that initially invited the believer into the faith.

Each time another believer causes you discomfort or even suffering, it is an opportunity for you to respond with a fruit of the Spirit that demonstrates the power of Christ working within you for the purpose of reconciliation. To do otherwise would be to "accept the grace of God in vain" (v. 1).

Mark 4:35-41

Teacher, do you not care that we are perishing? — Mark 4:38b

The experience of the disciples on the wind-tossed lake may have a more familiar ring to it than we first recognize. The disciples had made their commitment to Jesus and were doing their best to follow him. But now their very life was being threatened by something they could not control. When they looked to the very one who was their Savior, they discovered that he was fast asleep. What could they possibly think other than that he was either ignorant of or unconcerned with their predicament? We think we are living a relatively faithful life. Then suddenly a windstorm arrives and begins to beat upon our boat. We begin to sink under the weight of all the threats to our life. Where is Jesus when our life is being swamped by the storm? Where is Jesus when life is falling apart and returning to chaos?

According to the gospel, Jesus has not disappeared. Rather Jesus is asleep as if nothing is wrong. Do we not want to join the disciples and with righteous anger rouse Jesus from his sleep to make him aware of our situation? Is this not what our loud prayers are all about? Just in case Jesus does not fully understand, do we not want to lecture him on what appears to be irresponsibility on his part? Don't we want to cry out, "Don't you care?" What type of Christ is worth following and what type of God is worth believing in that does not help us when life's storms come along? The story has a distinct echo of the beginning of the story of Jonah. When Jonah was fleeing from God, his ship was also caught in a storm. The other sailors were struggling to survive, and when they went to find Jonah, he was in the hold fast asleep. The sailors awakened him and said, "What are you doing sound asleep? Get up, call on your God" (Jonah 1:6).

Such a story may cause us to reflect on whether the storms arise in our lives precisely because we are going away from God. Jesus' response to the disciples when they awakened him was, "why are you afraid? Have you still no faith?" Does Jesus sleep because we have been lulled into complacency? Is the chaos in our lives only restrained when we hear God speak a word as Jesus did? There is comfort in the fact that despite the disciples' lack of faith, Jesus said to the storm, "Peace! Be still!" (v. 39).

Proper 8
Pentecost 6
Ordinary Time 13

2 Samuel 1:1, 17-27

Your glory, O Israel, lies slain upon your high places! — 2
Samuel 1:19a

The story behind this lamentation is quite significant. David has
just received the report of the death of Saul and Saul's son, Jonathan.
By his behavior, Saul had become David's enemy. Saul had attempted
to kill David several times; yet twice when he had the opportunity,
David refused to kill Saul. Despite their estrangement, David revered
Saul as the Lord's anointed or the messiah. He took no pleasure in
hearing that the one who had sought his life and had driven him into
exile was now dead. Saul was God's chosen one and that deserved
human reverence and respect. "Your glory, O Israel, lies slain upon
your high places," laments David upon hearing of Saul's death. This
becomes a very significant image for those who would disparage
the body of Christ for its failures. There are many who have been
estranged, driven into exile, from the church. One does not need to
excuse the church's behavior in such cases to recognize that it remains,
even in its sinfulness, the body of Christ. If a particular expression of
that body is so resistant to the grace of God in its presence that it
fails to proclaim the resurrection life, then a lament for its death is
appropriate.

But that lament should never be spoken in glee or in a way that
gives comfort to the secular world that has opposed the faith. "Tell it
not in Gath, proclaim it not in the streets of Ash'kelon; or the daughters
of the Philistines will rejoice, the daughters of the uncircumcised will
exult" (v. 20). The Christian is inextricably linked to the body of Christ
and must always remember that it is the church that has provided us
with the word by which we live. "O daughters of Israel, weep over
Saul, who clothed you with crimson, in luxury, who put ornaments of

gold on your apparel" (v. 24). David will proceed to become the new king of Israel. The very ones who are estranged from the church may become the chosen ones to renew the body. This only happens if we remember that even in our estrangement, we revere the body as the true choice of God to proclaim a light unto the nations.

Psalm 130

O Israel, hope in the Lord! For with the Lord there is steadfast love, and with him is great power to redeem. — Psalm 130:7

It is so easy for the church to grow dispirited and discouraged in the face of all that troubles the world. What does it mean for the church to cry out, "Out of the depths I cry to you, O Lord! Lord, hear my voice!" (vv. 1-2). Does it not mean that the church is joining the rest of the world in struggling with the reality of evil? Like Christ, does the body of Christ need to identify with the pain and fear of people's lives? Does the church need to confess its inability to rise above its own tendency to serve itself? Is it only when we are boldly honest about our sinfulness as a church, that we can recognize our need of God? "If you, O Lord, should mark iniquities, Lord who could stand? But there is forgiveness with you, so that you may be revered" (vv. 3-4). Is it only from repeated experiences from the depth of despair that we can have the illusion of self-sufficiency shattered? It is then that, instead of planning God's agenda, we can say, "I wait for the Lord, my soul waits, and in his word I hope" (v. 5).

It is so hard for the church to wait for the Lord. Waiting seems like such a useless waste of time when there is so much to be done. Our impatience is like that of a watchman waiting for the morning. Yet, our hope, our only sustaining hope, is in "the steadfast love" of the Lord, and it is by experiencing that love out of our depths that we have hope to offer others. Waiting seems so beyond our control. There is no way to measure it. Like Christ, the body of Christ is totally dependent on God and our hope is that God "will redeem (the church) from all his iniquities" (v. 8).

2 Corinthians 8:7-15

For if the eagerness is there, the gift is acceptable according to what one has — not according to what one does not have. — 2 Corinthians 8:12

The people living in Jerusalem are apparently suffering from extreme poverty, and Paul has committed himself to raising an offering from the Gentile churches to respond to their needs. The year before, the church at Corinth had accepted the challenge of the offering (1 Corinthians 16:1-4). As happens in many financial campaigns, there appears to be some falling off of the initial enthusiasm, and Paul is writing to encourage the completion of the offering. It may be that the economic climate of the people of Corinth has changed and caused them to question whether they are able to respond as they intended. Paul encourages them to complete what they have started but is insistent that the real issue is one of attitude that is reflective of the faith in their lives.

The way of the Christian is to recognize that their lives are to be reflective of Christ. "For you know the generous act of our Lord Jesus Christ, that though he was rich, yet for your sakes he became poor, so that by his poverty you might become rich" (v. 9). But Jesus, who they are urged to imitate, did not give of himself reluctantly but rather with joy. It is not enough for someone to make a generous offering but to internally feel angry, self-righteous, or manipulated into doing so. Paul is quite clear that one should not give out of guilt nor should they give what they cannot afford. "For if the eagerness is there, the gift is acceptable according to what one has — not according to what one does not have."

The challenge for Christians is to honestly evaluate what they do have rather than to assume a false air of neediness. Far too often we fail to recognize the abundance that we do have because we have simply adjusted our expenditures up according to our income. Most surveys clearly indicate that poor people within the community of faith give a far larger percentage of their income to the church than do those with greater wealth. When one is offered the opportunity to respond to the needs of others, it is an opportunity to utilize the resources with which God has blessed that person, trusting that God will continue to bless him or her in the future. As Paul suggests, "It is a question of fair balance between your present abundance and their need, so that their abundance may be for your need, in order that there may be a fair balance" (vv. 13-14). We must trust that God is as capable of working within the heart of our neighbor when we are in need as God has worked in our heart to respond to their need.

Mark 5:21-43

Your daughter is dead, why trouble the teacher any further?
— Mark 5:35b

This passage contains two stories of desperation. First we are introduced to a father who is deeply concerned about his daughter who is critically ill. But while Jesus is journeying toward their home, he encounters a woman whose hemorrhages were destroying her health. Both were desperate enough to take risks in coming to Jesus. The father, Jairus, was a leader of the synagogue. What dignity and even reputation does he endanger by falling at the feet of a controversial rabbi and begging him repeatedly to help his daughter? The woman had been bleeding for twelve years. Such bleeding would have made her ritually unclean, and she clearly risked rebuke by touching a rabbi in a manner that would make him unclean, as well. In addition to the two individual stories, the interweaving of them reflects the way in which people can often pit one need against another in the church. Since addressing either need requires energy, we are faced with an issue of which one deserves our attention first. In both stories the practical solutions had failed, and they now were turning to Christ in desperation. One goes directly to Jesus, and the other tries to draw strength from him in an indirect manner. In both cases, Jesus responds to their needs but in his own timing. While the daughter is critically ill, Jesus feels free to interrupt his response to her by stopping to have a conversation with the woman who was already healed. Then while he was talking to the woman, some members of Jairus' household came and told him that his attempt to acquire Jesus' help was wasted effort. His little daughter was already dead. Yet Jesus neither feels the need to hurry nor is he constrained by the limits of death. If these stories and their relationship to each other interpret Jesus' response to our prayers when we come to Jesus seeking help, what do we learn about God's response?

Proper 9
Pentecost 7
Ordinary Time 14

2 Samuel 5:1-5, 9-10

*And David became greater and greater, for the Lord, the
God of hosts, was with him.* — 2 Samuel 5:10

Contained in these verses is the story of David uniting all Israel under his rule and making Jerusalem the capital of his kingdom. For the community of faith, it is more than a political history. David, who had been anointed by the prophet Samuel, traveled a long journey before he was recognized as king. After Saul's death, he became king of Judah in the south, but one of Saul's sons was made king of Israel. It was seven years and six months later that the people of Israel finally acknowledged David as king over all of Israel. God's purpose took time to unfold. It was worked out in what would seem to be some rather unsavory events such as the assassination of Abner and the assassination of Saul's son, Ishbosheth.

There is no suggestion that God was instrumental in the assassinations, but it is clear that God was not absent from the events and allowed them to become part of the events that led to the fulfillment of the divine intention. It is difficult for the church to recognize that even less than admirable events can be transformed within the church to bring about God's purpose. It often requires both faith and patience to trust in the unfolding purpose of God within a church when you believe that the people are making decisions that are not consistent with God's intentions. Yet this is what Paul was talking about when he said, "We know that all things work together for good for those who love God, who are called according to his purpose" (Romans 8:28).

David would proceed from his anointing by the people of Israel to establish his capital in the formerly Jebusite city of Jerusalem. Here was a city that had been occupied by people that were neither part of Israel nor Judah. It became a city that could serve to unite the formerly divided people. Sometimes, in order to unite factions within the community of faith, it is necessary to provide the people with a higher loyalty than that reflected by any of their positions. Jerusalem was established as the city of peace. It became David's city, and it was only by the hand of God that David was able to unite all of Israel.

Psalm 48

We ponder your steadfast love, O God, in the midst of your temple. — Psalm 48:9

Psalm 48 is a song of victory to be sung at the return of a conquering hero. In the flush of victory, the hero's city basks in the fame of victory. "Within its citadels, God has shown himself a sure defense" (v. 3). When the military forces assembled against the warrior (v. 4), they immediately were thrown into panic (vv. 5-7). The conquering warrior that Israel celebrates is God whose power extends to the control of nature: "... as when an east wind shatters the ships of Tarshish" (v. 7). Unlike ordinary military heroes, God's victory reflects a steadfast love (v. 9), God's very name evokes praise that "reaches to the ends of the earth" (v. 10), and God's judgments are cause for rejoicing (v. 11). The place of God's presence evokes a sense of security (vv. 12-13) that can be confidently passed on from generation to generation (v. 14).

While the military imagery is at first difficult for the Christian, it becomes important when we acknowledge our fear of the power of evil to work its will in this world. The psalmist contrasts the power of this world reflected in the assembled kings (v. 4) with God's power. While we are too often ready to concede to worldly displays of power, the psalmist sees the kings trembling in panic before God (v. 6). It is in assembling in the place of worship and reflecting on the steadfast love of God (v. 9) that we discover a true sense of security (vv. 12-14) and so are delivered from evil. Evil in this world is very real, but it is always subordinate to God. Worship becomes our continual reminder that God, and not the powers of this world, is still in charge.

2 Corinthians 12:2-10

Therefore, to keep me from being too elated, a thorn was given me in the flesh, a messenger of Satan to torment me, to keep me from being too elated. — 2 Corinthians 12:7b

There is no common agreement as to what the thorn was that Paul is referring to. It has become a familiar metaphor for many who are burdened by a particular malady or weakness in their journey of faith. Because Paul was not writing an autobiography but rather a letter to the church, it is important to apply the metaphor to the church as well. It is easy to look with envy on what outwardly appear to be very successful churches. More than one staff change has taken place within churches because the people compared what was happening within their church to what was happening to some other church that appeared more successful. More than a few clergy and members have grown greatly discouraged in their spiritual journey because of what they failed to see taking place within their church.

Rarely do we recognize what Paul is referring to as the danger of being too successful. Yet, the arrogant behavior of churches more frequently results from the churches' successes than from their failures. Churches rarely approach problems or failures as faith opportunities. Paul was willing to affirm that a "messenger of Satan" was actually an instrument of God in reminding him that his hope was not in his greatness but in the sovereignty of God. It is perhaps in the midst of struggle, conflict, and even failure that as Christians we are most willing to learn again, "My grace is sufficient for you, for power is made perfect in weakness" (v. 9). What are the faith opportunities that you can discern in the areas of weakness that are most obvious in your faith community?

Mark 6:1-13

And he was amazed at their unbelief. — Mark 6:6

Do we sometimes become so familiar with the trappings of faith that we are resistant to the miracle of God in our midst? Could Jesus' neighbors not get beyond the familiar to recognize the divine in their midst? Why were the people of Jesus' hometown so skeptical? What were they afraid of that made them so resistant to responding in faith? They had heard his words as he taught them in the synagogue and were astounded. "Where did this man get all this?" (v. 2). Immediately they began to question how the son of a local carpenter with whom they were neighbors could possibly have such wisdom and power. Could they not believe that it was possible for God to speak to them through the familiar? Do we insist that God can only come to us through the dark and mysterious?

What if Christ were to meet us in our neighbor or a brother or sister, could we hear God in such a familiar person whose weaknesses we know? How do we listen to God in those who live everyday lives near us? For many Christians, the experience of the divine in their lives is not through the miraculous but through the ordinary experiences of life. It is in the regular gathering for worship that we experience strength from God. It is the daily strength of friends that provide us with a taste of God's grace. It is in the practice of forgiveness for the small hypocrisies in the church that we recognize God's forgiveness in our own lives. It is not in the miraculous events but in the daily routine of faith through which we recognize Christ's presence.

Proper 10
Pentecost 8
Ordinary Time 15

2 Samuel 6:1-5, 12b-19

David danced before the Lord with all his might. — 2 Samuel 6:14a

Many Christians could more easily identify with Michal than David in this scene. We take our religion seriously and are reluctant to allow our enthusiasm to get the best of us. David is worshiping God with abandon. In a sense, he is loving God with all his heart, soul, mind, and strength. When we think of people worshiping God with such enthusiasm and using their bodies to do so, like Michal, we tend to be disdainful. What would it mean for us to give ourselves over to God with such abandon? First, it would mean that we were more focused on expressing ourselves in praise to God than we were worried about what others were thinking. Second, note that when David releases himself in such a manner in worship, it also results in a generosity toward others as well. "When David had finished offering the burnt offerings and the offerings of well-being, he blessed the people in the name of the Lord of hosts, and distributed food among all the people...."

When you give yourself to God, it overflows toward your neighbor. Thus the second commandment is like the first: "You shall love your neighbor as yourself." David's intention was to find an appropriate place on earth for the ark of God. The ark symbolized God's presence. Our churches are testimony to God fleshed out on earth in the person of Jesus. We are to point to God's presence in the body of Christ. Yet our restraint may reflect our reluctance to recognize God among us.

Psalm 24

Who shall ascend the hill of the Lord? — Psalm 24:3a

Psalm 24 appears to consist of three sections. Verses 1-2 establish God's relationship to creation. Verses 3-6 describe the one worthy to enter God's presence. Verses 7-10 talk of how to receive the king of glory. If the earth is the Lord's and all who dwell therein (vv. 1-2), then as several of Jesus' parables suggest, we need to think of how we will receive the Lord when he returns to his own and asks how we have handled the talents entrusted to us. The dual focus of God and neighbor is enjoined in saying we should not lift up our soul to what is false nor swear deceitfully. Such people will receive both blessing and vindication (v. 5). The third section may well reflect on how we respond to our fear that we may not have clean hands and a pure heart (v. 4) to receive the Lord. We are told to lift up our heads and be lifted up in order to receive the king of glory.

There is something we must do and something we must allow to be done for us. The God who is Lord of hosts, the powers that structure our universe, both awaits our reception and helps prepare us to receive him. While we need to prepare to come into God's presence, we also have an advocate preparing us. There is both a responsibility and a lifting of a burden in this psalm. As a church we need to focus not only on what we should be doing but also on what we have received from God in preparation for our ministry. A church, as well as its individual members, needs to both lift up its head and be lifted up in order to receive the king of glory.

Ephesians 1:3-14

Just as he chose us ... to be holy and blameless before him in love. — Ephesians 1:4

We live in a society that is dominated by a critical spirit. We expend far more energy and seem to relish the result of finding out what is wrong with a person or institution than we ever do in finding out what is right. Stories about scandals get far more space in the media and generate far more gossip than stories about what people are doing right. Ephesians says God made a decision to find us holy and blameless before him in love. Since we are all so aware of our own and others' failures, the idea that we could be holy and blameless seems impossible. Yet God approaches this task not by identifying and weeding out our faults but by making us so strong by God's grace that our faults fade away.

Unlike our negative spirit, God catches us in doing something right. In finding us to be blameless, God does not overlook our sins but entices us to live beyond them. God determines to find in us the diamond that needs polishing. Imagine the body of Christ embodying members in their life together God's gracious will toward each other. What if an entire church determined to find and nurture the best that was in each of their members? When members exhibited less than admirable qualities, the church would praise them for their gifts and invite them to live beyond their failings. Would not such a church be a living testimony to the grace of God? To do so is to rise above our negative spirit and, therefore, would require lots of prayer. But when it happened, it could evoke praise for God who has enabled them to see "every spiritual blessing" (v. 3) that God has given the church.

Mark 6:14-29

The king was deeply grieved; yet out of regard for his oaths and for the guests, he did not want to refuse her. — Mark 6:26

This story exemplifies the forces and power that we contend with in this world. King Herod had arrested John the Baptist and put him in prison. John had lectured the king on ethics and declared that "it is not lawful for you to have your brother's wife" (v. 18). Clearly the legal system allowed the king to marry Herodias, but John was declaring the king in violation of God's law. Despite his secular power, Herod apparently had a measure of respect and even fear of John "knowing that he was a righteous and holy man ..." (v. 20). While it is not part of the secular understanding of power, there is power in the ethical that impinges upon ruling authority. But then on his birthday, Herod threw a party for all the people who served him. It was clearly an opportunity for them to express admiration of Herod.

During the party, his daughter danced for them and clearly pleased Herod. He made a grandiose offer in response to her dance to fulfill whatever request she would make of him. Upon consulting with her mother who had been offended by John's condemnation of her marriage, she returned and asked for John's head on a platter. When he heard this, "the king was deeply grieved; yet out of regard for his oaths and for the guests, he did not want to refuse her" (v. 26). The king was not only affected by ethical considerations but even more so by appearances. All the guests heard him make his oath, and his ego would not let him back down on his promise. He ordered John to be executed against his better judgment because he feared letting others see that he did not keep his promise to his daughter.

How often are major decisions made both in the church and in our society not on the basis of rational thought but because of the force of ego or appearances? "For our struggle is not against enemies of blood and flesh, but against the rulers, against the authorities, against the cosmic powers of this present darkness, against the spiritual forces of evil in the heavenly places" (Ephesians 6:12).

Proper 11
Pentecost 9
Ordinary Time 16

2 Samuel 7:1-14a

But I will not take my steadfast love from him, as I took it from Saul, whom I put away from before you. Your house and your kingdom shall be made sure forever before me, your throne shall be established forever. — 2 Samuel 7:15-16

Given the human capacity for disobeying God, the lingering insecurity that pervades the spiritual life is whether God will get disgusted with humanity and give up on them. Many non-Jewish religions of the region perceived their god as someone who needed to be continually appeased or mollified. Human sacrifice was based on the understanding that only such a great sacrifice would satisfy the gods and convince them to share their beneficence with humanity. We see Israel's struggle with this question in both the story of Noah and the flood and the sacrifice of Isaac. Even closer to this event, the scriptures describe Saul as having been chosen by God and then rejected. While one could describe Saul as having been disobedient and therefore rejected, the haunting question was when would the next human rebellion result in God's rejection? Part of the mystery was and is that the behavior of God is never fully predictable. Why did God choose a people in the first place? What causes God to choose one person and not another? God's very freedom to be God was unsettling.

The promise to David was an answer to this insecurity. If God was unpredictable, God's promises were sure. What the Israelites, and later the Christians, counted on was that God had made an irrevocable promise to be their God. Once God made a promise, humans could count on it being fulfilled. A major theme of scripture is the often surprising yet consistent ways in which God keeps promises. When Jesus promises to be with the disciples even to the end of the world, it was a commitment never to turn the divine Spirit away from the church. Of course, this promise does not mean that behavior is unimportant. "I will be a father to him, and he shall be a son to me. When he commits iniquity, I will punish him with a rod such as mortals use, with blows inflicted by human beings" (v. 14). The community of faith is accountable for their acts of unfaithfulness, but through it all, they can count on the fact that God will never abandon them.

Psalm 89:20-37

I will make him the firstborn, the highest of the kings of the earth ... I will establish his line forever, and his throne as long as the heavens endure. — Psalm 89:27, 29

In scripture, God uses language in ways that contradict the ordinary meaning of words. Who is the firstborn of God? In Exodus 4:22, God says, "Thus says the Lord: Israel is my firstborn son." Now in Psalm 89 God declares of David, "I will make him the firstborn...." Later Christians would say of Jesus that he is the Son of God, and the implication is clearly that Jesus is God's first-born and only son (John 3:16). Clearly the term is used metaphorically and not literally. Drawing on the tradition of the favor shown to the firstborn son, we are speaking of those who clearly experience the favor of God. This David is so favored that God makes an eternal promise that his reign, in terms of his family line, will last forever.

During the destruction of Israel and the exile of the people, this divine promise was clearly in danger. Of course, as the scriptures continually describe, God fulfills the divine promise but often not in the manner that mortals expect. This is why, despite the confusion of the birth narratives, it was important for the early church to demonstrate how Jesus was of the house and lineage of David. The importance of these verses from Psalm 89 is the affirmation that God always keeps the promises he made.

As we read the scriptures and recognize the unbelievable birth of Isaac, the remarkable escape from Egypt, the survival of Israel despite political disaster, and the exceptional birth of Jesus, we are constantly confronted with our need to reinterpret our previous understanding as we confront the faithful, yet often unique, fulfillment of the promises of God. Eventually we are humbled by our inability to predict the acts of God and our need to simply trust that God will, in God's own way, be faithful to the promises God has made. In our journey of faith, it is important to review the promises of God, which enable us to face the future unafraid, but then it is incumbent on us to wait for its fulfillment with a mind open to the unexpected.

Ephesians 2:11-22

So then, remember that at one time you Gentiles by birth ...
remember that you were at that time without Christ, being
aliens from the commonwealth of Israel. — Ephesians
2:11a, 12a

The majority of Christians were Gentiles by birth and, according to Paul, we were "strangers to the covenants of promise, having no hope and without God in the world" (v. 12). I suspect that it is rare that a Christian enters a church aware of how tenuous his or her claim is to the promises of God. We are guests invited in rather than the owners of the house. Not only that, but also the rules had to be changed to make allowance for us. "He has abolished the law with its commandments and ordinances, that he might create in himself one new humanity in place of the two, thus making peace" (v. 15). When we speak of grace, we are talking about an incredible allowance made for our sakes.

As Paul makes clear in Romans 9 through 11, there are no grounds for the invited guests to eject the homeowners. Yet even today there is at best an uneasy alliance between Christians and Jews. If it is true that Christ intended to "reconcile both groups to God in one body through the cross, thus putting to death that hostility through it" (v. 16), then any attitude of hostility between Christian and Jew would be to make a mockery of the cross. While we, as Christians, cannot speak for Jews, it is clear that we have an obligation to honor the peace that Christ created between us. "So he came and proclaimed peace to you who were far off and peace to those who were near, for through him both of us have access in one Spirit to the Father" (vv. 17-18).

The question that Christians must ponder is: What is the nature of the peace that Christ proclaimed to us? If we come, not on the basis of our having achieved acceptance through obedience, but solely on the basis of God's grace, then do we reject that grace when we deny that grace to others? It is a scary world if we accept that our very worth and value is not dependent on what we do or who we are but is solely dependent on God's freely given love for us. Legalisms have been as much a problem for Christians as they have for Jews. If there were absolutely no requirement that you had to meet to be saved and the same were true of your neighbor, how would that affect your ability to judge them?

Mark 6:30-34, 53-56

> *... they were like sheep without a shepherd; and he began*
> *to teach them many things.* — Mark 6:34

Sometimes the way in which passages of scripture are placed can reveal part of their message. In these verses, Mark has chosen to bracket two miracle stories with descriptions of Jesus' compassion for both his disciples and for a crowd of Gentiles from the land of Gennesaret. The first miracle is the feeding of the 5,000 people with five loaves and two fish, and the second describes Jesus walking on water in the midst of a storm. On either side of these miracles, we are told that Jesus, who is Lord over the power of nature, allows himself to be affected by the cry of the people.

A constant theme throughout the Hebrew scriptures is that God is responsive to the cry of human need. The God who brought order out of chaos in Genesis and "causes the oaks to whirl and strips the forest bare" (Psalm 29:9) is also the God who is responsive to the basic human needs of slaves in Egypt and throughout their journey. Jesus, who demonstrates a power reflective of God, also reveals the capacity to have his actions altered in response to the basic cry of human need.

He has just heard of the death of his cousin, John, by the hands of Herod and recognizes the needs of his disciples to have some time apart to reflect and be nurtured, but his plans are changed by a crowd who cries out to him. Even in the Gentile land of Gennesaret, "wherever he went, into villages or cities or farms, they laid the sick in the marketplaces, and begged him that they might touch even the fringe of his cloak; and all who touched it were healed" (v. 56).

Jesus' actions become a cautionary judgment against a community of faith that is tempted to care for itself rather than respond to the needs of others around them. One can hear the judgment of Ezekiel: "Ah, you shepherds of Israel who have been feeding yourselves! Should not shepherds feed the sheep? ... You have not strengthened the weak, you have not healed the sick, you have not bound up the injured, you have not brought back the strayed, you have not sought the lost, but with force and harshness you have ruled them" (Ezekiel 34:2b-4). For Israel and for the church, the needs of the people who come to them take priority over all else.

Proper 12
Pentecost 10
Ordinary Time 17

2 Samuel 11:1-15

So David sent messengers to get her, and she came to him,
and he lay with her. (Now she was purifying herself after
her period.) — 2 Samuel 11:4a

David is one of the key figures of our faith. So central was he that it became critical to the completion of God's intention that the Christ be born from the line of David. Yet here is the story of David's adultery displayed for the entire world to see. In addition to adultery, he commits several other sins, as well. Since he involves messengers to bring Bathsheba to him, it is clear that it is David's power as king that not only commands Bathsheba's presence but also involves others in a conspiracy of silence. While we are not told what Bathsheba is feeling about all of this, we do see that David is perfectly willing to bring Uriah, her husband, back to sleep with her to cover up his sin. Both Bathsheba and Uriah become mere pawns in the political maneuvering to protect the king's reputation.

As if this were not bad enough, we discover that Uriah, a foreigner, has more respect for the faith and simple human decency than David, the leader. We are told that out of respect for both the Ark and the soldiers, Uriah is unwilling to take advantage of his trip home to sleep with his wife. Even when he is drunk, he has more honor than King David. So finally, in order to protect his reputation, David engages his commander, Joab, in a conspiracy to have Uriah killed in battle. This is God's chosen one, the anointed, or in Greek, the Christ. It is from David's family line that Jesus the Christ will be born.

Sexuality is a powerful and good gift of God, but it can also be extremely destructive to the faithfulness of relationships. In our denial of its power in our lives, we often engage in deception that is more concerned with protecting our reputation than with the pain in other people's lives. Like the larger society, we engage in hot debates about homosexuality when the major problem threatening the integrity of our faith is how to deal with sexuality in all our lives. David's story does suggest that God is not defeated by adultery, but it also challenges us to recognize our need for help from beyond ourselves to maintain the integrity of our relationships.

Psalm 14

Have they no knowledge, all the evildoers who eat up my people as they eat bread, and do not call upon the Lord?
— Psalm 14:4

Tradition suggests that the psalmist was thinking of the Hebrew children as slaves in Egypt as he prayed this psalm. When God looked down upon the Egyptian society that had enslaved the Hebrews, God saw evidence of the denial of the existence of God. When a society denies there is a God to whom they are accountable, then their actions toward others become corrupt (v. 1). From God's viewpoint, like the Egyptian's treatment of their slaves, in such a society people lack the necessary impetus to do good when doing good requires any sacrifice of personal comfort and security (vv. 2-3). Such a society eats up people like they eat bread (v. 4). We cannot treat the poor and the needy in society with disdain or neglect without experiencing the terror of God who is the refuge of the weak (vv. 5-6 and Matthew 25:31 ff).

The lectionary places this psalm in relation to the story of David's adultery with Bathsheba. David was behaving as if there were no God when he treated Bathsheba like an object for his pleasure. After this act, Uriah became a problem to be solved rather than a person with integrity. Both Bathsheba and Uriah became the poor whose only refuge was God. Like the slaves in Egypt whose cry was heard by God, their only hope in the face of royal power was God. In a world in which many people are treated as mere economic resources, our prayer is that deliverance would come out of Zion (v. 7), that people would look again to the source of God's revelation for a way out of the morass in which they find themselves. The great struggle for the church is how to be a witness to such a faith in an increasingly secular society. If the fool says in his heart there is no God, how do we demonstrate by our lives that God indeed reigns?

Ephesians 3:14-21

Now to him who by the power at work within us is able to accomplish abundantly far more than all we can ask or imagine, to him be glory in the church and in Christ Jesus to all generations forever and ever. Amen. — Ephesians 3:20-21

Stop and think for a moment about the state of the church in our present day. What is your hope for the church? What confidence do you have that the church will be able to contribute to God's transformation of the world? Can you think of any sin or failure of the present church that Paul did not have to confront in the early church? As you read the letters of Paul, it is clear that the early church faced problems dealing with greed, sexuality, division, envy, doctrinal disputes, immorality, persecution, and the list could go on. He constantly had to both correct the church and pray that they not lose heart. But his source of hope was not in their progressive morality or wisdom, although he clearly urged improvement in both areas. He prayed to God that they "may be strengthened in [their] inner being with power through [God's] Spirit" (v. 16). He also prayed that they might be granted all knowledge (3:18). But the center of his hope was that "Christ may dwell in [their] hearts, as [they] are rooted and grounded in love" (v. 17).

As Paul would say in 1 Corinthians 13, you can have all those things that we strive for in this world, but if they are not shaped by love, they are worthless. Think of all the disputes, divisions, and corruptions that have occurred in the history of the church or are present in our contemporary church. Which of those could have been avoided if the church was "rooted and grounded in love" as is made possible when we allow Christ to dwell in the heart of the church? It is this power of Christ's love, which dwells within us, that is capable of accomplishing "far more than all we can ask or imagine." Reflect again concerning your hope for the church and your confidence that the church will be able to contribute to God's transformation of the world. If you consider the future of the church in light of your faith in God, are you not filled with more hope than before?

John 6:1-21

But he said to them, "It is I; do not be afraid." — John
6:20

The gospel of John placed the stories of the feeding of the five
thousand and Jesus' walking on water next to each other. Both of them
were miracles. In both cases, Jesus was demonstrating the power of
God to overcome the threat of nature to the human species. In the
first story, it was the threat of hunger and in the second, the chaos of
a storm at sea. Both events took place near the time of Passover when
Jews celebrate the liberating power of God to triumph over human
suffering (slavery) and the forces of nature (the crossing of the Red
Sea). The response of the crowd to the first event was to want to make
him king. The response of the disciples to the second event was the
experience of terror.

The juxtaposition of the two stories engages us in a reflection on
what we seek from our faith. Do we simply want a faith that meets our
most basic needs? Many of the cults in our contemporary society make
their appeal through addressing our strong physical and communal
needs. Even our churches design their programs to respond to the
felt needs of the community. It is certainly true that Jesus addressed
those needs in his ministry. Yet there was something more to Jesus
that confounded and even terrified his closest followers. In Jesus
they experienced a mystery that they could neither control nor fully
understand. What does it mean for a church to truly worship Christ who
sometimes withdraws from their felt needs (vv. 3, 14) but is present in
the most unexpected ways when they are really threatened? Can we
face the rough and stormy seas resting in the assurance of Jesus, "It is
I, do not be afraid"? Would not such a faith alter the context of many
of our churches' discussions?

Proper 13
Pentecost 11
Ordinary Time 18

2 Samuel 11:26—12:13a

Then David's anger was greatly kindled against the man.
He said to Nathan, "As the Lord lives, the man who has
done this deserves to die," ... Nathan said to David, "You
are the man!" — 2 Samuel 12:5, 7a

It is so much easier to judge others with righteous anger than it is to recognize our own sins. We have such a capacity to rationalize our own behavior that we can rarely see it for what it is. The prophet Nathan did not directly confront David with his sin but presented it under the guise of a judicial case that needed a ruling. It was not uncommon for people to bring their concern for justice to the king for a hearing. David was quickly seduced by the story because it appealed to his sense of righteous indignation and did not threaten his position of power. Yet considering all of the ways in which David broke the commandments of God by his behavior, when he is finally confronted with his own sins, he demonstrated a remarkable courage in accepting the judgment. "David said to Nathan, 'I have sinned against the Lord' " (v. 13).

David did not rationalize or excuse his acts but boldly confessed them to God. It is when we stand defenseless before God that we are open to the cleansing forgiveness of God. It is one of the mysteries of our faith that David was so favored by God despite his behavior. A clue, which is important for all people of faith, is that David's ultimate trust was not in his own goodness but in the goodness of God. It is not unusual for people to conclude that they have so offended God that they have no hope. This is a reflection of our assumption that it is our behavior that must earn God's favor. It is very difficult for us to so trust in the love of God that we are willing to face our shadow side and recognize that God is capable of transforming the worst within us for a redeeming purpose. This does not excuse our behavior, and we still have to live with the consequences of our actions, but it does open up God's future for us.

Psalm 51:1-12

Create in me a clean heart, O God, and put a new and right spirit within me. — Psalm 51:10

There is a sense in which we have trivialized guilt and failed to recognize its enormous cost in our lives. We have so psychologized our society that all guilt is to be resolved by making an adjustment of our mental attitude. We have so rationalized our society that all bad behavior is simply a problem of miseducation and is to be resolved by enlightening our society or ourselves. The superscription to this psalm suggests that as we pray it we keep the story of David's adulterous affair with Bathsheba in mind. By doing so, we enlarge the boundaries of sin to include adultery, false witness, coveting, murder, indeed almost all of the Ten Commandments.

As we pray this psalm we recognize the true dimension of both our sin and our hope. Guilt cannot be resolved by some psychological adjustment or new enlightenment. Because God is the author of life, all that mars the perfection of life is a sin finally against him. It is not enough to adjust. Our dispute is with God. Only God can create in us a clean heart and put a new and right spirit within us. To recognize our need for God's cleansing is our first step toward healing. To attempt to resolve our sin on our own is to rely on the same ego problem that created our sin in the first place. In the same way that our sin has separated us from God and neighbor, so only by his cleansing us can we be restored to God and neighbor. Our hope is in God's steadfast love and abundant mercy.

Ephesians 4:1-16

But speaking the truth in love, we must grow up in every way into him who is the head, into Christ, from whom the whole body, joined and knit together by every ligament with which it is equipped, as each part is working properly, promotes the body's growth in building itself up in love. — Ephesians 4:15-16

Paul would not have had to make this appeal if there was not the threat of schism within the early church. Yet because his appeal is included in our scripture, it stands as a challenge to much of our behavior within the church today. On the one hand, it is comforting to realize that God has faced this type of behavior in the church before and triumphed over it. On the other hand, it should make most of us pause and examine our true loyalties within the church. Paul was appealing to the Christians in Ephesians to "lead a life worthy of the calling to which you [we also] have been called" (v. 1). Paul repeatedly lifted up what, in other contexts, he called the "fruits of the Spirit" as a measure of faithfulness to Christ's call in the church.

For Paul the fruits of the Spirit became one of the true marks of the church. When we raise our voices within the church, either locally or on a denominational level, are we doing so "with all humility and gentleness, with patience, bearing with one another in love, making every effort to maintain the unity of the Spirit in the bond of peace"? (vv. 2-3). While we may feel very passionately about a particular issue, do we demonstrate, even as we give voice to our opinions, that we believe that "there is one body and one Spirit, just as you were called to the one hope of your calling, one Lord, one faith, one baptism, one God and Father of all, who is above all and through all and in all"? (vv. 4-6). It is so difficult to maintain this spirit when we see people advocating things with which we passionately disagree. Yet Paul was quite adamant that our task is to "equip the saints for the work of ministry, for building up the body of Christ, until all of us come to the unity of the faith and the knowledge of the son of God, to maturity, to the measure of the full stature of Christ" (vv. 12-13).

Doctrine and right belief are very important, and Paul certainly was not shy about challenging what he believed to be errors in the faith. But it is Christ, not our beliefs, that is the head of the church. It is only as we recognize that our loyalty to Christ is above all else that we will have the courage to live together in unity in a way that causes the world to notice that there is something different about our faith. All the world knows how to fight and to divide, but Christ provides us with a different way of living that the world desperately needs to see.

John 6:24-35

*I am the bread of life. Whoever comes to me will never be
hungry, and whoever believes in me will never be thirsty.*
— John 6:35

It is so hard to believe that this verse is true. The crowd, who had
just witnessed the miracle of the feeding of the 5,000, was attracted by
the miracle and wanted to follow one who could so easily satisfy their
hunger needs. When they found Jesus, he said, "Very truly, I tell you,
you are looking for me, not because you saw signs, but because you
ate your fill of the loaves" (v. 26). While Jesus was sensitive to their
hunger, he wanted to direct them to a higher need in their lives. "Do
not work for the food that perishes, but for the food that endures for
eternal life, which the Son of Man will give you" (v. 27). We seem, so
often, to be satisfied to get our most basic physical needs and desires
met but are unwilling to confront the spiritual hunger that is gnawing
at our soul. Jesus challenged the crowd to look beyond the miracle to
the one who performed the miracle. "Jesus answered them, 'This is
the work of God, that you believe in him whom he has sent' " (v. 29).

Can a church be satisfied with providing programs that attract new
members or must it insist that there is more to faith than having our
immediate needs met? Jesus spoke of the "bread of God" as "that
which comes down from heaven and gives life to the world" (v. 33). If
the mandate of Christ for the church is to be the instrument by which
the world receives life, then the programmatic life of the church
cannot rest with feeding its members only but must turn outward to
the needs of the world. If Jesus is the "bread of life," then the church
must reveal the connection between the human spirit and God's Spirit
that breathes the breath of life into all people and frees them to be the
human beings that God has created them to be (Genesis 2:7). Only
when the world is truly connected with God's Spirit will humanity
never hunger and thirst again. But first people must learn again that
"one does not live by bread alone, but by every word that comes from
the mouth of the Lord" (Deuteronomy 8:3b).

Proper 14
Pentecost 12
Ordinary Time 19

2 Samuel 18:5-9, 15, 31-33

O my son, Absalom, my son, my son Absalom! Would that I had died instead of you, O Absalom, my son, my son! — 2 Samuel 18:33b

We are often caught in dual loyalties in our lives. David was king, but David was also a father. As king he was fighting for the preservation of his kingdom that had been challenged by the rebellion of his son, Absalom. As a father, he yearned to protect the life of his son that he loved. He sent his army out with an impossible task: defeat the rebellion but preserve the life of his son. His armies went out and at great cost — 20,000 slaughtered — they won the victory. At the same time, the son, Absalom, was killed. When David heard of his victory at the cost of his son, instead of rejoicing over the hard fought victory of his army, he went into mourning for his son. There is a proleptic echo here of the struggle that would take place in God's heart. The people will continue to become involved in rebellion against God's kingdom. The contrast is also important to note. In Absalom's case, he led the rebellion, and in Jesus' case, he was willing to give of his life in order to defeat the rebellion. Still, God would be caught in the same impossible bind that David experienced in choosing between the good of the people and the preservation of the life of his own son.

David had to pay the price of the life of Absalom, his son, for the sake of the people. God paid the price of the death of Jesus for the sake of the people. Can you not hear the tearing of God's heart as his own Son goes to the cross? In David's case, thousands of his soldiers gave their lives for the sake of the kingdom, and, yet, they felt shame because the king was in mourning for the sake of his son. In God's case, thousands would give their lives for the sake of the kingdom,

180

but they could celebrate because God raised up his Son to lead them forward.

We live in a world still caught in a rebellion against God's kingdom. At times, like David, it appears that God is driven from his throne but we know at what cost God was restored to his throne. Now, the question remains whether we will invite God back to rule in our lives.

Psalm 130

I wait for the Lord, my soul waits, and in his word I hope.
— Psalm 130:5

If Psalm 130 is heard in the context of that agonizing wait that David experienced as his army went out to confront the army of his son Absalom, we hear the pain of waiting in impossible circumstances for some healing word from God. Many a believer has known the depth of agony out of which they have cried out to God when they could not see any solution to their suffering. Some of the deepest of human agonies, like that of David's, is caused by conflict within the family. Again, like David, family situations can place us in a terrible bind between what we believe to be right and a love for a family member that we cannot give up on. "Out of the depths I cry to you, O Lord. Lord, hear my voice! Let your ears be attentive to the voice of my supplications!" (vv. 1-2). David's inability to handle his own lusts and desires had infused his family and resulted in the rape of his daughter, Tamar, and violence among his sons.

When a family member goes astray, it is not unusual for family members to become aware of their own guilt in the situation. Yet that retrospective awareness will not solve the problem. The psalmist recognized that the solution could only come in the hands of a forgiving God. "If you, O Lord, should mark iniquities, Lord, who could stand? But there is forgiveness with you, so that you may be revered" (vv. 3-4). Many a pastor has experienced this same agony within the family of the church that tears itself apart because it cannot get beyond its own lusts and desires. Sometimes the church even engenders guilt in the pastor as she or he examines the things that they have not been able to accomplish. It is difficult to wait for the Lord when your heart is being torn apart. Yet such a situation again reminds us of our true dependence on God. "O Israel, hope in the Lord! For with the Lord there is steadfast love, and with him is great power to redeem. It is he who will redeem Israel (or the church) from all its iniquities."

Ephesians 4:25—5:2

So then, putting away falsehood let all of us speak the truth to our neighbors, for we are members of one another. — Ephesians 4:25

It is clear from Paul's instructions that the new life in Christ is not automatic. Like the church today, so Paul's church wrestled with the negative human behaviors that tore at community. The central core of Paul's instructions was a reminder that our faith is lived out in relationships. We are to measure our individual behavior in terms of how it affects the bonds of community. "Let no evil talk come out of your mouths, but only what is useful for building up, as there is need, so that your words may give grace to those who hear" (v. 29). At the same time, this is not avoiding conflict through the hiding of our true feelings. That type of peace leads to a false sense of community which is finally destructive to truth. "So then, putting away falsehood let all of us speak the truth to our neighbors, for we are members of one another" (v. 25).

If we are truthful with our neighbor, sometimes our differences will result in anger. If we bury that anger so as not to cause conflict, we will, in Paul's words, be making "room for the devil" (v. 27). Such repressed anger continues to work within us and will lead to a life of lies that is destructive to community. Drawing upon the wisdom of the psalms, Paul encouraged people to "be angry but do not sin; do not let the sun go down on your anger ..." (v. 26; see Psalm 4:4 footnote).

Anger is a natural human emotion generated by our independent spirits rubbing up against each other. Facing anger honestly and immediately, keeping the value of the building up of the community primarily in mind, we have the opportunity to grow in relationship to each other. Living in the kingdom is not an easy task, and it is a continual challenge for the church. What church has not experienced periods when the negative spirits seemed to dominate? Can you not hear Paul speaking directly to your church when he says, "Put away from you all bitterness and wrath and anger and wrangling and slander, together with all malice..."? (v. 31). But when Paul urged us "to be kind to one another, tenderhearted, forgiving one another ..." (v. 32), it was more than just pragmatic advice. God in Christ, having formed us through forgiveness, established the foundation for our community. The heart of authentic community rests on our recognizing that God has forgiven us, and, therefore, to be true to God, we must forgive each other. This will continually require sacrifice on each individual's part on behalf of the others in the community. In doing so, we are imitating God as we seek to "live in love, as Christ loved us and gave himself up for us, a fragrant offering and sacrifice to God" (v. 2).

John 6:35, 41-51

> *Jesus said to them, "I am the bread of life. Whoever comes to me will never be hungry, and whoever believes in me will never be thirsty." —* John 6:35

The church continually experiences the tension of wanting her practical needs met while at the same time realizing that there is a deeper hunger that yearns to be fed. Jesus had previously performed the miracle of the feeding of the 5,000 (6:1-14), and they responded to Jesus as someone who could meet their immediate needs which were the continual challenge of their daily lives. The popularity of sermons that offer practical advice on daily living is testimony to that continual hunger among believers. Yet the authority of such preaching is the experience of the believer who finds it applicable to his or her life. In this passage, Jesus used the people's hunger for bread to point to a deeper hunger. He drew a contrast between the physical need of bread and a deeper hunger that was also a life hunger. "Your ancestors ate the manna in the wilderness, and they died. This is the bread that comes down from heaven, so that one may eat of it and not die" (vv. 49-50).

When Deuteronomy commented on the feeding of manna in the wilderness, it recognized that same dual hunger. "He humbled you by letting you hunger, then by feeding you with manna, with which neither you nor your ancestors were acquainted, in order to make you understand that one does not live by bread alone, but by every word that comes from the mouth of the Lord" (Deuteronomy 8:3). But when Jesus began to speak of things eternal, the question of authority was again raised. "Is not this Jesus, the son of Joseph, whose father and mother we know? How can he now say, 'I have come down from heaven'?" (v. 42).

For many people in our society, even those in the church, they can accept the practical ways the church helps them, but it is more difficult to believe that what the church has to offer can affect them eternally. People are free to be offended in the church and leave the community without any great concern that they may be risking anything eternal. Yet at the same time there is a continual hunger in our society that has made materials on spirituality a growth industry. Jesus offered himself as the bread that feeds that deeper hunger: "... and the bread that I will give for the life of the world is my flesh" (v. 51). It is as one seeks to live the life of faith within the body of Christ, the church, that one is both offended by its human nature and drawn to the truth of our full dependence on God for eternal life.

Proper 15
Pentecost 13
Ordinary Time 20

1 Kings 2:10-12; 3:3-14

God said to him, "Because you have asked this, and have not asked for yourself long life or riches, or for the life of your enemies, but have asked for yourself understanding to discern what is right, I now do according to your word."
— 1 Kings 3:11-12a

It was a time of transition of leadership for Israel. David had been king for forty years. A whole generation of people had never known any other king. What would it be like to be under a new king? What would it be like for Solomon to assume the leadership of God's people? Many a church has faced the anxious time of transition of leadership when one pastor leaves and another arrives. It is especially difficult when the previous pastor has had a long pastorate. There is both the issue of continuity and of newness that confronts the new pastor. If the new pastor moves too fast to change things, people may see it as a negative judgment on the previous pastor or on them.

Yet, because each pastor has his or her own unique calling and personality, it is both impossible and ineffective to maintain things exactly as they were. If the previous pastorate was a strong one, the new person may even feel inadequate in the face of the challenge. Like Solomon, his prayer may be, "O Lord my God, you have made your servant king in place of my father David, although I am only a little child; I do not know how to go out or come in" (v. 7). At the same time, such modesty may drive one to want to establish himself or herself and prove that the new pastor can be as successful as the previous pastor. Since the church will have conflicting desires and expectations for the new pastor, it is a time that requires of both of them a great deal of prayer in discerning God's purpose for the church.

Most churches and pastors feel the pressure of wanting to be successful in worldly terms of budget, reputation, and membership. These are not unlike what God recognized Solomon could have prayed for — long life, riches, or the life of his enemies. Solomon's prayer was, "Give your servant therefore an understanding mind to govern your people, able to discern between good and evil; for who can govern this your great people?" (v. 9). Should this not be the prayer of any pastor and any congregation as they seek to be faithful to God who has gathered them together as a "great people?"

Psalm 111

The fear of the Lord is the beginning of wisdom; all those who practice it have a good understanding. — Psalm 111:10

The fear that the psalmist referred to was less a sense of threat than a sense of awe and respect for God. This sense of awe and respect is often diluted in a society that is so concentrated on the immanence or presence of God that it neglects his transcendence or eternal nature. It is in balancing the immanence and transcendence of God that the believer comes to a full respect and awe of God. For the psalmist, this was expressed in a praise of God in the midst of the company of believers (v. 1). Praise was a rehearsal of the greatness of God as experienced in the way in which God had continued to express faithfulness to God's people. "Great are the works of the Lord, studied by all who delight in them" (v. 2). Imagine the impact on a congregation who regularly rehearses how God is gracious and merciful in their lives (v. 4) and has provided food for those who fear him (v. 5). In the same way that Israel saw the greatness of God "in giving them the heritage of the nations" (v. 6), consider the effect of a congregation reading the history of their own congregation for signs of how God had shaped their heritage. It was as Israel rehearsed God's faithfulness in their past that they grew confident in their relationship with God for the future. "The works of his hands are faithful and just; all his precepts are trustworthy. They are established forever and ever, to be performed with faithfulness and uprightness" (vv. 7-8).

The more a congregation rehearses the presence of God in their community, the more they will develop an awe and respect for the way that God works with us. This same sense of God's presence also confronts us with the mystery of God's transcendence. Who are we that the God of the universe takes note of our lives and pays attention to our hungers? "The fear of the Lord is the beginning of wisdom; all those who practice it have a good understanding. His praise endures forever."

Ephesians 5:15-20

Be careful then how you live, not as unwise people but as wise, making the most of the time, because the days are evil. — Ephesians 5:15

There is a casualness about the practice of the faith that seems to infect many contemporary Christians. When life is fairly comfortable, it is too easy for believers to see faith as just an add on to an otherwise fairly good life. As many have pointed out, we no longer live in a society that naturally supports the practice of the faith. Not only are the many demands of life in competition for the time we might devote to the nurture of our faith in ourselves and in the lives of our children, but also time for worship itself has to compete against many other attractive activities. When nothing catastrophic occurs in our lives when we neglect the practice of our faith, we begin to treat it as one among many alternatives for how we spend our time. Then a tragedy occurs that shatters the illusion that our society is continuing to make positive progression, and we are suddenly faced with the fact that there is real evil in our world. That can be a cause for panic and despair. Paul, however, admonishes us to "make the most of the time, because the days are evil."

The word that is translated "time" is *kairos*. *Kairos* carries the connotation of a pregnant opportunity filled with potential for new life. Those moments when we are shaken out of our complacency are God-given moments for us to realize his purpose in our lives. "So do not be foolish but understand what the will of the Lord is" (v. 17). Shaky moments in our lives, or in the society around us, are precisely the time when we should gather together as a community and "... be filled with the Spirit, as you sing psalms and hymns and spiritual songs among yourselves, singing and making melody to the Lord in your hearts ..." (vv. 18-19). Worship, above all else, refocuses our attention on the one who is able to redeem all moments and fill our lives with purpose and significance.

John 6:51-58

Those who eat my flesh and drink my blood have eternal life, and I will raise them up on the last day.... — John 6:54

If many Christians partake in communion without giving deep consideration to what is taking place, this raw language confronts them with its stark reality. It was one of the accusations against the early church that they secretly participated in cannibalistic rites. If a nonbeliever overheard such language as the above quote, it is certainly understandable how one might get the wrong impression. It is also understandable how some very sincere Jews, with their almost reverent attitude about the life-giving power of blood, could be offended.

Unlike the other gospels, John did not portray Jesus as keeping the Passover before his death because, for John, Jesus was the Pass-over. He was the Lamb of God without blemish whose blood warned off the angel of death and provided the passage to freedom for God's people (Exodus 12:1-13). A meal was considered a very intimate activity. When people had eaten at the table together, they had a responsibility for each other. This is what made Judas' betrayal all the more heinous.

Here, John was trying to impress upon us the intimate connection between Jesus and those who participated with him at the table. "Those who eat my flesh and drink my blood have eternal life, and I will raise them up on the last day; for my flesh is true food and my blood is true drink. Those who eat my flesh and drink my blood abide in me, and I in them" (vv. 54-56). Perhaps contemporary Christians need to once again face the offense of the table so that they might experience the power of what is taking place in this event. By ingesting Christ, we are becoming one with him. By eating his body and drinking his blood, we are becoming his body.

Proper 16
Pentecost 14
Ordinary Time 21

1 Kings 8:(1, 6, 10-11) 22-30, 41-43

But will God indeed dwell on the earth? Even the heaven and the highest heaven cannot contain you, much less this house that I have built! — 1 Kings 8:27

There is always a need for particular places to remind us of what is true in all places. We build churches hoping that by setting aside special places to worship God, we will be reminded of his presence in all places. We recognize the human need of the particular to remind us of the universal. If we simply said that God was everywhere, we might forget that he is anywhere. Yet, there is always the danger that in building a particular place, we might develop the illusion that we can contain God in that building and hide from him when we are far from the building.

In the story of Israel, there was a clear tension between the God who dwelt in a tent and therefore moved from place to place and the God who dwelt in a temple. From a human standpoint, we can understand why David might have been embarrassed to build himself a beautiful palace but to have the ark, which represented the presence of God, residing in a tent. We build beautiful cathedrals in order to broadcast our praise of God.

Yet, scripture continues to remind us that the true praise of God is revealed by how we live our lives. In Solomon's prayer, he both recognized the transcendence of God and the power of having a place toward which people can focus their attention. He pleaded "... that your eyes may be open night and day toward this house, the place of which you said, 'My name shall be there,' ..." (v. 29). We build our churches and lift our spires so that the name of God may be made visible to the community around us. As Solomon prayed, so we pray that when people are caught in distress, they will turn to the place where God is named. We believe that God, who dwells everywhere, will hear such prayers and respond.

Psalm 84

My soul longs, indeed it faints for the courts of the Lord; my heart and my flesh sing for joy to the living God. — Psalm 84:2

The psalmist recognized the centrality of worship in the fulfillment of the restlessness of his soul. As he gazed on the temple, he was drawn to the very presence of God that completed his joy in life (v. 2). This was not something unique to the priest but was so much a part of creation that even the sparrow found a home within the temple (v. 3). All of creation was meant to live a life that gave praise to its maker. Those who found a place of praise in their lives discovered that it went with them as they journeyed through life. "As they go through the valley of Baca they make it a place of springs; the early rain also covers it with pools. They go from strength to strength; the God of gods will be seen in Zion" (vv. 6-7).

Much of our population has lost their connection with the purpose or meaning that gives their lives value. People learn how to live for fleeting pleasures or even just to survive, but they lack the zest derived from knowing that their lives make a real difference in the unfolding of the universe. It is central to the truth of the psalms that the Lord reigns and that the truth of our lives is discovered in relationship to the God of the universe. "For the Lord God is a sun and shield (protection); he bestows favor and honor (purpose and respect). No good thing does the Lord withhold from those who walk uprightly" (v. 11) — (ethics is important). A life worth living is continually buffeted by the forces of society and can only stay connected with the truth at the center of life through regular gathering together with the community to offer worship and praise.

Ephesians 6:10-20

Put on the whole armor of God, so that you may be able to stand against the wiles of the devil. — Ephesians 6:11

It is one of the illusions of Western society that evil is the result of ignorance or misunderstanding. We continue to believe that we can educate ourselves out of the evils that beset us. For those who believe in a society of progress, it is difficult to accept that we are confronted with real forces of evil. "For our struggle is not against enemies of blood and flesh, but against the rulers, against the authorities, against the cosmic powers of this present darkness, against spiritual forces of evil in the heavenly places" (v. 12). This is more than individuals with mistaken ideas. Paul asserted that the capacity for evil was inherent in the institutions and cosmic structures that shaped people's lives.

If we are going to resist the power of evil in our lives, we need truth, but we also need a commitment to righteousness and a willingness to proclaim "a gospel of peace. With all of these, take the shield of faith, with which you will be able to quench all flaming arrows of the evil one. Take the helmet of salvation, and the sword of the Spirit, which is the word of God" (vv. 15-17).

Western society has tended to emphasize the rational at the expense of the spiritual. This was perhaps in reaction to the Middle Ages that tended to lean in the opposite direction. The "armor of God" includes both truth and spirit in its struggle against the evil that exists in this world. Churches that emphasize the intellectual side of faith often run the danger of quenching the Spirit and becoming rather bland echoes of the larger society that also uses the intellect to combat the evils of society. Churches that have their emphasis on the purely spiritual side of faith often run the danger of denying the gifts of intelligence that God has granted so that we can bring order to our world. Neither seems to have the full armor of God with which to combat the evil that besets us. When people of faith take evil with its full seriousness, they have resources that the world dearly needs to combat that evil.

John 6:56-69

> *So Jesus asked the twelve, "Do you also wish to go away?"*
> *Simon Peter answered him, "Lord, to whom can we go?*
> *You have the words of eternal life."* — John 6:67-68

Jesus had been pressing the larger group of his disciples to move from an understanding of faith as a means to acquire the necessities of life (bread) to an understanding that the meaning of life was drawn

191

from the word of God. The gospel of John made very clear that Jesus was the Word of God made flesh (1:14). Here in the physical life of this man, Jesus, is the true expression of God. In the intimate connection between Christ and the believers we are to discover the eternal truths of life. Jesus' suggestion that they would eat his flesh and drink his blood was too offensive for many of them to comprehend, and they began to complain. He said to them, "Does this offend you? ... The words that I have spoken to you are spirit and life" (vv. 61, 63). Many of his followers turned away because they could not accept what he was asking of them.

The church is filled with people who come because they want what the church offers them. Yet they wish to be the one who establishes the criteria of what is and is not acceptable. When they are asked to accept that Jesus is the criterion of all truth, this confronts them with a different canon than they wish to accept. Now there is a criterion of truth outside of themselves to which they are answerable. It is interesting to note that when Jesus confronted the twelve and said, "Do you also wish to go away?" they did not deny that they had had such thoughts. Still, they recognized that in Jesus they had encountered "words of eternal life." In this person of Jesus they had experienced the connection between their finite lives and the eternal truth of the universe. In Jesus their lives had meaning that extended beyond their earthly existence. "We have come to believe and know that you are the Holy One of God" (v. 69).

It is instructive for the church, however, to recognize that there is a shadow side to this discovery as well. Among the twelve, the foundation of the new community of hope, resided the betrayer as well. The church must never grow so confident of their grasp of the truth that they forget that within their own understanding the seeds of betrayal are also present.

Proper 17
Pentecost 15
Ordinary Time 22

Song Of Solomon 2:8-13

> *Arise, my love, my fair one, and come away; for now the winter is past, the rain is over and gone.* — Song Of Solomon 2:10b-11

The Song of Solomon is a love song that celebrates the gift of love. It is rich poetry that evokes in us the power of love. It is like the rush of delight with the first sign of spring. When we come into the presence of the one that we love, a power wells up within us almost involuntarily. While Christians have allegorized the book as a reflection of God's love for Israel or Christ's love for the church, one needs to approach it first as a celebration of the gift of love of one person for another. We deny its power if we do not first recognize its celebration of the power of love. It is a reminder of that most basic need within us to love and be loved by another. Like any powerful gift, love can, and often is, used superficially or destructively. We continually see the power of love used in a superficial manner in order to sell products. Sadly, we see the hunger for love cause people to act in ways that destroy their careers, reputation, and often even a family that they value.

Yet, love is also the core gift of life. The scriptures do not shy away from recognizing the physical nature of the expression of love. Especially in this poem, it is very explicit. Love is so rooted in the core of our being that it demands physical as well as emotional expression. Life yearns for touch and a desire to be embraced. Love also allows us to recognize our need to both surrender to and be surrendered to. Our bodies are so designed as to find fulfillment in that surrender that allows us to be completely vulnerable to another. It is here that we discover this poem's connection with God. In our human yearning to find someone with whom we can safely surrender, we discover our deeper longing to surrender to God and to love and be loved.

Psalm 45:1-2, 6-9

Your royal scepter is a scepter of equity; you love righteousness and hate wickedness. — Psalm 45:6b-7a

This psalm was apparently intended as a poem to be read at a king's wedding. If we only read it in that light, it might have little other than historical interest for us. For Christians, however, we proclaim Christ as our Lord and king. Therefore the celebration of the king at his wedding can speak to us of Christ's marriage to his bride, the church. When the psalmist proclaims that "grace is poured upon your lip; therefore God has blessed you forever" (v. 2), we are aware of the grace of Christ who speaks words of love and forgiveness even to his enemies.

We are drawn to Luke's recording of the words of Jesus on the cross: "Father, forgive them; for they do not know what they are doing" (Luke 23:34). As we continue with the verses that are indicated for us, we hear, "Your throne, O God, endures forever and ever" (v. 6), and we are reminded of the eternity of Christ's rule. In the same manner that Christians saw in the words of Isaiah 9:6-7 reflections of Christ as king, so we are led to see Christ in the psalmist words: "Your royal scepter is a scepter of equity; you love righteousness and hate wickedness." We hear the echo of the church's praise in the words "from ivory palaces stringed instruments make you glad ..." (v. 8). The church as the bride of Christ is dressed to honor Christ even as the bride of the king is dressed in the gold of Ophir. What we are reminded of in the psalm is the necessity of celebrating Christ as the husband of the church and appearing before our Lord in a manner that does him honor.

James 1:17-27

If any think they are religious, and do not bridle their tongues but deceive their hearts, their religion is worthless.
— James 1:26

The letter of James stands as a challenge to any Christian who, having been saved by grace, does not then allow his or her life to be transformed into a life of generosity and love. James will not allow Christians to be casual about the grace by which they are saved. It should result in fruits of the Spirit if it is to be a testimony of gratitude to what God has done for them. "Religion that is pure and undefiled before God, the Father, is this: to care for orphans and widows in their distress, and to keep oneself unstained by the world" (v. 27). In fact, James would go so far as to suggest that "every generous act of giving, with every perfect gift, is from above ..." (v. 17). God's intention, according to James, is to make us "a kind of firstfruits of his creatures" (v. 18). James did not deny that salvation was by grace alone, but he was clear that it should then result in a changed life. "But be doers of the word, and not merely hearers who deceive themselves. For if any are hearers of the word and not doers, they are like those who look at themselves in a mirror, for they look at themselves and, on going away, immediately forget what they were like" (vv. 22-24).

It would be like a Christian who experiences the grace of God moving in his or her life but then forgets that graciousness in his or her relationship with others. Such Christians would be denying themselves the blessing of their salvation. James' instruction to the church is to remember that having received the grace of Christ, we then experience the continued blessing of Christ when we "look into the perfect law, the law of liberty, and persevere, being not hearers who forget but doers who act — they will be blessed in their doing" (v. 25).

Mark 7:1-8, 14-15, 21-23

This people honor me with their lips, but their hearts are far from me; in vain do they worship me, teaching human precepts as doctrines. — Mark 7:6b-7

Throughout its entire history, the church has wrestled with the discrepancy between outward acts and inward spirit. The church has often accused the Jewish faith of being a religion of law while the church was founded on grace. The prophet Jeremiah proclaimed that God would create a new covenant that would be based not on external laws but an inner transformation of the heart (Jeremiah 31:33). Christians frequently saw Jesus' establishment of the church as the creation of the new covenant or New Testament. We even use that term to refer to the scriptures that we added to the Bible. Yet immediately, as we can see in this earliest of gospels, the church had to be reminded of the same problem of external behavior versus inner transformation.

Rituals and traditions can do much to nurture us in the framework of the faith. Yet, many people grow satisfied with these externals and forget that they are only the outer framework for an inner transformation that is necessary. "For it is from within, from the human heart, that evil intentions come: fornication, theft, murder, adultery, avarice, wickedness, deceit, licentiousness, envy, slander, pride, folly" (vv. 21-22). When the church fails to recognize the essential nature of this inner transformation, it often settles for the repression of outward appearances of sin. Then, when the church least expects it, the outward manifestation of such evil bursts forth in a scandal that shames the church and therefore mocks Christ. The confession of sins is a critical part of the community of faith's worship experience. Here is an opportunity for us to face honestly our own inner sins and seek a cleansing that enables us to live together without shame.

Proper 18
Pentecost 16
Ordinary Time 23

Proverbs 22:1-2, 8-9, 22-23

A good name is to be chosen rather than great riches and favor is better than silver or gold. — Proverbs 22:1

The wisdom of Proverbs is a summary of wisdom gathered from an intense observation of life. It is a very familiar form of wisdom treasured in most cultures. It is the golden nugget mined from the flowing stream of life. It is not meant to be a truth imposed on life like a commandment but rather a truth deduced by observing life. For example, we have popular sayings such as, "A stitch in time saves nine." "If we could just learn the right religious formula, then we could be healers as well." "A penny saved is a penny earned." None of these maxims is in the form of a commandment. They are observations that have their authority in people's acknowledgment.

Consider two contrasting examples. Arthur set out to become a rich man, and he was not concerned about who he stepped on to get there. He described himself as a bottomline guy. He forgot that "a good name is to be chosen rather than great riches." He did not have many close friends since he assumed that other people were a lot like him and were basically after his money. He was a rich, lonely, unhappy man. Eloise was always able to find time for other people. People intuitively trusted her. She did not have much money. She cleaned other people's houses for a living and put two children through school. When she fell ill, people from all over offered to help her with expenses. At such times, she knew that "favor was better than silver or gold." Of course, one can think of exceptions to the truth of such proverbs, but they represent a truth that has stood the test of time.

Psalm 125

> *Those who trust in the Lord are like Mount Zion, which cannot be moved, but abides forever.* — Psalm 125:1

This is a difficult psalm because it seems to challenge our very experience. The message is clear. We are to trust in the Lord, and God will surround us with protection in the same way that Jerusalem is surrounded by mountains that protect it. The analogy is based on the assumption that in the same way that the topography of Jerusalem builds in a natural protection that makes it impregnable, so our trust in God will make us impregnable. The problem is that foreigners have conquered Jerusalem several times. The very analogy can make us insecure about our faith. Perhaps from a longer historical perspective, we can recognize that given the continual attacks on our faith and the occasional occupation of our faith by the enemies of doubt and fear, our only protection is the Lord.

While, like the mountains that surround Jerusalem, the active practice of our faith can provide us a shield, we cannot assume that the natural trappings of faith will ultimately protect us. There will be times when our only source of help will rest beyond whatever we can do. We need to continually pray, "Do good, O Lord, to those who are good, and to those who are upright in their hearts" (v. 4). Our faith does not protect us from challenges internally and externally, but when we are attacked, we can learn again and again to trust in the one who is faithful to us even when we fail in our own faithfulness. It is our one and only hope.

James 2:1-10 (11-13) 14-17

> *My brothers and sisters, do you with your acts of favoritism really believe in our glorious Lord Jesus Christ?* — James 2:1

James continues his assault on "people who talk the talk but don't walk the walk." He is unrelenting and not very kind in his challenge to behavior that he is seeing among Christians. For middle-class Christians, his words strike at the heart of class and economic differences within our society. Who is this preacher who challenges our social graces by pointing out that we are showing favoritism to those who are dressed richly over against those who come into our churches dressed in dirty clothes? He even goes further and suggests that God may have an option for the poor: "Has not God chosen the poor in the world to be rich in faith and to be heirs of the kingdom that he has promised to those who love him?" (v. 5). Then he really shows his prejudice by suggesting that if we were to be wary of anyone, we should be wary of the wealthy: "Is it not the rich who oppress you? Is it not they who drag you into court? Is it not they who blaspheme the excellent name that was invoked over you?" (vv. 6-7).

For those who have worked hard to acquire whatever possessions they have, James' words seem harsh and offensive. They certainly are not designed to attract the wealthy members of the community to join the church. Unless, of course, those of us who have been blessed with material goods experience a transformation of the heart that recognizes that what we have is a blessing that allows us to be generous with those who have less. By James' challenge, we are invited to examine the living out of our faith as it shapes our use of the resources with which we have been blessed. "If a brother or sister is naked and lacks daily food, and one of you says to them, 'Go in peace; keep warm and eat your fill.' And yet you do not supply their bodily needs, what is the good of that? So faith by itself, if it has no works, is dead" (vv. 15-17).

Since most of us have seen and perhaps participated in acts of discrimination in our lives, we recognize how difficult it is to live the Christian faith. We are always in need of the grace of God and the vision of what it is that God asks of us.

Mark 7:24-37

Sir, even the dogs under the table eat the children's crumbs.
— Mark 7:28

Here are two stories of Jesus healing people outside the faith community. In both cases, they violated Jesus' desire for obscurity. In the first case, Jesus had entered a house to find some quiet, and a foreign woman violated his privacy to seek assistance for her daughter. In the second, Jesus asked the man and his friends to keep the healing quiet, but they immediately go out and spread the word about his healing power. In both cases, the ones seeking the healing did not feel any necessity in accepting what Jesus told them. In the first story,

Jesus made it very clear that his time needed to be focused on his ministry to the Jewish community. He even used what appears to be an insulting proverb. "Let the children be fed first, for it is not fair to take the children's food and throw it to the dogs" (v. 27). But the woman refused to be offended by the proverb and turned it to her own favor. "Sir, even the dogs under the table eat the children's crumbs" (v. 28).

In the second story, though he had received the favor of Jesus' healing, the man and his friends refused to keep quiet about what had happened. And in both cases, Jesus was clearly exercising his ministry outside the bounds of the Jewish community. Clearly, the second story reflects the prophet Isaiah's grand vision of the day of salvation where "the eyes of the blind shall be opened, and the ears of the deaf unstopped; then the lame shall leap like a deer, and the tongue of the speechless sing for joy" (Isaiah 35:5-6a). Perhaps the first story reflects Isaiah 49:6: "It is too light a thing that you should be my servant to raise up the tribes of Jacob and to restore the survivors of Israel; I will give you as a light to the nations, that my salvation may reach to the end of the earth."

For Mark's church, and perhaps ours, the stories push the church beyond normal assumptions of what is acceptable and reminds the church that God is outside the church responding to the needs of others who seek new beginnings for themselves or their loved ones.

Proper 19
Pentecost 17
Ordinary Time 24

Proverbs 1:20-33

How long, O simple ones, will you love being simple? How long will scoffers delight in their scoffing and fools hate knowledge? — Proverbs 1:22

At least in American society, there has always been an anti-intellectual strain. This manifests itself within the Christian community through a disparaging of the hard intellectual wrestling with the faith. This has been exacerbated in recent times by a culture that demands fast foods and responds well to politicians who offer simple answers and easy slogans. The growth of churches that offer "the simple faith" or, as it is sometimes called, "the old time religion" is quite apparent in our society. The tragedy is that this leaves us very unprepared for the tougher challenges of our society that are being raised by our advancement in technology and genetics. Wisdom declares, "Because I have called and you refused, have stretched out my hand and no one heeded, and because you have ignored all my counsel and would have none of my reproof, I also will laugh at your calamity; I will mock when panic strikes you ..." (vv. 24-26).

The book of Proverbs is a compilation of wisdom drawn from keen observation of life. It is based on the assumption that a measure of God's truth is expressed through the creation and can be grasped by those who are willing to read the "signs of the times." Proverbs are not necessary conclusions but likely possibilities. Wisdom observes that those who have disparaged wisdom "shall eat the fruit of their way and be sated with their own devices. For waywardness kills the simple, and the complacency of fools destroys them; but those who listen to me will be secure and will live at ease without dread of disaster" (vv. 31-33). These observations stand as a challenge to the churches. Will we repent of our refusal to do the hard work of wrestling with the challenges of our age and therefore be prepared to offer good news in the face of the challenges of our age?

Psalm 19

Let the words of my mouth and the meditation of my heart
be acceptable to you, O Lord, my rock and my redeemer.
— Psalm 19:14

Many a preacher has begun his sermon with this simple prayer either uttered or unuttered. There is an awareness of our own inadequacy in the task of preaching no matter how smooth we are in the process. Psalm 19 celebrates the revelation of God in two ways. In the first, the psalmist celebrates the revelation of God through creation. For him, the heavens tell "the glory of God" (v. 1). It is as if the creation is speaking of God even though "there is no speech, nor are there words ..." (v. 3). As John Calvin said, there are two books of revelation, and one of them is the creation itself. "There is no speech, nor are there words; their voice is not heard; yet their voice goes out through all the earth and their words to the end of the world."

We may pay too little attention to how the very wonder of creation speaks of God. While the character of God may depend more on the revelation of scripture, the work of God in creation displays the wonder of his work. It is hard to look at the pictures of the universe taken by the Hubble telescope or to see the delicate yet marvelously made structure of a newborn without being awed by the wisdom contained in nature. None of it insists on God as creator, but to believe it is the result of pure chance takes a larger leap of faith than to believe that intelligence is behind the creation.

If we hunger to know more of God, we turn to the law of God. It is important to note that when the scriptures speak of the law of God, they are speaking of more than a set of rules. They are speaking of the stories and commandments that reveal the character of the one who chose to reveal the divine self to us. These scripture stories provide wisdom for the simple, a rejoicing of the heart to know that we are not alone, and an enlightening of the heart for those who desire to know the true way of life. "More to be desired are they than gold, even much fine gold; sweeter also than honey, and drippings of the honeycomb" (v. 10). These stories of the people of God and the commandments that they derived from God convey to us that we are not alone and that there is purpose and direction for our lives if we choose to follow them.

At the same time, if there is a creator that expects something of us and there is a way of life that is better than others, then we have to confront the fact that we do not always live in the way of truth. "Moreover by them is your servant warned; in keeping them there is great reward. But who can detect their errors? Clear me of hidden faults" (vv. 11-12). Our lives are dependent on the grace of God to watch over us and redeem us from all errors. The preacher comes to his task fully aware of the responsibility and of his or her own inadequacy to the task of lifting up the truth of both revelations of God in a way that directs people in the right paths. "Let the words of my mouth and the meditation of my heart be acceptable to you, O Lord, my rock and redeemer."

James 3:1-12

How great a forest is set ablaze by a small fire! And the tongue is a fire. — James 3:5b-6a

Any person who has ever become involved in the workings of a church knows the power of the tongue to be destructive to the community of the church. It is little wonder that Paul named gossip as one of the fruits of the flesh that will bar one from the kingdom of heaven. Yet despite that clear warning, a church seems incapable of curbing the gossip of its members.

At the center of gossip is the tongue that makes it all possible. James begins with a reminder of the heavy responsibility of teachers. Those who have taught know how often something they have said can have a profound effect on one of their students. More often than not, they discover that the person interpreted what they said in a quite different way than they intended it. The responsibility of teaching is a heavy and often frightening responsibility. James then proceeds to suggest that though the tongue seems a very small organ in the body, it is like a bridle that guides a horse or even a rudder that guides a ship. Who has not experienced the difficulty of taming their own tongue, let alone the tongue of another?

The church, because it invites a diverse community together to pursue the faith, is subject to multiple tongues, each of which can start a series of fires. Like most powerful gifts, the tongue can become either a blessing or a curse to a community of faith. "With it we bless the Lord and Father, and with it we curse those who are made in the likeness of God. From the same mouth come blessing and cursing" (vv. 9-10). The constant challenge of the church is to modify the damage that is caused by a loose tongue and to enhance the blessing possible through the proper use of the tongue.

In the final analysis, we are to gauge what we say by the criterion of whether it will result in the blessing of God or the cursing of a member. It is not an easy task for pastor or member, and they need each other's support in the continual struggle.

Mark 8:27-38

He asked them, "But who do you say that I am?" Peter answered him, "You are the Messiah." — Mark 8:29

This passage marks the turning point in the gospel of Mark. Prior to this, most of Jesus' ministry was focused on the public ministry. After this, he spent more time instructing the disciples. There are turning points in any ministry. There is the public side of ministry that is focused on demonstrating the love of God for humanity through your service to their needs. But then comes a time when people do have to answer the question of who they believe Jesus to be. Peter represents the church in his response, "You are the Messiah." Having acknowledged that truth, it is incumbent on the church to then face a deeper responsibility of faith.

As Peter also demonstrated, the more complex issues of faith are also the more frightening aspects of faith. It is one thing to acknowledge that Jesus is the Christ, but then we have to answer whether we are willing to follow him as our Lord, even if it means suffering. Most people initially want to have a faith that fulfills their needs. It is the next stage of faith that allows us to recognize that we are called to respond to the needs of others. The scary part is that we are asked to do that even at the cost of our own comfort and security. "If any want to become my followers, let them deny themselves and take up their cross and follow me. For those who want to save their life will lose it, and those who lose their life for my sake, and for the sake of the gospel, will save it" (vv. 34-35). This is a counterintuitive truth. Our whole inclination is to want to preserve our life and to prosper in it. While we know that there are risks involved in achieving our goals, it runs counter to our intuition to believe that we should be willing to risk our safety and security on behalf of the needs of others. Yet by Jesus' own life, he demonstrated that this was the path that leads to eternal life.

The life we lead is our wilderness experience in which we have the opportunity to learn that we are dependent on God. Along the way, precisely because of the gifts and benefits that God has blessed us with, we are tempted to conclude that we can make it on our own. At the same time, we are presented opportunities that are beyond our control, and these demonstrate God's faithfulness to us. Jesus faced the ultimate test with the cross. Here he would suffer death while witnessing the abandonment of the very disciples that he had taught. All his efforts and ideas would be wasted unless God could redeem this moment. It is with the resurrection that we learn that God, not death, has the final word.

Proper 20
Pentecost 18
Ordinary Time 25

Proverbs 31:10-31

A capable wife who can find? She is far more precious than jewels. The heart of her husband trusts in her, and he will have no lack of gain. — Proverbs 31:10-11

This is one of the more famous or infamous of the writings of Proverbs. On the one hand, it paints a picture of a perfect companion. She is perfect because she tirelessly devotes herself to taking care of others. It would seem, at first, to be the clear expression of a patriarchal society in which the woman's purpose is to serve her husband, whose main duty seems to be to take "his seat among the elders of the land" (v. 23) at the city gate. Yet on closer examination, it paints a picture of a woman who has power, authority, and a strong business sense. She is clearly in charge of her household (v. 15), but she is also adept in the business world (v. 16). She demonstrates the gift of compassion (v. 20), and is the one who has the foresight to plan for the future (v. 21). On top of all of this, she demonstrates excellent parental skills (v. 28).

If one is not exhausted by this picture of the perfect wife, one can pause to reflect on how her well-rounded personality not only gains her respect within the society around her (v. 31), but also demonstrates the faithful life to which we are all called (v. 30). The negative reaction to this passage may well reflect the chauvinism of our own society. Had it been a picture of a man of faith, we might have urged it as a picture of perfection towards which we all should strive. Here is a person who cares deeply and responsibly for her family, utilizes her considerable gifts for the sake of others, and is comfortable with the gift of wisdom that God has given her. Her very life, lived to its fullest, is a praise of God.

Psalm 1

They are like trees planted by streams of water, which yield their fruit in its season, and their leaves do not wither. — Psalm 1:3

This psalm, which introduces the whole book of Psalms, contrasts two ways of life. The one way is what might be called the way of the independent. This person is the one who desires to be the center of his or her own universe. Such a person does not need God and is skeptical of those who do. The problem for such people is that life is too short and our place in it too insignificant to make a lasting impression by ourselves. The self-contained individual is "like chaff that wind drives away ..." (v. 4). In contrast, there are those who attach their lives to the story of the universe that is unfolding in time. This is the story that God is telling. They look to the revelation of God's truth in scripture, and they discover happiness or satisfaction in finding a way to make their contribution to this unfolding story. "... Their delight is in the law of the Lord, and on his law they meditate day and night" (v. 2). Such people find their roots in something that is more substantial than a fleeting moment of time. "They are like trees planted by streams of water, which yield their fruit in its season, and their leaves do not wither" (v. 3).

A central challenge for many in our Western society is that they lack purpose in their lives. Many of the bizarre turns in people's lives are generated from people's discovery that they have achieved many of the initial goals that they set out to accomplish and that they still have very little meaning in their lives. What seemed like worthy goals are found to be too limited. They are in need of a higher purpose that makes their struggle and sacrifice worthwhile. The psalmist suggests that such purpose can be discovered only in the way of the eternal God. It is in meditating on the purposes of God that we discover our own purpose and the true meaning of our life.

James 3:13—4:3, 7-8a

But the wisdom from above is first pure, then peaceable, gentle, willing to yield, full of mercy and good fruits, without a trace of partiality or hypocrisy. — James 3:17

We live in a society that is cynical about experts and disdainful of the intellect. We are confused as to where we find truth and yet we hunger for wisdom. James suggested that there are two kinds of wisdom. He distinguished between wisdom from above and wisdom from below. We are very familiar with what he suggested is wisdom from below. It is generated by "bitter envy and selfish ambition in [our] hearts," and causes us to "be boastful and false to the truth" (v. 14). This kind of wisdom results in "disorder and wickedness of every kind" (v. 16).

At times, however, we experience what he called "wisdom from above." This wisdom is "first pure, then peaceable, gentle, willing to yield, full of mercy and good fruits, without a trace of partiality or hypocrisy" (v. 17). When we experience such wisdom, we know it immediately. It does not need proof texts or credentials. It allows us to feel good about ourselves and valued by our community. We may only experience it intermittently, but in those moments we do experience God's shalom. "And a harvest of righteousness is sown in peace for those who make peace" (v. 18).

James was very clear that the source of our conflicts and tensions within the church or in the world have their origins in the "cravings that are at war within [us]" (v. 1). When you consider your own church and any disputes or tension that has arisen within it, would you agree with James that at the center of our disputes and tension is covetousness? "And you covet something and cannot obtain it; so you engage in disputes and conflicts" (v. 2). This is in contrast to a people who are "gentle, willing to yield, full of mercy and good fruits, without a trace of partiality or hypocrisy."

James assumed that such attributes were a reflection of God and that "God yearns jealously for the Spirit that he has made to dwell in us" (v. 5). The difficulty is that it is more than a case of willpower. We demonstrate the earthly manner of self-centeredness despite our best intentions. Yet recognition of this fact is the first step toward availing ourselves of "wisdom from above." "God opposes the proud, but gives grace to the humble" (v. 6).

Mark 9:30-37

When he was in the house, he asked them, "What were you arguing about on the way?" But they were silent, for on the way they had argued with one another who was the greatest. — Mark 9:33b-34

Despite the fact that Jesus had been teaching them about the servant ministry of the church and had predicted a second time that as servant he was going to suffer arrest and death on the cross, the disciples were still caught up in the dream of success and fame. The insatiable need of the ego to be affirmed and praised has plagued the church from its very beginning. Even in this community bound together by the self-giving love of Christ, we are constantly torn apart by the competing egos of the members of the community. It is almost impossible for the church to comprehend the clear teaching of Jesus to his disciples: "Whoever wants to be first must be last of all and servant of all" (v. 35).

It is hard to comprehend the transformation that would take place in a church if every member were committed to the task of serving the other members of the church. Especially in our individualistic culture, the thought of being so devoted to the well-being of others seems to challenge our very understanding of life. Then to develop the teaching further, Jesus took a very dramatic action. "Then he took a little child and put it among them; and taking it in his arms, he said to them, 'Whoever welcomes one such child in my name welcomes me, and whoever welcomes me welcomes not me but the one who sent me' " (vv. 36-37).

We tend to romanticize children in our society and therefore miss the challenge that Jesus was presenting. In that culture, the child was considered to be of only potential value. As a child he was only a burden to be cared for. He was a very vulnerable member of society. Jesus was taking this most vulnerable member of society and saying that to welcome this person in all the person's dependency was to welcome not only Jesus but also God. As a church, we cannot escape the challenge that God is present in the most vulnerable of our society. Like a drumbeat throughout scripture, the message rings forth again and again. God identifies with the most vulnerable and needy of our society. If we want to welcome God, we must reach out to them.

Proper 21
Pentecost 19
Ordinary Time 26

Esther 7:1-6, 9-10; 9:20-22

Then King Ahasuerus said to Queen Esther, "Who is he, and where is he, who has presumed to do this?" Esther said, "A foe and enemy, this wicked Haman!" Then Haman was terrified before the king and the queen. — Esther 7:5-6

These few verses scarcely do justice to this delightful story of Esther. It is a classic folktale of good versus evil, which has been repeated again and again in various guises. While it scarcely mentions God, it is designed to reveal the providential hand of God working behind the scenes, incognito, to bring about justice in this world.

The Jews were living quietly in a foreign land. An incident, which seemed far removed from them, took place in the king's palace that resulted in the deposing of the queen. A plan was put forth whereby the king could view all of the eligible young women in his kingdom and choose from among them a new queen. Esther was among the young women who were brought to the palace. Mordecai, her uncle, being aware of the prejudice against the Jews, warned her not to reveal her identity. Esther won the beauty contest and became the new queen. In the meantime, we are introduced to the classically evil Haman who advised the king. Haman was offended by the Jews' refusal to bow down to him and proceeded to develop a plot that would result in their destruction as a people. Mordecai asked Esther to intervene, but she was frightened.

Then we hear the classic line suggesting the providential hand of God in this opportunity. "Do not think that in the king's palace you will escape any more than all the other Jews. For if you keep silence at such a time as this, relief and deliverance will rise for the Jews from another quarter, but you and your father's family will perish. Who knows? Perhaps you have come to royal dignity for just such a time as this" (Esther 4:13-14). Esther gathered up her courage and developed an elaborate plan to win the king's favor and expose Haman and his plot against her people.

Undergirding the story is a confidence in the providence of God that is working behind the scenes to accomplish the divine purpose. There is also a belief that as believers we are placed in positions to assist God in defeating evil in this world. If we refuse to participate, God's purpose will be accomplished in another way, but we will suffer the consequences of our refusal. Both the providence of God and the capacity of human free will are preserved in this story. For churches that refuse to become involved in correcting injustice, it is a cautionary tale. For humans who suffer from those injustices, it is a story of hope.

Psalm 124

Our help is in the name of the Lord, who made heaven and earth. — Psalm 124:8

The Bible is quite clear that we are continually in a struggle between good and evil in our lives. It was important for Israel, situated as they were in a crossroads between superpowers that sought to conquer their world, to believe that someone greater than any power on earth protected them. While God was an invisible presence, signs of that help were often hidden in the mysterious ways in which events unfolded. The seemingly miraculous way in which they continued to escape the threats to their existence over time gave them confidence that God was faithful to them. They told and retold the formative story of their escape from Egypt, but then they included other stories of rescue both in the country and even later in exile, as with the story of Esther. Each time they rehearsed their history, they could say again, "If it had not been the Lord who was on our side, when our enemies attacked us, then they would have swallowed us up alive ..." (vv. 2-3). They knew that they could not explain the miracle of their existence by virtue of their cleverness, strength, or resources.

Their own history reminded them that they existed due to the grace of God and not by their works lest anyone should boast (Ephesians 2:9). It was almost with a sense of giddy unbelief that they could say, "Blessed be the Lord who has not given us as prey to their teeth. We have escaped like a bird from the snare of the fowlers; the snare is broken and we have escaped" (vv. 6-7). The temptation of life is to assume that we are in charge of our own future and that we shape our own destiny. Often that illusion is created by virtue of a selective amnesia that overlooks the many ways in which our life is gifted. It is in rehearsing the memory of our life that, with eyes of faith, we can join the psalmist in saying, "If it had not been the Lord who was on our side...." It is that awareness that enables us to affirm again and again, "Our help is in the name of the Lord, who made heaven and earth."

James 5:13-20

The prayer of the righteous is powerful and effective. —
James 5:16b

In a time when people, even believers, are quick to dismiss the church as a nonessential add-on to the more important personal journey of faith, the words of James are instructive. It is the communal gathering of the people of faith that encourages and nurtures our life in faith. It is too easy as an individual to allow our sufferings to throw us into despair. It is equally tempting in good times to forget the source of our blessings. It is the community of faith that reminds us that if we are suffering, we should pray; and if we are cheerful, we should sing songs of praise.

When we are ill, we are not left alone. It is the responsibility of the elders to bring the resources of faith to bear on our illness. At the same time, it is the church to which we should come to seek forgiveness for our sins. There is a power in the community of faith that is not available to the individual. "Therefore confess your sins to one another, and pray for one another, so that you may be healed" (v. 16). It is popular in our individualistic society to excuse our dismissal of the church through pointing out the failures of the church. While most churches provide plenty of evidence of their failure to demonstrate the faith they proclaim, they also provide the arena in which we can grow in the faith.

Paul recognized from the beginning that the treasure of the faith was contained in the clay jars of the church (2 Corinthians 4:7), but he saw in that very fact the power of God at work. James had admonished his people for their many shortcomings. Yet it is to the church, with all its frailties, that he called the people. It is the church that preserves the scriptures, the rituals that nurture us, and the opportunity for praise that points us to the giver of all that we have. It is the church that both invites and offers forgiveness as we grow in our understanding of the grace of God. It is the church that reminds us that "the prayer of the righteous is powerful and effective."

Mark 9:38-50

Teacher, we saw someone casting out demons in your name, and we tried to stop him, because he was not following us.
— Mark 9:38

The issue of inclusion and exclusion has plagued the church from its beginning and continues today. Denominational divisions have solidified around who has proper beliefs or practices. Churches have shown far less openness than the one that they affirm as their Lord has. "Do not stop him; for no one who does a deed of power in my name will be able soon afterward to speak evil of me" (v. 29). What a prescription for ecumenical cooperation! Imagine the impact of all Christian communities recognizing and affirming the ministry we share in the name of our Lord. The sense of competition, even among churches of the same denomination, continues to demean the testimony of our faith. These verses follow immediately upon the story of the disciples arguing about who is the greatest and seem to reflect this same attitude of competition. To our shame, we need to recognize that more than one potential believer has been discouraged by this very attitude among the churches.

It makes Jesus' warning very potent. "If any of you put a stumbling block before one of these little ones who believe in me, it would be better for you if a great millstone were hung around your neck and you were thrown into the sea" (v. 42). But the question always arises as to how far we should carry this openness. Many of the issues we argue about are very important. Jesus took a very strong stand against such reasoning. It is clear in Leviticus 21:16-24 that certain imperfections in the body made one unworthy to approach God. Now Jesus instructed his disciples to mutilate their body in precisely the manner that Leviticus warned about rather than to cause them to stumble in their faith. It is better to risk our own purity than to have that purity be the cause of our stumbling in the faith.

In the end, we are all dependent on the grace and forgiveness of God. Of course this will mean a lot of variety among Christians, but it could lend itself to the vitality of the community as a whole. It is like salt that flavors our food. "Salt is good; but if salt has lost its saltiness, how can you season it? Have salt in yourselves, and be at peace with one another" (v. 50). It is a prescription worthy of the churches of Christ.

Proper 22
Pentecost 20
Ordinary Time 27

Job 1:1; 2:1-10

There was once a man in the land of Uz whose name was
Job. That man was blameless and upright, one who feared
God and turned away from evil. — Job 1:1

The story of Job is an examination of the issue of the suffering of the righteous and of how we should respond to a God who allows such suffering to take place. The story line that sets up the question can raise some troubling questions for the believer if it is taken literally. Satan, in this story, was a member of the heavenly court and assumed the role of the prosecutor who was simply searching for the truth. God was very proud of his servant, Job, and believed he was the example of right living. Satan, as the advocate for truth, questioned whether Job was not righteous because it benefited him rather than because of some internal integrity.

God permitted Satan to test the theory that even right living is, at its core, based on self-interest. First, disaster struck his family and his possessions, but still Job maintained his faith even as he mourned his loss. Satan pushed further and attacked Job's health. The story line clearly could pose the problem of why God would permit such a monstrous contest to take place. The intention of the story, however, was to pose the question of how the faithful were to respond to suffering that obviously falls on the righteous and the unrighteous alike. Still, lingering in the background, was the question of the nature of God who permitted such suffering.

It was not uncommon for people to challenge the justice of God as they observed the sufferings of the world. It was the mirror image of the question posed by Satan. Satan suggested that Job was good because it benefited him to be good. The frequent human response, which affirms Satan's challenge, is: Why should people be good if it does not benefit them? Is there a reason to be faithful to God if being faithful does not protect you against the threats of life? Job's initial response was, "Shall we receive the good at the hand of God, and not receive the bad?" (v. 10). The question for the believer is whether he or she can trust God to be faithful when it is clear from life's experience that such trust does not guarantee a trouble free life?

Psalm 26

> *Vindicate me, O Lord, for I have walked in my integrity, and I have trusted in the Lord without wavering.* — Psalm 26:1

The setting for this psalm would seem to reflect a trial in which the petitioner would like to be declared innocent. If it is read with the story of Job in mind, it reflects the cry to God of any sufferer. The Hebrews were very clear from the beginning of their tradition that God was moved by the cry of injustice that comes up to heaven. It was the cry of Abel's blood, after having been slain by Cain, that cried out to God. It was because God had heard the sufferings of the people in slavery that he approached Moses to be a liberator. God was known not only as a God of justice, but also as a God who was moved by the cry of the sufferer.

The psalmist felt comfortable in putting his case before God. "Vindicate me ... prove me ... try me ... test my heart and mind" (vv. 1-2). Like all believers who lift their case to God, the petitioner presented the evidence. His evidence consists of his relationship with others and his relationship with God. On the assumption that we are judged by the company we keep, the psalmist asserts, "I do not sit with the worthless nor do I consort with hypocrites; I hate the company of evildoers, and will not sit with the wicked" (vv. 4-5). Since our life is also shaped by our connection with God through worship, the psalmist further asserted, "I wash my hands in innocence, and go around your altar, O Lord, singing aloud a song of thanksgiving, and telling all your wondrous deeds" (vv. 6-7).

This prayer was an affirmation of the value of a life lived with integrity. In other places there is opportunity to acknowledge our need of forgiveness, but here we have our dignity affirmed and our effort at living with integrity acknowledged. "But as for me, I walk in my integrity; redeem me, and be gracious to me. My foot stands on level ground; in the great congregation I will bless the Lord."

Hebrews 1:1-4; 2:5-12

He is the reflection of God's glory and the exact imprint of God's very being, and he sustains all things by his powerful word. — Hebrews 1:3a

In our increasingly pluralistic world in which we are acquiring more respect for people of other faiths, this passage from Hebrews raises significant questions as to our understanding of Christ as the finality of God's revelation. While Hebrews emphasized the humanity of Jesus, it began with cosmic claims for Christ. Jesus was not just a great teacher or a good man but "a Son ... appointed heir of all things" (v. 2). And Jesus was not just the result of a sudden decision by the eternal God, but he was one "through whom [God] also created the worlds." Jesus was not even one revelation among many but "the reflection of God's glory and the exact imprint of God's very being...." There were present and future implications to Jesus because "he sustains all things by his powerful word." Finally, lest there be any misunderstanding for what was affirmed, this passage declared, "When he had made purification for sins, he sat down at the right hand of the majesty on high, having become as much superior to angels as the name he has inherited is more excellent than theirs" (vv. 3-4).

It has to be admitted that where Christians have dominated in the past, they have often used such cosmic claims as justification for seeking to eliminate other religions. As we come into an era where people of other faiths have become our neighbors whom we have grown to admire and respect, do such cosmic claims take on a different meaning? One approach, following the pattern that Hebrews sets, is to distinguish between the cosmic Christ and the earthly Jesus. While Jesus is recognized as the Christ who was "crowned with glory and honor" (v. 9), this came to him because he was willing to suffer and die on behalf of the world. Jesus did not approach people from a position of superiority, which demanded their compliance, but rather from a humility that sought to serve them at their point of need. The commonality among our faiths is the desire to address people at their point of human need.

The truth of Christ is proclaimed through our transformed lives rather than the imposition of our understanding of Christ on others. Also, the image of Christ as assistant at creation is drawn from the wisdom tradition. (See the parallels in Proverbs 8:22-31 as well as the Wisdom of Solomon 9:2.) The suggestion is that the truth of Christ is built into the creation (Colossians 1:15-17). Is it then possible for us to approach other faiths with a humility that seeks to learn as well as share, since they, too, are part of creation? Could God not speak to us through the spirit that moves within their faiths even as God speaks to them through ours? This is an incomplete response, but it bears continued reflection.

Mark 10:2-16

For this reason a man shall leave his father and mother and be joined to his wife, and the two shall become one flesh. — Mark 10:7-8a

Marriage, in Jesus' eyes, was more than a societal convention or even a means to provide for the protection and nurture of children. It was the custom at the time that a woman left her family and was joined to her husband's family. In a patriarchal society, this was a means of shifting responsibility for protection from one man to another. Jesus challenges this position by quoting Genesis 2:24 that says in marriage a man left his family and was joined to his wife. This must have come as a shock to his hearers. Jesus seemed to develop the idea found in story in Genesis 1:27 in which the image of God was reflected in the differentiation of the sexes. This creation story declared that the image of God was reflected in both maleness and femaleness. Further, it was in the coming together in total commitment that the image was complete.

The focal point of the image of God is in the power released in relationship. It is not easy for two such different creatures, male and female, to be totally committed to each other. The church, being more instructed by Moses' teachings than those of Jesus, has recognized divorce as an option resulting from our hardness of heart. But, as Jesus makes clear in his uncompromising statement about divorce, we can never enter into marriage with that as an assumption. Marriage must begin as a total commitment to discovering the heart of God through reaching across the bridge of our differences. God is reflected, or imaged, in the reconciliation of that which has been separated in creation.

The final verses in this reading are a reminder that families do not split up without affecting the children. By the very fact that they are so powerless in such a situation, we are reminded that God's commitment is to the powerless ones among us. "Let the little children come to me; do not stop them; for it is to such as these that the kingdom of God belongs" (v. 14). While the church needs to demonstrate the grace and forgiveness of Christ in welcoming those who have been divorced, it should not fool itself. Divorce is a sin that needs the love of God if its very real wounds are to be healed.

Proper 23
Pentecost 21
Ordinary Time 28

Job 23:1-9, 16-17

God has made my heart faint; the Almighty has terrified me; If only I could vanish in darkness and thick darkness would cover my face! — Job 23:16-17

While a major theme of scripture is that God is a compassionate God who hears the cry of those who suffer, Job was faced with a situation in which he was no longer confident that God did indeed hear his cry. "Oh, that I knew where I might find him, that I might come even to his dwelling!" (v. 3). Job gives voice to the complaint of all those who feel that they have suffered a great injustice in their life. While the suffering is bad, what is even worse is the inability to get a fair hearing. When we suffer unfairly, we want our "day in court." "I would lay my case before him, and fill my mouth with arguments" (v. 4). If we are going to have to suffer, we at least want our suffering to make sense. "I would learn what he would answer me, and understand what he would say to me" (v. 5).

Job trusted in the character of a God of justice if he could just find him. "(In the presence of God,) an upright person could reason with him, and I should be acquitted forever by my judge" (v. 7). People of faith are instructed by scripture to lay their complaint before God. All meaningless suffering is a threat to the orderliness of the universe. Suffering can be endured if it is for some higher purpose. Rob it of that purpose, and suffering becomes unbearable. What appeared to be suffering without purpose had terrified Job. "God has made my heart faint; the almighty has terrified me" (v. 16). What appeared to be purposeless suffering was such a threat to the foundation of his faith that he wanted to vanish. "If only I could vanish in darkness, and thick darkness would cover my face!" (v. 17). For those who believe in a just and merciful God, the absence of God is the most terrifying experience that we can imagine.

Psalm 22:1-15

My God, my God, why have you forsaken me? Why are you so far from helping me, from the words of my groaning? — Psalm 22:1

These words have become so intimately attached to Jesus' cry on the cross that it is hard to separate them from the cross. Whether it is Jesus, Job, or any person who is suffering, it is the cry of a soul in torment. For Christians, the recognition that Jesus prayed this prayer provides permission for us to cry out to God in uncensored honesty when we are suffering torment. If there are times when it appears that our life is in personal chaos and that emotionally we are at a breaking point, it does not suggest a lack of faith that we are experiencing the abandonment of God. It is clear that this sufferer has a faith of long-standing. "Yet it was you who took me from the womb; you kept me safe on my mother's breast. On you I was cast from my birth, and since my mother bore me you have been my God" (vv. 9-10).

Yet the combination of his torment together with the experience of divine silence has shaken not only his faith but also his sense of humanity. "But I am a worm, and not human; scorned by others, and despised by the people" (v. 6). This prayer offers us a map for the turmoil of one in deep grief over his or her situation. It is not wrong for believers to voice their feelings of disappointment when they do not sense God's presence. The failure of a once firm faith to address a situation is naturally discouraging. Normal faithful people feel demeaned in their humanity when they feel surrounded on every side by vicious evil and cannot find the physical strength to endure. What is helpful for the believer is the recognition that not only the psalmist but also Christ, through his use of this prayer, encourages us to express all of those feelings to God who has the capacity to transform them and fill them with new meaning.

Hebrews 4:12-16

And before him no creature is hidden, but all are naked and laid bare to the eyes of the one to whom we must render an account. — Hebrews 4:13

In light of the previous readings from Job and Psalm 22, this emphasis on the fact that we are completely "laid bare to the eyes of the one to whom we must render an account" can be seen as liberating rather than terrifying. It is clear that all humans have a shadow side to their personality that can find its expression in strong negative feelings and strange uncontrolled desires. Too often, Christians fall under the illusion that such shadows are so shameful that they need to expend energy in hiding them from others and from God. Here, in Hebrews, as elsewhere, we are reminded that God already knows all about our whole self, shadows and all. Therefore, it is a useless expenditure of energy to try to fool ourselves into believing that we can hide that part of us from God or to believe that we can rid ourselves of that aspect of our personality. "Indeed, the word of God ... is able to judge the thoughts and intentions of the heart" (v. 12). But then comes the wonderful news. The one to whom we must render account of ourselves is none other than Jesus who has become our high priest. Only, this high priest is not one who is removed from the struggles of our lives but rather is one who is able "to sympathize with our weaknesses ... because he too has been tested as we are ..." (v. 15).

Since God knows who we are, and we are accountable to one who has shared in our struggles, we are invited to "approach the throne of grace with boldness, so that we may receive mercy and find grace to help in time of need" (v. 16). This is the message of grace that we need to proclaim in our churches. We do not need to come to worship pretending that we are better than we are. Rather we can come boldly, acknowledge our shadow sides as well as our strengths, and count on the grace that releases our full potential to the service of God.

Mark 10:17-31

Then Jesus looked around and said to his disciples, "How hard it will be for those who have wealth to enter the Kingdom of God!" — Mark 10:23

222

This verse comes right after the incident in which a rich man came up and asked him, "What must I do to inherit eternal life?" (v. 17). Jesus at first directed him toward the last six of the Ten Commandments that focus on our relationship with others. When he declared that he had kept these from the time he was a youth, Jesus turned to focus in an indirect way on the first commandment, "You shall have no other gods before me" (Exodus 20:3). He asked the young man to go and sell what he had and give the money to the poor. Then we are told, "When he heard this, he was shocked and went away grieving, for he had many possessions" (v. 22).

Are we led to assume that if he had not had many possessions, he might have been able to comply with Jesus' request more easily? If so, this suggests that his possessions were what came between him and God. To enter the kingdom of God is to live a life in harmony with his purposes. "Thy kingdom come, thy will be done on earth as it is in heaven." Jesus painted a picture of that being almost impossible if you had become rich.

Think of how this challenges the normal assumptions of our society. Large portions of our energies are directed at acquiring possessions. We are interested not only in our daily bread but also in having abundance far beyond our daily needs. When we hear Jesus' words, we rationalize that we are not rich and that he surely cannot be talking about us. Yet there are few of us who are free to come and follow Jesus if it means even giving up our savings. We know that wealth cannot guarantee health, happiness, or security. Yet we cling to the hope that it can. Because we cannot control God, we are unwilling to trust him for our future. God asks that we begin with a tithe as a down payment.

Proper 24
Pentecost 22
Ordinary Time 29

Job 38:1-7 (34-41)

Then the Lord answered Job out of the whirlwind ... Where were you when I laid the foundation of the earth? — Job 38:1, 4a

With the exception of the opening scenes where we hear the conversation between God and Satan, God had not been an active part of the story of Job's wrestling with the issue of evil until now. While Job had declared his desire to question God directly, up until now we have only heard conversations about God among humans. That is the way it usually is for humans who seek to understand the reasons why things happen as they do in this universe. Then, suddenly, God spoke to Job out of the whirlwind. Despite all he had suffered, here was a sign of the favor with which God held Job. Still, God did not come to Job as a defendant who needed to answer Job's questions. God was still God. God was the one in charge of this conversation. "Gird up your loins like a man, I will question you, and you shall declare to me," he said.

In one sense God responded to Job's question by revealing the vast complexity of creation and the impossibility of a human even beginning to comprehend the mystery of the universe. "Where were you when I laid the foundation of the earth? ... Or who shut in the sea with doors when it burst out from the womb?" (vv. 4, 8). But, in another sense, God's very description of God's creative presence in every aspect of creation from the beginning of time provided a reassurance that despite Job's inability to understand the mystery of the universe, he could trust that there was one who did understand. God asked rhetorical questions such as "Do you know the ordinances of the heavens? Can you establish their rule on the earth?" (v. 33). Behind those questions was the fact that there was one who did hold

224

that power and that one had chosen out of freedom to address Job. The first part of our struggle to answer the question of why evil and suffering exist in this life is the belief that there is someone who is in charge and evil does not have free range.

Psalm 104:1-9, 24, 35c

You set the earth on its foundations, so that it shall never be shaken. — Psalm 104:5

This psalm is a celebration of God as creator and provider for all of creation. The verses that we read celebrate the cosmic dimensions of God's creative care. Other verses celebrated how God had ordered this universe so that water was available for the wild animals and "plants for people to use to bring forth food from the earth and wine to gladden the human heart ..." (vv. 14-15). This was a rehearsal of the greatness of the creator and the care with which God had ordered the forces of this universe to provide for life in all its forms.

Sometimes we take the nature of our universe as a given and forget how intricately interwoven creation is. For the psalmist, a close observation of life around us cannot help but cause us to burst forth in a song of praise. "Bless the Lord, O my soul. O Lord my God, you are very great. You are clothed with honor and majesty, wrapped in light as with a garment" (vv. 1-2). It is so easy to become consumed by our immediate problems that we forget the grandeur of creation. This psalm, and others like it, could serve as a valuable reminder to the congregation of faith that we daily live in the presence of expressions of the majesty of God.

Creation is not immortal. It depends on God's sustaining care and our recognition of its giftedness. We daily live in need of offering our thanks to God. "O Lord, how manifold are your works! In wisdom you have made them all; the earth is full of your creatures" (v. 24).

Hebrews 5:1-10

In the days of his flesh, Jesus offered up prayers and supplications, with loud cries and tears, to the one who was able to save him from death, and he was heard because of his reverent submission. — Hebrews 5:7

Unless the author is drawing upon traditions that have since been lost, he must be referring to Jesus' prayers in the Garden of Gethsemane prior to his arrest. Luke records that his anguish was so great that "sweat became like great drops of blood falling down on the ground" (Luke 22:44). Yet, even in that anguish, he could both acknowledge his desire to escape the cross and his willingness to submit to the higher will of God.

Hebrews reported that "he was heard because of his reverent submission." The human Jesus achieved his purpose because he was willing to learn "obedience through what he suffered; and having been made perfect, he became the source of eternal salvation for all who obey him ..." (vv. 8-9). While it is natural to want to avoid suffering, as Jesus demonstrated through his prayers, it is through trusting God in the midst of suffering that one perfects one's faith. There is no evidence that Jesus sought out suffering as some noble pursuit, but it is clear that when suffering was thrust upon him, he did not turn away from God but rather sought to trust God in the midst of the experience.

Mark 10:35-45

You know that among the Gentiles those whom they recognize as their rulers lord it over them, and their great ones are tyrants over them. But it is not so among you; but whoever wishes to become great among you must be your servant, and whoever wishes to be first among you must be slave of all. — Mark 10:42b-44

Jockeying for positions of prominence seemed to be a favorite pastime of the disciples, as Mark described it. Whether it is members or pastors, that game seems to be a continuing facet of church life. We never seem to be able to get this power thing right in the church. It is not as if Jesus was vague about how we should behave. Both by his words and by his actions we are clearly told that "... the Son of Man came not to be served but to serve, and to give his life as a ransom for many" (v. 45). Each time Mark described Jesus as trying to prepare his disciples for his death and resurrection, they reacted by trying to maneuver for leadership positions. The first time in Mark 8:31 ff, after he told them of his coming fate, Peter immediately assumed the position of spokesman and tried to dissuade him of taking actions that would lead to his death. The next time he told them of his coming death in Mark 9:30 ff, the disciples reacted by arguing about who was the greatest. In Mark 10: 32 ff, he tells them for a third time, and immediately James and John approached him about securing positions of power in the coming kingdom.

The first time, Jesus tried to tell the disciples and the crowd that true discipleship did not mean positions of leadership but the willingness to take up your cross and forsake the normal pursuits of life. The second time, he tried to illustrate by taking a child among them and suggest that "whoever wants to be first must be last of all and servant of all" (Mark 9:35). In this passage, he compares what they want to the tyrants among the pagan Gentiles. The continual struggle within the Christian community is not discovering the proper approach to attract new members but discovering the proper humility to become servants one of another.

Each time a person or a community imitates Jesus' ministry of servanthood, people are attracted to the community of faith.

Proper 25
Pentecost 23
Ordinary Time 30

Job 42:1-6, 10-17

I had heard of you by the hearing of the ear, but now my eye sees you.... — Job 42:5

The book of Job struggles with the problem of innocent suffering. It is not uncommon when a person experiences great tragedy that the person's friends seek to comfort the individual by explaining why this tragedy came upon him. As did Job's friends, we seek explanations that will help maintain the sense of order in our universe. If suffering comes about because of ignorance, then the solution for the future is to learn from our mistakes what to avoid the next time. If we suffer because we are being punished for our sins, then the solution is to repent and be more faithful. If the cause of our pain is the evil of someone else, then the solution is to defeat the evil person. If we can discern a cause-and-effect relationship that explains the tragedy or suffering, then our universe still makes sense to us.

This is why Job and his friends struggled so hard to come to terms with Job's tragedy. If there is no rational explanation, then none of us is safe in the future. Instead of living in an ordered universe, we stare into the abyss of pure chaos, and all of us are vulnerable. Job's answer was not an explanation that restored order to his universe but rather Job discovered a relationship with the one who could "by a word" give order to chaos. Job's anger and willingness to quarrel with God was affirmed not because of his arguments but because of his trust in a God with whom he could be honest. "After the Lord had spoken these words to Job, the Lord said to Eliphaz the Temanite: 'My wrath is kindled against you and against your two friends; for you have not spoken of me what is right, as my servant Job has' " (vv. 7).

In the end, we are not given an explanation that explains the cause of innocent suffering. Rather we are offered a relationship with a God that comprehends what we can never understand who is present to us and can redeem us even from the chaos that strips us of all that we have. "And the Lord restored the fortunes of Job when he had prayed for his friends; and the Lord gave Job twice as much as he had before" (v. 10).

Psalm 34:1-8 (19-22)

Depart from evil, and do good; seek peace, and pursue it.
The eyes of the Lord are on the righteous and his ears are
open to their cry. — Psalm 34:14-15

This psalm is a prayer of trust in the face of trouble. As Job discovered in his experience, there is no secret to life that will protect you from all trouble and suffering. There is, however, a way of life that prepares you if trouble should arise. In this psalm, you are offered a continual relationship with the one who will be present to you in times of trouble. We maintain that relationship through our continual worship of God. "I will bless the Lord at all times; his praise shall continually be in my mouth" (v. 1). We build our confidence for the future by rehearsing in our prayers how God has been faithful to us in the past. "I sought the Lord, and he answered me, and delivered me from all my fears" (v. 4). We develop courage for living by reminding ourselves of the character of God. "O taste and see that the Lord is good; happy are those who take refuge in him" (v. 8). We seal our relationship with God by living a life that is worthy of such trust. "Depart from evil, and do good; seek peace, and pursue it."

Our relationship is with a God that we know is responsive to what is happening to us. "The eyes of the Lord are on the righteous, and his ears are open to their cry." Our hope is not in the avoidance of trouble but in a God who can save us when we encounter trouble. "When the righteous cry for help, the Lord hears, and rescues them from all their troubles. The Lord is near to the brokenhearted, and saves the crushed in spirit" (vv. 17-18). Early Christians saw in this psalm help in understanding the events of the cross. John quoted a witness at the cross testifying to the fact that instead of breaking Jesus' legs to assist in his dying, the soldier pierced his side to confirm his death. John saw this as fulfilling the words of this psalm, "He keeps all their bones; not one of them will be broken" (v. 20 and John 19:36). Jesus, as the innocent one, did experience suffering, but he also experienced the faithfulness of God. "The Lord redeems the life of his servants; none of those who take refuge in him will be condemned" (v. 22). The answer to our fears of the future is not a secret to life but a relationship that we can trust.

Hebrews 7:23-28

Unlike the other high priests, he has no need to offer sacrifices day after day, first for his own sins, and then for those of the people; this he did once for all when he offered himself. — Hebrews 7:27

The author of Hebrews saw in the office of Christ as high priest an answer to the uncertainties presented by the constantly changing life around us. In the face of this constant change, the church is called to be priests for the world. "But you are a chosen race, a royal priesthood, a holy nation, God's own people, in order that you may proclaim the mighty acts of him who called you out of darkness into his marvelous light" (1 Peter 2:9). Like the Levitical priests, we have the responsibility of making intercession on behalf of the world and on behalf of ourselves. Even the best of pastors or the best of lay leaders is subject to their own finitude. Church members are aware of the uncertainties that arise whenever they welcome a new pastor to lead them. Most pastors continually face the vagaries of the turnover of leadership among the lay members of the church. Even our understanding of truth is affected by the changing circumstances of our lives. What worked in the past is not necessarily good for the future. Yet, whatever else changes, Hebrews offers Christ as the constant in our life that is always available to intercede for us.

While the church continues to change in this evolving world, the head of the church remains a constant. "For it was fitting that we should have such a high priest, holy, blameless, undefiled, separated from sinners, and exalted above the heavens."

While we are called to act as priests, we are subject to the high priest who understands our weaknesses and is continually available to make intercession for us. As Paul would remind us, the miracle of the church is seen in the fact that God's grace is sufficient for us, "for power is made perfect in weakness" (2 Corinthians 12:9).

Mark 10:46-52

As he and his disciples and a large crowd were leaving Jericho, Bartimaeus son of Timaeus, a blind beggar, was sitting by the roadside. — Mark 10:46b

Jesus was leaving Jericho headed for Jerusalem. His ministry was coming to a climax, and this was a significant part of his journey. He knew what was ahead of him, and he had tried three times to prepare his disciples for these events. It was a tense time, and it was important that they stay focused to what lay ahead. Suddenly there was this shouting from the side of the road. "Jesus, Son of David, have mercy on me!" (v. 47). Not only was this an interruption in the journey, but also the shouts were messianic claims that could easily draw a response from the Roman soldiers who were already tense because of the events of Passover. The crowd recognized the problem and tried to hush the blind beggar.

As with the entire gospel, this story is told for the sake of the church. There always seems to be a Bartimaeus interrupting the important plans of the church. The church makes plans to serve the needs of the many, and then its plans are interrupted by the cry of an insignificant beggar that is not even a part of the community of faith. Jesus, the head of the church, told his disciples to bring the blind beggar to him. He not only interrupted his very valid journey, but he paid attention to the needs of one whose cries might endanger the fulfillment of those plans. "Then Jesus said to him, 'What do you want me to do for you?' "

Despite the much larger problems that were facing Jesus, he paid direct attention to the beggar and his perceived needs. The beggar was equally direct. "My teacher, let me see again" (v. 51). Jesus did not ask for any commitments from him but simply said, "Go; your faith has made you well" (v. 52). While the church has a larger ministry of proclaiming the good news of Christ to the world, it must always be ready to respond to the direct needs of those who come to it in hope.

Proper 26
Pentecost 24
Ordinary Time 31

Ruth 1:1-18

Where you go, I will go ... your people shall be my people and your God my God. — Ruth 1:16b

The land of Moab was a totally separate culture from the land of Judah. Historically they were enemies, but in a time of famine, Moab had become a land of refuge for Naomi's family. They had raised their family there, and their two sons had found wives. But tragedy struck, and Naomi was left without husband or sons. Bereft of husband and sons, she decided to return to Judah. Her daughters-in-law began to go with her, but she told them to return to their own people. It was appropriate advice. Women without men were defenseless, and the normal prejudices of a foreign culture would make them even more vulnerable.

One daughter-in-law, Orpah, decided to join her own people, and scripture does not fault her choice. But Ruth chose to venture into a new land and risk building relationships with a group of people who often considered her people the enemy. It was from Ruth that God would form the body of Christ. She was not even aware of what was happening, but she would become the great-grandmother of David and would provide the line by which the Christ would come.

The body of Christ would exist in a world of prejudice, but it would proclaim a faith in which there was neither Greek nor Jew, slave nor free, male nor female, but, rather, Christlike persons. The body of Christ would call its members to take the risk, like Ruth, of reaching across the divisions of this world and proclaiming a truth that challenged our prejudices. Like Ruth, in doing so, we become the mother of new life.

Psalm 146

Praise the Lord! Praise the Lord, O my soul! I will praise the Lord as long as I live; I will sing praises to my God all my life long. — Psalm 146:1-2

The book of Psalms builds to a crescendo with its last six psalms of praise. The last five all begin with the command to praise the Lord. The psalms begin with a mixture of laments and praises but with an emphasis on the lament. It is a reflection of the continuum of life that stretches from our experiences of pain to pleasure. Our experiences of suffering cause us to cry out with the question of whether there is any justice in the universe. Almost all of the individual psalms of lament conclude in words of praise. They seem to testify to the experience of the believer that when we are honest with our petitions of anguish, there is someone who listens and responds. As you read in the psalms, the early grouping of psalms has a significant number of laments, but later on the balance of lament and praise shifts toward the expression of praise.

In this psalm, it is declared that true happiness finally culminates in the experience of praise. God is praised as the creator "who made heaven and earth, the sea, and all that is in them" (v. 6a). In contrast to mortals who will ultimately die, God is praised as one who "keeps faith forever" (v. 6b). It is this God who "executes justice for the oppressed; (and) who gives food to the hungry" (v. 7). This is a God who has heard the cry and responded to the lament of the prisoner, the blind, those bowed down, the stranger, the orphan, and the widow.

As we lift our voice in praise, we recall the sensitivity of God to the most vulnerable of our society. We are released to praise God not only with voice and song but also in service to the very ones whom God seeks to minister to in our society.

Hebrews 9:11-14

Then through the greater and perfect tent (not made with hands, that is, not of this creation), he entered once for all into the Holy Place. — Hebrews 9:11b-12a

The author of Hebrews continued to explore the significance of Christ as our high priest. Recalling the tent or tabernacle that was constructed according to God's instructions to accompany the Hebrews in their wilderness journey, the author suggested that Christ has created a "greater and perfect tent." The tabernacle was the place that signaled God's presence with the people (Exodus 40). The Ark of the Covenant, which contained the stone tablets upon which God had written the Ten Commandments, was placed in a separate section of the tent known as the holy of holies. This place was the most sacred part of the entire tabernacle and was to be approached only once a year by the high priest.

Christ, as our more perfect high priest had, by his resurrection, created a more perfect tabernacle. The entire created world had been purified by the blood of Christ and made into one great tabernacle of our God. Unlike previous high priests, Christ was always available to us and made the presence of God real to us. The tabernacle was a window into eternity through which people could approach the eternal God. In preparation for that approach, so that they might not be harmed by the holiness of God, the priest offered sacrifices of animals as an offering for the forgiveness of sins. Through Christ, that window had been expanded, and God had been made more approachable. Christ was both the high priest and the sacrifice that purified us and released us "to worship the living God!" (v. 14). The invitation was open to all who come in repentance. The promise was that in coming we might be in touch with the eternal God who provided meaning to our lives.

Mark 12:28-34

> *One of the scribes came near and heard them disputing with one another, and seeing that he answered them well, he asked him, "Which commandment is the first of all?"*
> — Mark 12:28

Jesus' response to this question is so familiar that we sometimes forget the significance of his response for the church. The question emerged in the midst of a religious dispute. People were arguing about the various points of religion. The history of the church is that it finds in such arguments reasons to split churches or even form different denominations. This scribe wanted to cut through all the arguments and identify what was really important. Jesus' response is a stark reminder to the church that many of our disputes are simply excuses for our self-centeredness.

Jesus identified two passages from the scriptures that for him summarized the essence of the faith. As had some other rabbis before him, he chose to combine what was referred to as the shema in Deuteronomy 6:4-5 with the command to love your neighbor in Leviticus 19:18b. It is significant that of the nineteen references to scribes by Mark, this is the only one that is shown in a positive light. The scribe was not testing or trying to entrap Jesus but sincerely seeking his understanding.

The fact that Mark portrayed the scribe as agreeing with Jesus suggests a bridge between the church and Judaism as offered by Jesus. Jesus, as Lord of the church, was declaring that all of religion is measured by its effect on our relationship with God and our relationship with our neighbor. Matthew, in telling this story, quoted Jesus as saying that all of the law and the prophets were summed up in these two commandments (Matthew 22:40). For a church involved in religious disputes, as were the Pharisees and the Sadducees in previous verses, this becomes the canon within the canon by which we measure the validity of our arguments. It is not only the disputes but also the manner in which we pursue the disputes that must be measured by how they reflect our love of God and neighbor.

Proper 27
Pentecost 25
Ordinary Time 32

Ruth 3:1-5; 4:13-17

My daughter, I need to seek some security for you, so that it may be well with you. — Ruth 3:1b

There is a certain earthy quality to this story that reminds us that God works through both the human inclinations and concrete realities of our world. Naomi was a schemer even if she schemed for a good purpose. She had recognized that her kinsman, Boaz, was attracted to her daughter-in-law, Ruth. She also recognized that in her society a woman without a man was very vulnerable. She devised a plan to provide for the daughter-in-law that had been so faithful in returning to Judah with her. It was the end of the barley and wheat harvests and the scene shifted to the threshing floor where Naomi knew that Boaz would be working into the night to winnow the barley.

In bold terms, she told Ruth to make herself attractive and to prepare to meet Boaz at night on the threshing floor. This is not a tale for the easily embarrassed. It is clearly a plan of seduction. Naomi even instructed Ruth to wait until Boaz had eaten a full meal and filled himself with wine. Ruth was to watch in secret and "When he lies down, observe the place where he lies; then, go and uncover his feet and lie down; and he will tell you what to do" (v. 4). The fact that in Hebrew the word for feet is often used as a euphemism for the male organ would not be lost on the reader of the Hebrew text.

Ruth was fully prepared to carry out the plan. "When Boaz had eaten and drunk, and he was in a contented mood, he went to lie down at the end of the heap of grain. Then she came stealthily and uncovered his feet and lay down" (v. 7). When he discovered her in the dark, he asked, " 'Who are you?' And she answered, 'I am Ruth, your servant; spread your cloak over your servant, for you are next-of-kin' " (v. 9). This latter statement was a reminder to Boaz that what

236

was intended was not simply a night of pleasure. Rather, it had long-range implications. The end result of this rather risqué tale was that Boaz did take her as his wife, and she produced a child who would become the grandfather of David. God was at work in the very human dimensions of life to bring about the divine purpose.

Psalm 127

Unless the Lord builds the house, those who build it labor in vain. — Psalm 127:1

This psalm is read as a response to the story of Ruth and Naomi's recognition that behind all of the events of her life was the hand of God. When Naomi heard that Ruth had met Boaz, her kinsman, her response was, "Blessed be he by the Lord, whose kindness has not forsaken the living or the dead!" (Ruth 2:19b). It is not a denial of the importance of hard work and striving but recognition that such efforts, no matter how earnest, are only part of what determines the outcome. We can become so caught up in our attempt to gain control of our lives and to secure our future that we fail to recognize the hand of God in what is happening. When we fail to recognize God's hand in our lives, we become consumed with the effort to control that which is uncontrollable. The result is the development of anxiety. "It is in vain that you rise up early and go late to rest, eating the bread of anxious toil; for he gives sleep to his beloved" (v. 2).

In many ways this is similar to Jesus' teachings about the cause of anxiety in our lives in Matthew 6:25-34. It is only when we learn to trust in the benevolent hand of God that we are able to rest at night without undue worry about tomorrow. "So do not worry about tomorrow, for tomorrow will bring worries of its own. Today's trouble is enough for today" (Matthew 6:34). The same, the psalmist reminds us, can be said about our worries about our family. We do what we can to care for them, but then we must recognize that they are a blessing from God and count on God to help us care for them.

Hebrews 9:24-28

But as it is, he has appeared once for all at the end of the age to remove sin by the sacrifice of himself ... so Christ, having been offered once to bear the sins of many, will appear a second time, not to deal with sin, but to save those who are eagerly waiting for him. — Hebrews 9:26b, 28

There is a stream of Christian thought that delights in picturing the end time as a time in which the saved will be separated from the lost and raptured into heaven while the sinners continue to suffer the torment of the damned. While the author of Hebrews expected an end time, he had a slightly different perspective that bears reflection by the church. The sanctuary of the tabernacle was meant to be a reflection of heaven in which one could draw closer to God. Christ, by his resurrection, has entered the true sanctuary, "now to appear in the presence of God on our behalf" (v. 24). Now we have an advocate who is not speaking from a distance to God on our behalf but is actually in the very presence of God.

Like all priests, Christ is charged with the responsibility of preparing us to enter into the presence of God by cleansing us of our sins. Unlike those who seem to delight in picturing a time when those who have sinned will finally have to pay, Hebrews said Christ "has appeared once for all at the end of the age to remove sin by the sacrifice of himself." According to Hebrews, there will be a second time in which Christ will appear, but it will not be to deal with our sins, which have already been taken care of. " ... So Christ, having been offered once to bear the sins of many, will appear a second time, not to deal with sin, but to save those who are eagerly waiting for him." This shifts the focus of the church from considering the end time as a time of judgment on those who do not believe properly to a time of final reconciliation with God who through Christ "was reconciling the world to himself, not counting their trespasses against them, and entrusting the message of reconciliation to us" (2 Corinthians 5:19).

Mark 12:38-44

For all of them have contributed out of their abundance; but she out of her poverty has put in everything she had, all she had to live on. — Mark 12:44

Mark placed two stories together to contrast models of discipleship. The first was about scribes who hold a place of honor in the society. These were the ones that interpreted the faith and nurtured the faithful.

The problem was, as had been amply demonstrated by the various previous attempts of the disciples to secure places of honor, that along with honor came temptation. Praise is a very seductive drug. Once you have experienced the pleasure of it, you want more. Jesus pointed to scribes who "like to walk around in long robes, and to be greeted with respect in the marketplaces, and to have the best seats in the synagogues and places of honor at banquets" (vv. 38-39).

One does not have to observe today's religious community for long in order to observe this temptation being played out among us. Sometimes it even results in our taking advantage of the most vulnerable of our community in order to advance ourselves. Jesus warned against those who "devour widows' houses and for the sake of appearance say long prayers" (v. 40). Mark juxtaposed this example with the story of a widow who became a model for discipleship. A widow was a very vulnerable individual in Jesus' society. This particular one had obviously fallen on hard times.

In the midst of the many who are making their offering at the temple, Jesus took note of her. He did not condemn those who made more generous offerings but only noted the relative impact of the offerings. Those who had much, even if they gave a generous offering, still had much left over for their own personal needs. The widow, on the other hand, while her offering was not very much in absolute terms, had nothing left over to attend to her own needs. She was demonstrating a total dependence on God while the rest were only giving what they could afford. It is significant that repeated studies of church giving reveal that as people's income increases, they tend to give a smaller proportion of their income to the church. It is as if the more God blesses them, the less they feel that they can trust God for their future.

Proper 28
Pentecost 26
Ordinary Time 33

1 Samuel 1:4-20

In due time Hannah conceived and bore a son. She named him Samuel, for she said, "I have asked him of the Lord."
— 1 Samuel 1:20

It is clear that God loves children because children, or the lack of them, play such an important role in the unfolding story of God in history. Abram and Sarai had to learn that nothing was impossible for God (Genesis 18:14), so they waited until their old age to bear Isaac. Then Rebecca was barren until Isaac petitioned God, and she bore twins. One of the twins was Jacob who would father twelve sons that would produce the twelve tribes of Israel. Later it would be the child, Moses, who had to be preserved through a series of unusual circumstances in order to prepare for the liberation of God's people from slavery in Egypt. Difficult, unusual, even seemingly impossible births became a continual theme of God's involvement in the world. They became, as Isaiah would tell the reluctant King Ahaz, a sign of Immanuel, or God with us (Isaiah 7:14). The birth of Samuel was seen as such a sign.

It also reaffirmed another theme of the biblical story. God heard the cry of the oppressed and was moved by their cry of anguish. In this case, it was an individual cry of lament as voiced by Hannah both in response to her barrenness and in reaction to the constant harassment by her rival, Peninnah. God was responsive to both personal anguish and the anguish brought on by the behavior of another. The misunderstanding of the priest, Eli, who, upon observing her silent prayer presumed that Hannah was drunk, is a cautious reminder that professional religious training can cause us to overlook the clear signs of piety in those among us. Later, it would be the religious professionals who were unable to recognize what God was doing when another baby was born in Bethlehem.

1 Samuel 2:1-10

The Lord will judge the ends of the earth; he will give strength to his king, and exalt the power of his anointed.
— 1 Samuel 2:10b

One can easily see why the church picked up Hannah's song and saw in it the same theme that was manifest in the birth of Jesus. While the births were different in many respects, the overarching truth was that both children were gifts from God. Each was dedicated to God's service. Both were heralds of a new era in God's unfolding plan of salvation. The people had been without a king, and Samuel would guide them into a new period when they would have a king to lead them. Jesus would guide them into a new understanding of God's grace in their lives and prepare them for inclusion of the Gentiles into God's people.

Both women, Hannah and Mary, broke into song in response to this surprise gift of God. Their songs affirmed God as a God who challenged the set values and understandings of the world and was particularly attentive to the needy and those who had been treated unjustly. As these songs have been sung in the community of faith, the God who is aware of the cries of the people is affirmed over and over again.

Hebrews 10:11-14 (15-18) 19-25

But when Christ had offered for all time a single sacrifice for sins, "He sat down at the right hand of God," and since then has been waiting "until his enemies would be made a footstool for his feet." — Hebrews 10:12-13

It is generally agreed that Hebrews was written to a Christian community that had grown dispirited and was in need of encouragement. A central theme had been that Christ, as their high priest, was far superior to the Levitical priests that had previously offered sacrifices on behalf of the faithful. When Christ had made his sacrifice on the cross, all that was necessary had been accomplished. There was no need for him to make repeated sacrifices for the new sins of the people. There was a period of waiting that was necessary, but the victory was not in doubt. Jesus was simply waiting until humanity realized the full implications of what he had accomplished. He continued to wait "until his enemies would be made a footstool for his feet" (v. 13).

Through Jesus the promise that had been made by Jeremiah had been fulfilled. God had established a new agreement or covenant with humanity. While previously people were incapable of coming into God's presence because of their sinfulness, now God "will remember their sins and their lawless deeds no more" (v. 17). So if God is not keeping score of our sins, what is there left for us to do? We are to trust what Christ has done for us. "Let us hold fast to the confession of our hope without wavering, for he who has promised is faithful" (v. 23). But this has implications for our life together in the meantime. "And let us consider how to provoke one another to love and good deeds, not neglecting to meet together, as is the habit of some, but encouraging one another ..." (vv. 24-25). The message for the church is the same today. We no longer have to focus on our sinfulness. Christ has taken care of that. Our focus now should be on how to provoke one another to love and good deeds.

Mark 13:1-8

> *For nation will rise against nation, and kingdom against kingdom; there will be earthquakes in various places; there will be famines but this is but the beginning of the birthpangs.* — Mark 13:8

There are many in our culture that would like to build on a partial reading of such apocalyptic passages and apply them to events in our world in order to convince people that we are now at the end time. Such scare tactics conveniently ignore the clear intention of Mark in this passage. The gospel says that the pain of our society, symbolized by wars, rumors of wars, and famine are birth pangs of something new God is giving birth to. One of the major images that early Christians used to interpret the meaning of suffering in this world was the image of God being a mother about to give birth. In the Old Testament, from Sarah to Hannah, God was seen as opening the womb and providing

242

birth where there was no possibility of birth. For the Israelites, that was their faith when the people faced impossible situations.

What was impossible for humans was possible for God. In the gospels, and for Paul, as the writers saw the constant failure of nations to live in peace and the famines that resulted from the greedy exploitation of nature, they built on this theme of giving birth to discern hope. A mother's birth pangs come with a mixture of fear, concern, and hope. It is the hope that enables a mother to endure the pain. She clings to the hope that she is the instrument of a whole new life. Mark offers that same image to us as Christians. The events that generate fear in those who have no hope should be interpreted as the quickening by God that is necessary in order to create something new. Life for a Christian has its share of tragedy, but it is a tragedy that is continually brushed by grace. Even in dark times, we are urged to "look up for your salvation is near" (Luke 21:28b).

Christ The King
Proper 29

2 Samuel 23:1-7

Is not my house like this with God? For he has made with me an everlasting covenant, ordered in all things and secure. — 2 Samuel 23:5a

This passage is chosen for Christ the King Sunday. This is the culmination of the liturgical year. All year long we have prepared for the coming of Christ, celebrated his birth, been guided by the meaning of his life and teachings, reflected on his suffering and death, rejoiced in his resurrection, and witnessed the extension of his life through the body of Christ. Now we recognize the goal toward which history is moving. This is the plan of his love: "to gather up all things in him, things in heaven and things on earth" (Ephesians 1:10).

In what could be seen as David's last will and testament, we hear David speak of how he had been the recipient of God's "everlasting covenant, ordered in all things and secure" (v. 5). For Christians that covenant finds its fulfillment in the rule of Christ as the everlasting king. There will continue to be many twists and turns in the unfolding of God's purpose, but "the God of Israel has spoken, the rock of Israel has said to me: One who rules over people justly, ruling in the fear of God, is like the light of morning, like the sun rising on a cloudless morning, gleaming from the rain on the grassy land" (vv. 3-4). The church looks for the rule of Christ in its life so that it might reflect that justice shaped by a fear of God.

In Christ, we will learn that the king is truly a servant who rules by love and compassion. David provided the initial image of one who "the spirit of the Lord speaks through" (v. 2). It was God's faithfulness to David in all his ups and downs that provides us an image of God's faithfulness to us. We look forward to a time when the whole world will recognize Christ's rule in their lives. In the meantime, we are provided the opportunity to demonstrate what that lordship looks like in our own lives.

Psalm 132:1-12 (13-18)

The Lord swore to David a sure oath from which he will not turn back: "One of the sons of your body I will set on your throne." — Psalm 132:11

As we turn to celebrate Christ the King Sunday, we are faced with the issue of the promises of God. Here and elsewhere we hear of God's promise to David. "The Lord swore to David a sure oath from which he will not turn back; 'One of the sons of your body I will set on your throne.'" This was fulfilled in the succession of Solomon to the throne. Then God made a further promise that seems to have a condition attached. "If your sons keep my covenant and my decrees that I shall teach them, their sons also, forevermore, shall sit on your throne" (v. 12). Eventually, the line of David's ancestors was broken with the conquest of Judah by Babylon. Yet the promise of God persisted in the minds of the people, and its fulfillment was sought in a Messiah that David would send among them. What they waited for was a person from the house and lineage of David who would keep God's covenant and decrees. Israel had long recognized two things about the character of God. First, God always kept his promises. Second, God often kept the divine promise in a way that was totally unexpected by the people. Thus, at Jesus' birth, it was important to affirm that he was of the house and lineage of David and that he lived a life in obedience to the covenant of God.

For those who saw Jesus as the Messiah, it was again important to count on the promises of God. "For your servant David's sake do not turn away the face of your anointed one" (v. 10). That was what was so shocking about the crucifixion. The resurrection was just another example of the way that God fulfills God's promises in totally unexpected ways. Christians were faced with a new challenge. We affirm that Christ is king, but he is such a strange king. He chooses to rule by service rather than force. He chooses to die on our behalf rather than conquer our enemies. The resurrection was an affirmation by God of his anointed one. With the ascension, we are faced with following a king who rules in absentia. This again confronts the believer with the issue of trust that God will fulfill God's promises. It also causes us to be alert to the signs of Christ's rule in the most unexpected ways.

Revelation 1:4b-8

To him who loves us and freed us from our sins by his blood, and made us to be a kingdom, priests serving his God and Father, to him be glory and dominion forever and ever. Amen. — Revelation 1:5b-6

To be part of a kingdom is to be part of a people that show obedience to a king. A warrior that conquerors an evil ruler and sets the people free from the tyranny of the previous rule may be hailed by the people as their new king. The book of Revelation proclaims that to be the case. The tyrant who previously ruled the people was sin. It enslaved people and made their lives miserable. Jesus gave his life and blood that the people might be set free from that tyranny. They were invited to accept him as king or ruler in their lives. His victory was accomplished by defeating the power of death that sin had used to maintain its power over them.

By demonstrating that death could not hold him, he revealed that the God of grace that he proclaimed had power even over death. But it was more than an individual victory. By conquering death, Jesus also demonstrated to the other rulers of the earth that he had authority over them as well. That is, Jesus had been given final authority over all those who had the power to govern on this earth. That was true even though many of them had not recognized his authority over them. To say, "He is coming with the clouds; every eye will see him, even those who pierced him ..." (v. 7) was to suggest that there would be a time when his authority would be recognized. To say that he was coming with the clouds was to say that God, who often spoke from the clouds, would make Jesus' authority so clear that even those who crucified him would recognize his authority.

The promise was not just a time of personal rule in individual hearts but a rule over the nations of the earth. There have been times in history when the church has tried to impose its rule over nations and rulers. From those experiences, we have learned that we are no better at exercising power than the secular rulers are. As we await the culmination of Christ's rule, we are given an opportunity to reflect on what it means to rule with service and love.

John 18:33-37

Pilate replied, "I am not a Jew, am I?" — John 18:35a

John delighted in the use of irony. Pilate played the role of the interrogator of the prisoner but soon became the one who was interrogated. He began by summoning Jesus and asking him, "Are you the King of the Jews?" (v. 33). But Jesus replied with a question that placed the responsibility back on Pilate. "Do you ask this on your own, or did others tell you about me?" (v. 35). The question seemed to imply that perhaps Pilate was not in charge of himself as he had supposed. Pilate tried to evade the question by asking another question. "I am not a Jew, am I?" Later, Christians would realize that they could not avoid making the decision as to their personal response to the lordship of Jesus by claiming that they were not Jews. By Christ we are all invited to answer the question for ourselves as part of the people of God. As some discovered in Nazi Germany, there comes a time when we are all challenged to be Jews in opposition to the evil before us. Jesus' kingship is not restricted to old world categories of who is in and who is out.

Pilate asked, "So you are a king?" Jesus transformed his question into an affirmation, "You say that I am a king ..." (v. 37). But then Jesus proceeded to redefine kingship from one who exercises power over others to one who leads by truth. "For this I was born, and for this I came into this world, to testify to the truth. Every one who belongs to the truth listens to my voice" (v. 37c). Now the question for Pilate and us is do we belong to the truth and listen to Christ's voice?

www.ingramcontent.com/pod-product-compliance
Lightning Source LLC
Chambersburg PA
CBHW071151130626
46553CB00004B/1611